# Problem-solving in High Performance Computing

## A Situational Awareness Approach with Linux

# Problem-solving in High Performance Computing
## A Situational Awareness Approach with Linux

**Igor Ljubuncic**

AMSTERDAM • BOSTON • HEIDELBERG • LONDON
NEW YORK • OXFORD • PARIS • SAN DIEGO
SAN FRANCISCO • SINGAPORE • SYDNEY • TOKYO

Morgan Kaufmann is an Imprint of Elsevier

Acquiring Editor: Todd Green
Editorial Project Manager: Lindsay Lawrence
Project Manager: Priya Kumaraguruparan
Cover Designer: Alan Studholme

Morgan Kaufmann is an imprint of Elsevier
225 Wyman Street, Waltham, MA 02451, USA

**British Library Cataloguing-in-Publication Data**
A catalogue record for this book is available from the British Library

**Library of Congress Cataloging-in-Publication Data**
A catalog record for this book is available from the Library of Congress

ISBN: 978-0-12-801019-8

For information on all Morgan Kaufmann publications
visit our website at http://store.elsevier.com/

*This book is dedicated to all Dedoimedo readers for their generous and sincere support over the years.*

# Contents

# Preface

I have spent most of my Linux career counting servers in their thousands and tens of thousands, almost like a musician staring at the notes and seeing hidden shapes among the harmonics. After a while, I began to discern patterns in how data centers work – and behave. They are almost like living, breathing things; they have their ups and downs, their cycles, and their quirks. They are much more than the sum of their ingredients, and when you add the human element to the equation, they become unpredictable.

Managing large deployments, the kind you encounter in big data centers, cloud setup, and high-performance environments, is a very delicate task. It takes a great deal of expertise, effort, and technical understanding to create a successful, efficient work flow. Future vision and business strategy are also required. But amid all of these, quite often, one key component is missing.

There is no comprehensive strategy in problem solving.

This book is my attempt to create one. Years invested in designing solutions and products that would make the data centers under my grasp better, more robust, and more efficient have exposed me to the fundamental gap in problem solving. People do not fully understand what it means. Yes, it involves tools and hacking the system. Yes, you may script some, or you might spend many long hours staring at logs scrolling down your screen. You might even plot graphs to show data trends. You may consult your colleagues about issues in their domain. You might participate in or lead task forces trying to undo crises and heavy outages. But in the end, there is no unifying methodology that brings together all the pieces of the puzzle.

An approach to problem solving using situational awareness is an idea that borrows from the fields of science, trying to replace human intuition with mathematics. We will be using statistical engineering and design of experiment to battle chaos. We will work slowly, systematically, step by step, and try to develop a *consistent* way of fixing identical problems. Our focus will be on busting myths around data, and we will shed some of the preconceptions and traditions that pervade the data center world. Then, we will transform the art of system troubleshooting into a product. It may sound brutal that art should be sold by the pound, but the necessity will become obvious as you progress throughout the book. And for the impatient among you, it means touching on the subjects of monitoring, change control and management, automation, and other best practices that are only now slowly making their way into the modern data center.

Last but not least, we will try all of the above without forgetting the most important piece at the very heart of investigation, of any problem solving, really: fun and curiosity, the very reason why we became engineers and scientists, the reason why we love the chaotic, hectic, frenetic world of data center technologies.

Please come along for the ride.

Igor Ljubuncic, May 2015

# Acknowledgments

While writing this book, I occasionally stepped away from my desk and went around talking to people. Their advice and suggestions helped shape this book up into a more presentable form. As such, I would like to thank Patrick Hauke for making sure this project got completed, David Clark for editing my work and fine-tuning my sentences and paragraphs, Avikam Rozenfeld who provided useful technical feedback and ideas, Tom Litterer for the right nudge in the right direction, and last but not least, the rest of clever, hard-working folks at Intel.

Hats off, ladies and gentlemen.

**Igor Ljubuncic**

# Introduction: data center and high-end computing

## DATA CENTER AT A GLANCE

If you are looking for a pitch, a one-liner for how to define data centers, then you might as well call them the modern power plants. They are the equivalent of the old, sooty coal factories that used to give the young, enterpreneurial industrialist of the mid 1800s the advantage he needed over the local tradesmen in villages. The plants and their laborers were the unsung heroes of their age, doing their hard labor in the background, unseen, unheard, and yet the backbone of the revolution that swept the world in the nineteenth century.

Fast-forward 150 years, and a similar revolution is happening. The world is transforming from an analog one to a digital, with all the associated difficulties, buzz, and real technological challenges. In the middle of it, there is the data center, the powerhouse of the Internet, the heart of the search, the *big* in the big data.

## MODERN DATA CENTER LAYOUT

Realistically, if we were to go into specifics of the data center design and all the underlying pieces, we would need half a dozen books to write it all down. Furthermore, since this is only an introduction, an appetizer, we will only briefly touch this world. In essence, it comes down to three major components: network, compute, and storage. There are miles and miles of wires, thousands of hard disks, angry CPUs running at full speed, serving the requests of billions every second. But on their own, these three pillars do not make a data center. There is more.

If you want an analogy, think of an aircraft carrier. The first thing that comes to mind is Tom Cruise taking off in his F-14, with Kenny Loggins' *Danger Zone* playing in the background. It is almost too easy to ignore the fact there are thousands of aviation crew mechanics, technicians, electricians, and other specialists supporting the operation. It is almost too easy to forget the floor upon floor of infrastructure and workshops, and in the very heart of it, an IT center, carefully orchestrating the entire piece.

Data centers are somewhat similar to the 100,000-ton marvels patrolling the oceans. They have their components, but they all need to communicate and work together. This is why when you talk about data centers, concepts such as cooling and power density are just as critical as the type of processor and disk one might use. Remote management, facility security, disaster recovery, backup – all of these are hardly on the list, but the higher you scale, the more important they become.

## WELCOME TO THE BORG, RESISTANCE IS FUTILE

In the last several years, we see a trend moving from any old setup that includes computing components into something approaching standards. Like any technology, the data center has reached a point at which it can no longer sustain itself on its own, and the world cannot tolerate a hundred different versions of it. Similar to the convergence of other technologies, such as network protocols, browser standards, and to some extent, media standards, the data center *as a whole* is also becoming a standard. For instance, the Open Data Center Alliance (ODCA) (Open Data Center Alliance, n.d.) is a consortium established in 2010, driving adoption of interoperable solutions and services – standards – across the industry.

In this reality, hanging on to your custom workshop is like swimming against the current. Sooner or later, either you or the river will have to give up. Having a data center is no longer enough. And this is part of the reason for this book – solving problems and creating solutions in a large, unique high-performance setup that is the inevitable future of data centers.

## POWERS THAT BE

Before we dig into any tactical problem, we need to discuss strategy. Working with a single computer at home is nothing like doing the same kind of work in a data center. And while the technology is pretty much identical, all the considerations you have used before – and your instincts – are completely wrong.

High-performance computing starts and ends with scale, the ability to grow at a steady rate in a sustainable manner without increasing your costs exponentially. This has always been a challenging task, and quite often, companies have to sacrifice growth once their business explodes beyond control. It is often the small, neglected things that force the slowdown – power, physical space, the considerations that are not often immediate or visible.

## ENTERPRISE VERSUS LINUX

Another challenge that we are facing is the transition from the traditional world of the classic enterprise into the quick, rapid-paced, ever-changing cloud. Again, it is not about technology. It is about people who have been in the IT business for many years, and they are experiencing this sudden change right before their eyes.

## THE CLASSIC OFFICE

Enabling the office worker to use their software, communicate with colleagues and partners, send email, and chat has been a critical piece of the Internet since its earlier days. But, the office is a stagnant, almost boring environment. The needs for change and growth are modest.

## LINUX COMPUTING ENVIRONMENT

The next evolutionary step in the data center business was the creation of the Linux operating system. In one fell swoop, it delivered a whole range of possibilities that were not available beforehand. It offered affordable cost compared to expensive mainframe setups. It offered reduced licensing costs, and the largely open-source nature of the product allowed people from the wider community to participate and modify the software. Most importantly, it also offered scale, from minimal setups to immense supercomputers, accommodating both ends of the spectrum with almost nonchalant ease.

And while there was chaos in the world of Linux distributions, offering a variety of flavors and types that could never really catch on, the kernel remained largely standard, and allowed businesses to rely on it for their growth. Alongside opportunity, there was a great shift in the perception in the industry, and the speed of change, testing the industry's experts to their limit.

## LINUX CLOUD

Nowadays, we are seeing the third iteration in the evolution of the data center. It is shifting from being the enabler for products into a product itself. The pervasiveness of data, embodied in the concept called the Internet of Things, as well as the fact that a large portion of modern (and online) economy is driven through data search, has transformed the data center into an integral piece of business logic.

The word *cloud* is used to describe this transformation, but it is more than just having free compute resources available somewhere in the world and accessible through a Web portal. Infrastructure has become a service (IaaS), platforms have become a service (PaaS), and applications running on top of a very complex, modular cloud stack are virtually indistinguishable from the underlying building blocks.

In the heart of this new world, there is Linux, and with it, a whole new generation of challenges and problems of a different scale and problem that system administrators never had to deal with in the past. Some of the issues may be similar, but the time factor has changed dramatically. If you could once afford to run your local system investigation at your own pace, you can no longer afford to do so with cloud systems. Concepts such as uptime, availability, and price dictate a different regime of thinking and require different tools. To make things worse, speed and technical capabilities of the hardware are being pushed to the limit, as science and big data mercilessly drive the high-performance compute market. Your old skills as a troubleshooter are being put to a test.

## 10,000 × 1 DOES NOT EQUAL 10,000

The main reason why a situational-awareness approach to problem solving is so important is that linear growth brings about exponential complexity. Tools that work well on individual hosts are not built for mass deployments or do not have the capability for cross-system use. Methodologies that are perfectly suited for slow-paced, local setups are utterly outclassed in the high-performance race of the modern world.

## NONLINEAR SCALING OF ISSUES

On one hand, larger environments become more complex because they simply have a much greater number of components in them. For instance, take a typical hard disk. An average device may have a mean time between failure (MTBF) of about 900 years. That sounds like a pretty safe bet, and you are more likely to decommission a disk after several years of use than see it malfunction. But if you have a thousand disks, and they are all part of a larger ecosystem, the MTBF shrinks down to about 1 year, and suddenly, problems you never had to deal with explicitly become items on the daily agenda.

On the other hand, large environments also require additional considerations when it comes to power, cooling, physical layout and design of data center aisles and rack, the network interconnectivity, and the number of edge devices. Suddenly, there are new dependencies that never existed on a smaller scale, and those that did are magnified or made significant when looking at the system as a whole. The considerations you may have for problem solving change.

## THE LAW OF LARGE NUMBERS

It is almost too easy to overlook how much effect small, seemingly imperceptible changes in great quantity can have on the larger system. If you were to optimize the kernel on a single Linux host, knowing you would get only about 2–3% benefit in overall performance, you would hardly want to bother with hours of reading and testing. But if you have 10,000 servers that could all churn cycles that much faster, the business imperative suddenly changes. Likewise, when problems hit, they come to bear in scale.

## HOMOGENEITY

Cost is one of the chief considerations in the design of the data center. One of the easy ways to try to keep the operational burden under control is by driving standards and trying to minimize the overall deployment cross-section. IT departments will seek to use as few operating systems, server types, and software versions as possible because it helps maintain the inventory, monitor and implement changes, and troubleshoot problems when they arise.

But then, on the same note, when problems arise in highly consistent environments, they affect the *entire* installation base. Almost like an epidemic, it becomes necessary to react very fast and contain problems before they can explode beyond control, because if one system is affected and goes down, they all could theoretically go down. In turn, this dictates how you fix issues. You no longer have the time and luxury to tweak and test as you fancy. A very strict, methodical approach is required.

Your resources are limited, the potential for impact is huge, the business objectives are not on your side, and you need to architect robust, modular, effective, scalable solutions.

## BUSINESS IMPERATIVE

Above all technical challenges, there is one bigger element – the business imperative, and it encompasses the entire data center. The mission defines how the data center will look, how much it will cost, and how it may grow, if the mission is successful. This ties in tightly into how you architect your ideas, how you identify problems, and how you resolve them.

## OPEN 24/7

Most data centers never stop their operation. It is a rare moment to hear complete silence inside data center halls, and they will usually remain powered on until the building and all its equipment are decommissioned, many years later. You need to bear that in mind when you start fixing problems because you cannot afford downtime. Alternatively, your fixes and future solutions must be smart enough to allow the business to continue operating, even if you do incur some invisible downtime in the background.

## MISSION CRITICAL

The modern world has become so dependent on the Internet, on its search engines, and on its data warehouses that they can no longer be considered separate from the everyday life. When servers crash, traffic lights and rail signals stop responding, hospital equipment or medical records are not available to the doctors at a crucial moment, and you may not be able to communicate with your colleagues or family. Problem solving may involve bits and bytes in the operating systems, but it affects everything.

## DOWNTIME EQUALS MONEY

It comes as no surprise that data center downtimes translate directly into heavy financial losses for everyone involved. Can you imagine what would happen if the stock market halted for a few hours because of technical glitches in the software? Or if the Panama Canal had to halt its operation? The burden of the task has just become bigger and heavier.

## AN AVALANCHE STARTS WITH A SINGLE FLAKE

The worst part is, it does not take much to transform a seemingly innocent system alert into a major outage. Human error or neglect, misinterpreted information, insufficient data, bad correlation between elements of the larger system, a lack of situational awareness, and a dozen other trivial reasons can all easily escalate into complex scenarios, with negative impact on your customers. Later on, after sleepless nights and long post-mortem meetings, things start to become clear and obvious in retrospect. But, it is always the combination of small, seemingly unrelated factors that lead to major problems.

This is why problem solving is not just about using this or that tool, typing fast on the keyboard, being the best Linux person in the team, writing scripts, or even proactively monitoring your systems. It is *all* of those, and much more. Hopefully, this book will shed some light on what it takes to run successful, well-controlled, well-oiled high-performance, mission-critical data center environments.

## Reference

Open Data Center Alliance, n.d. Available at: http://www.opendatacenteralliance.org/ (accessed May 2015)

# Do you have a problem?

1

Now that you understand the scope of problem solving in a complex environment such as a large, mission-critical data center, it is time to begin investigating system issues in earnest. Normally, you will not just go around and search for things that might look suspicious. There ought to be a logical process that funnels possible items of interest – let us call them events – to the right personnel. This step is just as important as all later links in the problem-solving chains.

## IDENTIFICATION OF A PROBLEM

Let us begin with a simple question. What makes you think you have a problem? If you are one of the support personnel handling environment problems in your company, there are several possible ways you might be notified of an issue.

You might get a digital alert, sent by a monitoring program of some sort, which has decided there is an exception to the norm, possibly because a certain metric has exceeded a threshold value. Alternatively, someone else, your colleague, subordinate, or a peer from a remote call center, might forward a problem to you, asking for your assistance.

A natural human response is to assume that if problem-monitoring software has alerted you, this means there is a problem. Likewise, in case of an escalation by a human operator, you can often assume that other people have done all the preparatory work, and now they need your expert hand.

But what if this is not true? Worse yet, what if there is a problem that no one is really reporting?

## IF A TREE FALLS IN A FOREST, AND NO ONE HEARS IT FALL

Problem solving can be treated almost philosophically, in some cases. After all, if you think about it, even the most sophisticated software only does what its designer had in mind, and thresholds are entirely under our control. This means that digital reports and alerts are entirely human in essence, and therefore prone to mistakes, bias, and wrong assumptions.

However, issues that get raised are relatively easy. You have the opportunity to acknowledge them, and fix them or dismiss them. But, you cannot take an action about a problem that you do not know is there.

In the data center, the answer to the philosophical question is not favorable to system administrators and engineers. If there is an obscure issue that no existing monitoring logic is capable of capturing, it will still come to bear, often with interest, and the real skill lies in your ability to find the problems despite missing evidence.

It is almost like the way physicists find the dark matter in the universe. They cannot really see it or measure it, but they can measure its effect indirectly.

The same rules apply in the data center. You should exercise a healthy skepticism toward problems, as well as challenge conventions. You should also look for the problems that your tools do not see, and carefully pay attention to all those seemingly ghost phenomena that come and go. To make your life easier, you should embrace a methodical approach.

## STEP-BY-STEP IDENTIFICATION

We can divide problems into three main categories:

- real issues that correlate well to the monitoring tools and prior analysis by your colleagues,
- false positives raised by previous links in the system administration chain, both human and machine,
- real (and spurious) issues that only have an indirect effect on the environment, but that could possibly have significant impact if left unattended.

Your first tasks in the problem-solving process are to decide what kind of an event you are dealing with, whether you should acknowledge an early report or work toward improving your monitoring facilities and internal knowledge of the support teams, and how to handle come-and-go issues that no one has really classified yet.

## ALWAYS USE SIMPLE TOOLS FIRST

The data center world is a rich and complex one, and it is all too easy to get lost in it. Furthermore, your past knowledge, while a valuable resource, can also work against you in such a setup. You may assume too much and overreach, trying to fix problems with an excessive dose of intellectual and physical force. To demonstrate, let us take a look at the following example. The actual subject matter is not trivial, but it illustrates how people often make illogical, far-reaching conclusions. It is a classic case of our sensitivity threshold searching for the mysterious and vague in the face of great complexity.

A system administrator contacts his peer, who is known to be an expert on kernel crashes, regarding a kernel panic that has occurred on one of his systems. The administrator asks for advice on how to approach and handle the crash instance and how to determine what caused the system panic.

The expert lends his help, and in the processes, also briefly touches on the methodology for the analysis of kernel crash logs and how the data within can be interpreted and used to isolate issues.

Several days later, the same system administrator contacts the expert again, with another case of a system panic. Only this time, the enthusiastic engineer has invested some time reading up on kernel crashes and has tried to perform the analysis himself. His conclusion to the problem is: "We have got one more kernel crash on another server, and this time it seems to be quite an old kernel bug."

The expert then does his own analysis. What he finds is completely different from his colleague. Toward the end of the kernel crash log, there is a very clear instance of a hardware exception, caused by a faulty memory bank, which led to the panic.

```
HARDWARE ERROR

CPU 6: Machine Check Exception:          5 Bank 3: be00000000200151

RIP !INEXACT! 10:<ffffffff8010bb4b> {apic_timer_interrupt+0x7f/0x8c}

TSC 2d363c5d00fb ADDR 109900 MISC 16485

This is not a software problem!

Run through mcelog -- ascii to decode and contact your hardware vendor

Kernel panic - not syncing: Machine check
```

You may wonder what the lesson to this exercise is. The system administrator did a classic mistake of assuming the worst, when he should have invested time in checking the simple things first. He did this for two reasons: insufficient knowledge in a new domain, and the tendency of people doing routine work to disregard the familiar and go for extremes, often with little foundation to their claims. However, once the mind is set, it is all too easy to ignore real evidence and create false logical links. Moreover, the administrator may have just learned how to use a new tool, so he or she may be biased toward using that tool whenever possible.

Using simple tools may sound tedious, but there is value in working methodically, top down, and doing the routine work. It may not reveal much, but it will not expose new, bogus problems either. The beauty in a gradual escalation of complexity in problem solving is that it allows trivial things to be properly identified and resolved. This saves time and prevents the technicians from investing effort in chasing down false positives, all due to their own internal convictions and the basic human need for causality.

At certain times, it will be perfectly fine – and even desirable – to go for heavy tools and deep-down analysis. Most of the time, most of the problems will have simple root causes. Think about it. If you have a monitor in place, this means you have a mathematical formula, and you can explain the problem. Now, you are just trying to prevent its manifestation or minimize damage. Likewise, if you have several levels of technical support handling a problem, it means you have identified the severity level, and you know what needs to be done.

Complex problems, the big ones, will often manifest themselves in very weird ways, and you will be tempted to ignore them. On the same note, you will overinflate simple things and make them into huge issues. This is why you need to be methodical and focus on simple steps, to make the right categorization of problems, and make your life easier down the road.

## TOO MUCH KNOWLEDGE LEADS TO MISTAKES

Our earlier example is a good example of how wrong knowledge and wrong assumptions can make the system administrator blind to the obvious. Indeed, the more experienced you get, the less patient you will be to resolving simple, trivial, well-known issues. You will not want to be fixing them, and you may even display an unusual amount of disregard and resistance when asked to step in and help.

Furthermore, when your mind is tuned to reach high and far, you will miss all the little things happening right under your nose. You will make the mistake of being "too proud," and you will search for problems that increase your excitement level. When no real issues of that kind are to be found, you will, by the grace of human nature, invent them.

It is important to be aware of this logical fallacy lurking in our brains. This is the Achilles's heel of every engineer and problem solver. You want to be fighting the unknown, and you will find it anywhere you look.

For this reason, it is critical to make problem solving into a discipline rather than an erratic, ad-hoc effort. If two system administrators in the same position or role use completely different ways of resolving the same issue, it is a good indication of a lack of a formal problem-solving process, core knowledge, understanding of your environment, and how things come to bear.

Moreover, it is useful to narrow down the investigative focus. Most people, save an occasional genius, tend to operate better with a small amount of uncertainty rather than complete chaos. They also tend to ignore things they consider trivial, and they get bored easily with the routine.

Therefore, problem solving should also include a significant effort in automating the well known and trivial, so that engineers need not invest time repeating the obvious and mundane. Escalations need to be precise and methodical and well documented, so that everyone can repeat them with the same expected outcome. Skills should be matched to problems. Do not expect inexperienced technicians to make the right decisions when analyzing kernel crashes. Likewise, do not expect your expert to be enthused about running simple commands and checks, because they will often skip them, ignore possibly valuable clues, and jump to their own conclusions, adding to the entropy of your data center.

With the right combination of known and unknown, as well as the smart utilization of available machine and human resources, it is possible to minimize the waste during investigations. In turn, you will have fewer false positives, and your real experts will be able to focus on those weird issues with indirect manifestation, because those are the true big ones you want to solve.

## PROBLEM DEFINITION

We still have not resolved any one of our three possible problems. They still remain, but at least now, we are a little less unclear how to approach them. We will now focus some more energy on trying to classify problems so that our investigation is even more effective.

## PROBLEM THAT HAPPENS NOW OR THAT MAY BE

Alerts from monitoring systems are usually an indication of a problem, or a possible problem happening in real time. Your primary goal is to change the setup in a manner that will make the alert go away. This is the classic definition of threshold-based problem solving.

We can immediately spot the pitfalls in this approach. If a technician needs to make the problem go away, they will make it go away. If it cannot be solved, it can be ignored, the threshold values can be changed, or the problem interpreted in a different way. Sometimes, in business environments, sheer management pressure in the face of an immediate inability to resolve a seemingly acute problem can lead to a rather simple resolution: reclassification of a problem. If you cannot resolve it, acknowledge it, *relabel* it, and move on.

Furthermore, events often have a maximum response time. This is called service level agreement (SLA), and it determines how quickly the support team should provide a resolution to the problem. Unfortunately, the word resolution is misused here. This does not mean that the problem should be fixed. This only means that an adequate response was provided, and that the next step in the investigation is known.

With time pressure, peer pressure, management mission statement, and real-time urgency all combined, problem resolution loses some of its academic focus and it becomes a social issue of the particular environment. Now, this is absolutely fine. Real-life business is not an isolated mathematical problem. However, you need to be aware of that and remember when handling real-time issues.

Problems *that may be* are far more difficult to classify and handle. First, there is the matter of how you might find them. If you are handling real-time issues, and you close your events upon resolution, then there is little else to follow up on. Second, if you know something is going to happen, then it is just the matter of a postponed but determined fix. Last, if you do not know that a future problem is going to occur in your environment, there is little this side of time travel you can do to resolve it.

This leaves us with a tricky question of how to identify possible future problems. This is where proper investigation comes into play. If you follow the rules, then your step-by-step, methodical procedures will have an expected outcome. Whenever the results deviate from the known, there is a chance something new and unanticipated may happen. This is another important reason why you should stick to working in a gradual, well-documented, and methodical manner.

Whenever a system administrator encounters a fork in their investigation, they have a choice to make. Ignore the unknown and close the loop, or treat the new development seriously and escalate it. A healthy organization will be full of curious and slightly paranoid people who will not let problems rest. They will make sure the issues are taken to someone with enough knowledge, authority, and company-wide vision to make the right decision. Let us explore an example.

The monitoring system in your company sends alerts concerning a small number of hosts that get disconnected from the network. The duration of the problem is fairly short, just a couple of minutes. By the time the system administrators can take a look, the problem is gone. This happens every once in a while, and it is a known occurrence. If you were in charge of the 24/7 monitoring team that handles this issue, what would you do?

- Create an exception to the monitoring rule to ignore these few hosts? After all, the issue is isolated to just a few servers, the duration is very short, the outcome is not severe, and there is little you can do here.
- Consider the possibility that there might be a serious problem with the network configuration, which could potentially indicate a bug in the network equipment firmware or operating system, and ask the networking experts for their involvement?

Of course, you would choose the second option. But, in reality, when your team is swamped with hundreds or thousands of alerts, would you really choose to get yourself involved in something that impacts 0.001% of your install base?

Three months from now, another data center in your company may report encountering the same issue, only this time it will have affected hundreds of servers, with significant business impact. The issue will have been traced to a fault in the switch equipment. At this point, it will be too late.

Now, this does not mean every little issue is a disaster waiting to happen. System administrators need to exercise discretion when trying to decide how to proceed with these unknown, yet-to-happen problems.

## OUTAGE SIZE AND SEVERITY VERSUS BUSINESS IMPERATIVE

The easy way for any company to prioritize its workload is by assigning severities to issues, classifying outages, and comparing them to the actual customers paying the bill for the server equipment. Since the workload is always greater than the workforce, the business imperative becomes the holy grail of problem solving. Or the holy excuse, depending on how you look at it.

If the technical team is unable to fix an immediate problem, and the real resolution may take weeks or months of hard follow-up work with the vendor, some people will choose to ignore the problem, using the excuse that it does not have enough impact to concern the customers. Others will push to resolution exactly because of the high risk to the customers. Most of the time, unfortunately, people will prefer the status quo rather than to poke, change, and interfere. After a long time, the result will be outdated technologies and methodologies, justified in the name of the business imperative.

It is important to acknowledge all three factors when starting your investigation. It is important to quantify them when analyzing evidence and data. But, it is also important not to be blinded by mission statements.

Server outages are an important and popular metric. Touting 99.999% server uptime is a good way of showing how successful your operation is. However, this should not be the only way to determine whether you should introduce disruptive changes to your environment. Moreover, while outages do indicate how stable your environment is, they tell nothing of your efficiency or problem solving.

Outages should be weighed against the sum of all non-real-time problems that happened in your environment. This is the only valuable indicator of how well you run your business. If a server goes down suddenly, it is not because there is magic in the operating system or the underlying hardware. The reason is one and simple: you did not have the right tools to spot the problem. Sometimes, it will be extremely difficult to predict failure, especially with hardware components. But lots of times, it will be caused by not focusing on deviations from the norm, the little might-be's and would-be's, and giving them their due time and respect.

Many issues that happen in real time today have had their indicators a week, a month, or a year ago. Most were ignored, wrongly collected and classified, or simply not measured because most organizations focus on volumes of real-time monitoring. Efficient problem solving is finding the parameters that you do not control right now and translating them into actionable metrics. Once you have them, you can measure them and take actions before they result in an outage or a disruption of service.

Severity often defines the response – but not the problem. Indeed, focus on the following scenario: a test host crashes due to a kernel bug. The impact is zero, and the host is not even registered in the monitoring dashboard of your organization. The severity of this event is low. But does that mean a problem severity is low?

What if the same kernel used on the test host is also deployed on a thousand servers doing compilations of critical regression tasks? What if your Web servers also run the same kernel, and the problem could happen anytime, anywhere, as soon as the critical condition in the kernel space is reached? Do you still think that the severity of the issue is low?

Finally, we have the business imperative. Compute resources available in the data center may have an internal and external interface. If they are used to enable a higher functionality, the technical mechanisms are often hidden from the customer. If they are utilized directly, the user may show interest in the setup and configuration.

However, most of the time, security and modernity considerations are often secondary to functional needs. In other words, if the compute resource is fulfilling the business need, the users will be apathetic or even resistant to changes that incur downtime, disruption to their work, or a breakage of interfaces. A good example of this phenomenon is Windows XP. From the technical perspective, it is a 13-year-old operating system, somewhat modernized through its lifecycle, but it is still heavily used in both the business and the private sector. The reason is that the users see no immediate need to upgrade because their functional requirements are all met.

In fact, in the data center, technological antiquity is highly prevalent and often required to provide the much-needed backward compatibility. Many services simply cannot upgrade to newer versions because the effort outweighs the benefits from the customer perspective. For all practical purposes, in this sense, we can treat the data center as a static component in a larger equation.

This means that your customers will not want to see things change around them. In other words, if you encounter bugs and problems, unless these bugs and problems are highly visible, critical, and with a direct impact on your users, these users will not see a reason to suspend their work so that you can do your maintenance. The business imperative defines and restricts the pace of technology in the data center, and it dictates your problem-solving flexibility. Often as not, you may have great ideas how to solve things, but the window of opportunity for change will happen sometime in the next 3 years.

Now, if we combine all these, we face a big challenge. There are many problems in the environment, some immediate and some leaning toward disasters waiting to happen. To make your work even more difficult, the perception and understanding of how the business runs often focuses on wrong severity classification. Most of the time, people will invest energy in fixing issues happening right now rather than strategic issues that should be solved tomorrow. Then, there is business demand from your customers, which normally leans toward zero changes.

How do we translate this reality into a practical problem-solving strategy? It is all too easy to just let things be as they are and do your fair share of firefighting. It is quick, it is familiar, it is highly visible, and it can be appreciated by the management.

The answer is, you should let the numbers be your voice. If you work methodically and carefully, you will be able to categorize issues and simplify the business case so that it can be translated into actionable items. This is what the business understands, and this is how you can make things happen.

You might not be able to revolutionize how your organization works overnight, but you can definitely make sure the background noise does not drown the important far-reaching findings in your work.

You start by not ignoring problems; you follow up with correct classification. You make sure the trivial and predictable issues are translated into automation, and focus the rest of your wit and skills on those seemingly weird cases that come and go. This is where the next severe outage in your company is going to be.

## KNOWN VERSUS UNKNOWN

Faced with uncertainty, most people gravitate back to their comfort zone, where they know how to carry themselves and handle problems. If you apply the right problem-solving methods, you will most likely be always dealing with new and unknown problems. The reason is, if you do not let problems float in a medium of guessing, speculation, and arbitrary thresholds, your work will be precise, analytical, and without repetitions. You will find an issue, fix it, hand off to the monitoring team, and move on.

A problem that has been resolved once is no longer a problem. It becomes a maintenance item, which you need to keep under control. If you continue coming back to it, you are simply not in control of your processes, or your resolution is incorrect.

Therefore, always facing the unknown is a good indication you are doing a good job. Old problems go away, and new ones come, presenting you with an opportunity to enhance your understanding of your environment.

# PROBLEM REPRODUCTION

Let us put the bureaucracy and old habits aside. Your mission is to conduct a precise and efficient investigation of your problem. You do that with the full understanding of your own pitfalls, of your environment complexity, the constraints, as well as the knowledge that most facts will be wired against you.

## CAN YOU ISOLATE THE PROBLEM?

You think there is a new issue in your environment. It looks to be a non-real-time problem, and it may come to bear sometime in the future. By now, you are convinced that a methodical investigation is the only way to do that.

You start simple, you classify the problem, you suppress your own technical hubris, and you focus on the facts. The next step is to see whether you can isolate and reproduce the problem.

Let us assume you have a host that is exhibiting nonstandard, unhealthy behavior when communicating with a remote file system, specifically network file system (NFS) (RFC, 1995). All right, let us complicate some more. There is also automounter (autofs) (Autofs, 2014) involved. The monitoring team has flagged the system and handed off the case to you, as the expert. What do you do now?

There are dozens of components that could be the root cause here, including the server hardware, the kernel, the NFS client program, the autofs program, and so far, this is only the client side. On the remote server, we could suspect the actual NFS service, or there might be an issue with access permissions, firewall rules, and in between, the data center network.

You need to isolate the problem. Let us start simple. Is the problem limited to just one host, the one that is shown up in the monitoring systems? If so, then you can be certain that there is no problem with the network or the remote file server. You have isolated the problem.

On the host itself, you could try accessing the remote filesystem manually, without using the automounter. If the problem persists, you can continue peeling additional layers, trying to understand where the root cause might reside. Conversely, if more than a single client is affected, you should focus on the remote server and the network equipment in between. Figure out if the problem manifests itself only in certain subnets or VLAN; check whether the problem manifests itself only with one specific file server or filesystem or all of them.

It is useful to actually draw a diagram of the environment, as you know and understand it, and then test each component. Use simple tools first and slowly dig deeper. Do not assume kernel bugs until you have finished with the easy checks.

After you have isolated the problem, you should try to reproduce it. If you can, it means you have a deterministic, formulaic way of capturing the problem manifestation. You might not be able to resolve the underlying issue yourself, but you understand the circumstances when and where it happens. This means that the actual fix from your vendor should be relatively simple.

But what do you do if the problem's cause eludes you? What if it happens at random intervals, and you cannot find an equation to the manifestation?

## SPORADIC PROBLEMS NEED SPECIAL TREATMENT

Here, we should refer to Arthur C. Clarke's Third Law, which says that any sufficiently advanced technology is indistinguishable from magic (Clarke, 1973). In the data center world, any sufficiently complex problem is indistinguishable from chaos.

Sporadic problems are merely highly complex issues that you are unable to explain in simple terms. If you knew the exact conditions and mechanisms involved, you would be able to predict when they would happen. Since you do not, they appear to be random and elusive.

As far as problem solving goes, nothing changes. But you will need to invest much time in figuring this out. Most often, your work will revolve around the understanding of the affected component or process rather than the actual resolution. Once you have full knowledge of what happens, the issue and the fix will have become quite similar to our earlier cases. Can you isolate it? Can you reproduce it?

## PLAN HOW TO CONTROL THE CHAOS

This almost sounds like a paradox. But you do want to minimize the number of elements in the equation that you do not control. If you think about it, most of the work in the data center is about damage control. All of the monitoring is done pretty much for one reason only, to try to stop a deteriorating situation as quickly as possible. Human operators are involved because it is impossible to translate most of the alerts into complete, closed algorithms. IT personnel are quite good at selecting things to monitor and defining thresholds. They are not very good at making meaningful decisions on the basis of the monitoring events.

Shattering preconceptions is difficult, and let us not forget the business imperative, but the vast majority of effort is invested in alerting on suspected exceptions and making sure they are brought back to normal levels. Unfortunately, most of the alerts rarely indicate ways to prevent impending doom. Can you translate CPU activity into a kernel crash? Can you translate memory usage into an upcoming case of performance degradation? Does disk usage tell us anything about when the disk might fail? What is the correlation between the number of running processes and system responsiveness? Most if not all of these are rigorously monitored, and yet they rarely tell anything unless you go to extremes.

Let us use an analogy from our real life – radiation. The effects of electromagnetic radiation on human tissue are only well known once you exceed the normal background levels by several unhealthy levels of magnitude. But, in the gray area, there is virtually little to no knowledge and correlation, partly because the environmental impact of a million other parameters outside our control also plays a possibly important role.

Luckily, the data center world is slightly simpler. But not by much. We measure parameters in a hope that we will be able to make linear correlations and smart conclusions. Sometimes, this works, but often as not, there is little we can learn. Although monitoring is meant to be proactive, it is in fact reactive. You define your rules by adding new logic based on past problems, which you were unable to detect at that time.

So despite all this, how do you control the chaos?

Not directly. And we go back to the weird problems that come to bear at a later date. Problems that avoid mathematical formulas may still be reined in if you can define an environment of indirect measurements. Methodical problem solving is your best option here.

By rigorously following smart practices, such as using simple tools for doing simple checks first, trying to isolate and reproduce problems, you will be able to eliminate all the components that do *not* play a part in the manifestation of your weird issues. You will not be searching for what is there, you will be searching for what is not. Just like the dark matter.

Controlling the chaos is all about minimizing the number of unknowns. You might never be able to solve them all, but you will have significantly limited the possibility space for would-be random occurrences of problems. In turn, this will allow you to invest the right amount of energy in defining useful, meaningful monitoring rules and thresholds. It is a positive-feedback loop.

## LETTING GO IS THE HARDEST THING

Sometimes, despite your best efforts, the solution to the problem will elude you. It will be a combination of time, effort, skills, ability to introduce changes into the environment and test them, and other factors. In order not to get overwhelmed by your problem solving, you should also be able to halt, reset your investigation, start over, or even simply let go.

It might not be immediately possible to translate the return on investment (ROI) in your investigation to the future stability and quality of your environment. However, as a rule of thumb, if an active day of work (that is, not waiting for feedback from vendor or the like) goes by without any progress, you might as well call for help, involve others, try something else entirely, and then go back to the problem later on.

## CAUSE AND EFFECT

One of the major things that will detract you from success in your problem solving will be causality between the problem and its manifestation, or in more popular terms, the cause and the effect. Under pressure, due to boredom, limited information, and your own tendencies, you might make a wrong choice from the start, and your entire investigation will then unravel in an unexpected and less fruitful direction.

There are several useful practices you should embrace to make your work effective and focused. In the end, this will help you reduce the element of chaos, and you will not have to give up too often on your investigations.

## DO NOT GET HUNG UP ON SYMPTOMS

System administrators love error messages. Be they GUI prompts or cryptic lines in log files, they are always the reason for joy. A quick copy-paste into a search engine, and 5 minutes later, you will be chasing a whole new array of problems and possible causes you have not even considered before.

Like any anomaly, problems can be symptomatic and asymptomatic – monitored values versus those currently unknown, current problems versus future events, and direct results versus indirect phenomena.

If you observe a nonstandard behavior that coincides with a manifestation of a problem, this does not necessarily mean that there is any link between them. Yet, many people will automatically make the connection, because that is what we naturally do, and it is the easy thing.

Let us explore an example. A system is running relatively slowly, and the customers' flows have been affected as a result. The monitoring team escalates the issue to the engineering group. They have some preliminary checks, and they have concluded that the slowness event has been caused by errors in the configuration management software running its hourly update on the host.

This is a classic (and real) case of how seemingly cryptic errors can mislead. If you do a step-by-step investigation, then you can easily disregard these kinds of errors as bogus or unrelated background noise.

Did configuration management software errors happen only during the slowness event, or are they a part of a standard behavior of the tool? The answer in this case is, the software runs hourly and reads its table of policies to determine what installations or changes need to be executed on the local host. A misconfiguration in one of the policies triggers errors that are reflected in the system messages. But this occurs every hour, and it does not have any effect on customer flows?

Did the problem happen on just this one specific client? The answer is no, it happens on multiple hosts and indicates an unrelated problem with the configuration rather than any core operating system issue.

Isolate the problem, start with simple checks, and do not let random symptoms cloud your judgment. Indeed, working methodically helps avoid these easy pitfalls.

## CHICKEN AND EGG: WHAT CAME FIRST?

Consider the following scenario. Your customer reports a problem. Its flows are occasionally getting stuck during the execution on a particular set of hosts, and there is a very high system load. You are asked to help debug.

What you observe is that the physical memory is completely used, there is a little of swapping, but nothing that should warrant very high load and high CPU utilization. Without going into too many technical details, which we will see in the coming chapters, the CPU %sy value hovers around 30–40. Normally, the usage should be less than 5% for the specific workloads. After some initial checks, you find the following information in the system logs:

```
BUG: soft lockup - CPU#8 stuck for 21s! [process.exe]

...

Call Trace:

[<ffffffff81135a69>] isolate_freepages+0x359/0x3b0

[<ffffffff81135b0e>] compaction_alloc+0x4e/0x60

[<ffffffff8113fc69>] unmap_and_move+0x49/0x180

[<ffffffff8113fe3e>] migrate_pages+0x9e/0x1b0

[<ffffffff811362f3>] compact_zone+0x1f3/0x300

[<ffffffff81136662>] compact_zone_order+0xa2/0xe0

[<ffffffff8113677f>] try_to_compact_pages+0xdf/0x110

[<ffffffff810f876e>] __alloc_pages_direct_compact+0xee/0x1c0

[<ffffffff810f8ba2>] __alloc_pages_slowpath+0x362/0x7f0

[<ffffffff810f9219>] __alloc_pages_nodemask+0x1e9/0x200

[<ffffffff81134cb0>] alloc_pages_vma+0xd0/0x1c0

[<ffffffff811440f8>] do_huge_pmd_anonymous_page+0x138/0x260

[<ffffffff81448617>] do_page_fault+0x1f7/0x4b0

[<ffffffff814453e5>] page_fault+0x25/0x30

[<00002aaaaba83a1d>] 0x2aaaaba83a1c
```

At this moment, we do not know how to analyze something like the code above, but this is a call trace of a kernel oops. It tells us there is a bug in the kernel, and this is something that you should escalate to your operating system vendor.

Indeed, your vendor quickly acknowledges the problem and provides a fix. But the issue with customer flows, while lessened, has not gone away. Does this mean you have done something wrong in your analysis?

The answer is, not really. But, it also shows that while the kernel problem is real, and that it does cause CPU lockups, indicating that it translates into the problem your customers are seeing, it is not the *only* issue at hand. In fact, it masks the underlying root cause.

In this particular case, the real problem here is with the management of Transparent Huge Pages (THP) (Transparent huge pages in 2.6.38, n.d.), and for the particular kernel version used, with high memory utilization, a great amount of the computing power would be wasted on managing the memory rather than actual computation. In turn, this bug would trigger the CPU lockups, which do not happen when the THP usage is tweaked in a different manner.

Compound problems with interaction can be extremely difficult to analyze, interpret, and solve. They often come to bear in strange ways, and sometimes a perfectly legitimate issue will be just a derivative of a bigger root cause, which is currently masked. It is important to acknowledge this and be aware that sometimes the problem you are solving is in fact the result of another. Sort of like the Matrioshka (Russian nesting) dolls; you do not have one problem and one root cause, you have multiple chickens and a whole basket of eggs.

## DO NOT MAKE ENVIRONMENT CHANGES UNTIL YOU UNDERSTAND THE NATURE OF THE PROBLEM

If you work under the assumption that there might be multiple layers of problem manifestation in your environment, and you are not completely certain how they are related to one another, it is important that you do not introduce additional noise factors into the equation and make an even bigger problem.

Ideally, you will want and be able to analyze the situation one component at a time. You will never want to make more than a single change until you have observed the behavior and ascertained the effect. However, this will not always be possible.

Regardless, if you do not fully understand your setup or the problem, making arbitrary changes will most definitely complicate things. This goes against our natural instinct to interfere and change the world around us. Moreover, without statistical tools and methods, this will be even trickier, unless you are really lucky and happen to be fixing only simple issues with a linear response.

When trying to fix a problem, temporary tweaks and changes can be a good indicator if you are making progress in the right direction, but there is a very thin line between a sound solution based on a hypothesis and even more chaos.

## IF YOU MAKE A CHANGE, MAKE SURE YOU KNOW WHAT THE EXPECTED OUTCOME IS

Business is not academia. Everyone will tell you that. You do not have the time and skill to invest in rigorous mathematics just to be able to even start your investigation. But the researchers have gotten one thing right, and that is the expected outcome to any proposed theory or experiment. It is not so much that you want to prove what you want to prove, but you need to be able to tell what it is you are looking for and then prove yourself either right or wrong. But testing without a known outcome is just as effective as random guessing.

If you tweak a kernel tunable, it must be done with the knowledge and expectation of just what this particular parameter is going to do and how it is going to affect your system performance, stability, and the tools running on it. Without these, your work will be arbitrary and based on chance, and sooner or later, you will get lucky, but in the long run, you will increase the entropy of your environment and make your problem solving much more difficult.

## CONCLUSIONS

This chapter is just a warm-up before we roll up our sleeves and start investigating in earnest. But, it is also one of the more important pieces of this book. It does not teach so much what you need to do, but rather how to do it. It also helps you avoid some of the classic mistakes of problem solving.

You need to be aware of the constraints in your business environment – and then to challenge them. You need to focus on the core issues rather than the easily visible ones, although sometimes they will go hand in hand. But most of the time, the problems will not wait for you to fix them, and they will not be obvious.

The facts will be against you. You will tend to focus on the familiar and known. Monitoring tools will be skewed toward the easily quantifiable parameters, and most of the metrics will not be able to tell you about the internal mechanisms for most of your systems, which means that you will not be able to predict failures. However, if you invest time in resolving future problems through indirect observation and careful, step-by-step study of issues, you should be able to gain an upper hand over your environment woes. In the end, it is about minimizing the damage and gaining as much control as you can over your data center assets.

## REFERENCES

Autofs., 2014. Ubuntu documentation. <https://help.ubuntu.com/community/Autofs/> (accessed 2014)

Clarke, A.C., 1973. Profiles of the Future: An Inquiry into the Limits of the Possible, revised ed Harper & Row, s.l., New York City, U.S.

RFC 1813, 1995. NFS version 3 protocol specification. <http://tools.ietf.org/html/rfc1813> (accessed April 2015)

Transparent huge pages in 2.6.38, n.d. <https://lwn.net/Articles/423584/>

# The investigation begins

2

The first chapter gave us a mostly philosophical perspective on how one should approach problem solving in data centers. We begin our work with preconceptions and bias, and they often interfere with our judgment. Furthermore, it is all too easy to get hung up on conventions, established patterns and habits, and available numbers – and we deliberately avoid using the word data because it may imply the usefulness of these numbers – which can distract us from problem solving even more.

Now, we will give our investigation a more precise spin. We will apply the concepts we studied earlier and apply them to the actual investigation. In other words, while working through the steps of identification, isolation of the problem, causality, and changes in the environment, we want to be able to make educated guesses and reduce the randomness factor rather than just follow gut feelings or luck.

## ISOLATING THE PROBLEM

If you suspect there is an anomaly in your data center – and let us assume you have done all the preliminary investigation correctly and avoided the classic pitfalls – then your first step should be to migrate the problem from the production environment into an isolated test setup.

### MOVE FROM PRODUCTION TO TEST

There are several reasons why you would want to relocate your problem away from the production servers. The obvious one is that you want to minimize damage. The more important one, as far as problem solving goes, is to be able to investigate the issue at leisure.

The production environment comes with dozens, maybe hundreds of variables, all of which affect the possible outcome of software execution, and you may not be able to control or change most of them, including business considerations, permissions, and other restrictions. On the other hand, in a test setup, you have far more freedom, which can help you disqualify possible reasons and narrow down the investigation.

For example, if you think there might be a problem with your remote login software, you cannot just simply turn it off, since you could affect your customers. In a laboratory environment or a sandbox, you can very easily manipulate the components.

Naturally, this means your test environment should mimic the production setup to a high degree. Sometimes, there will be parameters you might not be able to reproduce.

**17**

For instance, scalability problems that manifest themselves when running a particular software application on thousands of servers may never be observed in a small replica with a handful of hosts. The same goes for network connectivity and high-performance workloads. Still, inherent bugs in software and configurations will still occur, and you can then work toward finding the root cause, and possibly the fix.

## RERUN THE MINIMAL SET NEEDED TO GET RESULTS

In some cases, your problems will be trivial local runs, without any special dependences. On other occasions, you will have to troubleshoot third-party software running in a distributed manner across dozens of servers, with network file system access, software license leases across the WAN, dependences on hundreds of shared libraries, and other factors. In theory, this means you will have to meet all these conditions in your test setup just to test the customer tools and debug the problem. This will rarely be feasible. Few organizations have the capacity, both financial and technical, to maintain test settings that are comparable in scale and operation to the production environments.

This means you will have to try to reduce your problem by eliminating all noncritical components. For instance, if you see that a problem happens both during a local run and one where data are read from a remote file server, then your test load does not need to include the setup of an expensive and complex file server. Likewise, if the problem manifests itself on multiple hardware models, you can exclude the platform component and focus on a single server type.

In the end, you want to be able to rerun your customer tools with the fewest number of variables. First, it is cheaper and faster. Second, you will have far fewer potential suspects to examine and analyze later on, as you progress with your investigation. If you narrow down the scope to just a single factor, your solution or workaround will also be far easier to construct. Sometimes, if you are really lucky with your methodical approach, the very process of partitioning the problem phase space and isolating the issue to a minimal set will present you with the root cause and the solution.

## IGNORE BIASED INFORMATION; AVOID ASSUMPTIONS

We go back to what we learned in Chapter 1. If you ever witness yourself in a situation in which the flow of information begins with sentences such as *I heard that* or *They told me* or *It was always like that*, you will immediately know that you are on the wrong track. People seek the familiar and shun the unknown. People like to dabble in what they know and have seen before, and they will do everything, subconsciously, to confirm and strengthen their beliefs. Throw in the work pressure, tight timetables, confusion of the workplace, and the business impact, and you will be more than glad to proclaim the root cause even if you have done very little to prove it with real numbers.

Assumptions are not always wrong. But, they must be based on evidence. To give you a crude example, you cannot say there is a problem with the system memory (whatever that means), unless you have a good understanding of how the operating system kernel and its memory management facility works, how the hardware works, or how the actual workload supposed to be running on the system behaves – even if the problem supposedly manifests itself in high memory usage or any one monitor that flags the system memory figures as a potential culprit. Remember what we learned about monitoring tools?

Monitoring tools will be skewed toward the easily quantifiable parameters, and most of the metrics will not be able to tell you about the internal mechanisms for most of your systems, which means that you will not be able to predict failures. Monitoring is mostly reactive, and at best, it will confirm a change in what you perceive as a normal state, but not *why* it has changed. In this case, memory, if at all relevant, is a symptom of something bigger.

But assumptions are the very first thing people will do, drawing on their past experience and work stress. To help themselves decide, system administrators will use opinionated pieces of information, which also means very partial data sets, to determine the next step in problem solving. Often as not, these kinds of actions will be detrimental to the fast, efficient success of your investigation.

If you have worked in the IT sector, the following examples will sound familiar. Someone reports a problem, you open the system log, and you flag the first error or warning you see. Someone reports an issue with a particular server model, and you remember something vaguely similar from the last month, when half a dozen servers of the same model had a different problem. The system CPU usage is 453% above the threshold, and you think this is bad, and not how it should be for the current workload running on the host. An application struggles loading data from a database located on the network file system; it is a network file system problem.

All of these could be true, but the logic flow needs to be embedded in facts and numbers. Often, there will be too many of them, so you need to narrow it down to a humanly manageable set rather than make hasty decisions. Now, let us learn a few tricks for how you can indeed achieve these goals and form your investigation on information and assumptions that are highly focused and accurate.

## COMPARISON TO A HEALTHY SYSTEM AND KNOWN REFERENCES

Since production environments can be extremely complex and problem manifestation can be extremely convoluted, you need to try to reduce your problem to a minimum set. We mentioned this earlier, but there are several more conditions that you can meet to make your problem solving even more efficient.

### IT IS NOT A BUG, IT IS A FEATURE

Sometimes, the problem you are seeing might not actually be a problem, just an inherently counterintuitive way the system or one of its components behaves. You may not like it, or you may find it less productive or optimal than you want, or have seen in the past with similar systems, but it does not change the fact you are observing an entirely normal phenomenon.

In situations such as these, you will need to accept the situation, or work strategically toward resolving the problem in a way that the undesired behavior does not come to bear. But, it is critical that you understand and accept the system's idiosyncrasies. Otherwise, you may spend a whole lot of time trying to resolve something that needs no resolution.

Let us examine the following scenario. Your data center relies on centralized access to a network file system using the automounter mechanism. The infrastructure is set in such a way that autofs mounts, when not in use, are supposed to expire after 4 hours. This used to work well on an older, legacy version of the supported operating system in use in the environment. However, moving to version + 1 leads to a situation in which autofs paths are not expiring as often as you are used to. At a first glance, this looks like a problem.

However, a deeper examination of the autofs behavior and its documentation as well as consultation with the operating system vendors and its experts reveals the following information:

```
The timeout option specifies how long autofs will wait before trying to unmount a
volume. The default timeout is 600 seconds, or 10 minutes. Every $TIMEOUT/4 seconds,
autofs checks whether the volume is being used and updates the expiration timer
accordingly.

On the legacy version of the operating system, the expiration check queries the
kernel whether the mount point can be unmounted at the exact moment the check is
done. If there are processes (at least one) holding an open file or have current
working directory set to that mount point, there will be no expiration. The volume
will be marked as effectively busy, and autofs will reset the expiration time.

On the new version of the operating system, the expiration check is much broader.
Among other features, the system knows exactly when the volume was last accessed, and
it does not need to be busy at the time of the check for the timer to be reset. Every
file access will cause a reset of the timeout.

As a practical example, consider the following. Suppose /nfs is an automounted volume
with a timeout of 60 seconds and that /nfs/file is a regular text file. If you run
the following command:

$ while true; do cat /nfs/file; sleep 5; done

On the legacy systems, you will note that that approximately 60 seconds after /nfs
was mounted, it will be unmounted, regardless of the multiple accesses to /nfs/file.
A few seconds after the unmount, the cat command will trigger the mount again.
However, on the new version of the operating system, you will notice that as long as
the command is running, the volume will NOT be unmounted. To sum it up, on the new
system, expiration of mount points are less likely to happen. Expiration only happens
when no access to files or directories inside the mount point happened during
$TIMEOUT seconds. With long timeouts, like the 4-hour period mentioned earlier, it is
highly unlikely that something won't access the mount during that time and reset the
timer.
```

From this example, we clearly see how problem solving and investigation, if we ignore the basic premise of feature versus bug, could lead to a significant effort in trying to fix something that is not broken in the first place.

## COMPARE EXPECTED RESULTS TO A HEALTHY SYSTEM

The subtle matter of problem ambiguity means that potentially, many resources can be wasted just trying to understand where you stand, even before you start a detailed, step-by-step investigation. Therefore, it is crucial that you establish a clear baseline for what your standard should be.

If you have systems that exhibit expected, normal behavior, you can treat them as a control in your investigation and compare suspected, problematic systems to them across a range of critical parameters. This will help you understand the scope of the problem, the severity, and maybe determine whether you have a problem in the first place. Remember, the environment setup may flag a certain change in the monitored metrics as a potential anomaly, but that does not necessarily mean that there is a systematic problem. Moreover, being able to compare your existing performance and system health to an older baseline is an extremely valuable capability, which should help you maintain awareness and control of your environment.

This could be pass/fail criteria metrics, system reboot counts, a number of kernel crashes in your environment, total uptime, or maybe the performance of important critical applications, normalized to the hardware. If you have reference values, you can then determine if you have a problem, and whether you need to invest time in trying to find the root cause. This will allow you not only to more accurately mark instantaneous deviations, but also to find trends and long-term issues in your environment.

## PERFORMANCE AND BEHAVIOR REFERENCES ARE A MUST

Indeed, statistics can be a valuable asset in large, complex environments such as data centers. With so many interacting components, finding the right mathematical formula for precise monitoring and problem resolution can be extremely difficult. However, you can normalize the behavior of your systems by looking at them from the perspective of what you perceive to be a normal state and then by comparing it to one or more parameters.

Performance will often serve as a key indicator. If your applications are running fine, and they complete successfully and within the expected time envelope, then you can be fairly sure that your environment, as a whole, is healthy and functioning well. But then, there are other important, behavioral metrics. Does your system exhibit an unusual number, lower or higher than expected, of pass/fail tests like availability of service on the network, known and unknown reboots, and the like? Again, if you have a baseline, and you have acceptable margins, as long as your systems fall within this scope, you have a sane environment. However, that does not mean individual systems are not going to exhibit problems now and then. But you can correlate the current state to a known snapshot, as well as take into account your other metrics from the monitoring system. If you avoid hasty assumptions and hearsay and try to isolate and rerun problems in a simple, thorough manner, you will narrow down and improve your investigation.

## LINEAR VERSUS NONLINEAR RESPONSE TO CHANGES

Unfortunately, you will not always find it easy to debug problems. We already know that the world will be against you. Time, money, resource constraints, insufficient and misleading data, old habits, wrong assumptions, and user habits are only a few out of many factors that will stand in your way. But it gets worse. Some problems, even if properly flagged by your monitoring systems, will exhibit nonlinear behavior, which means we need to proceed with extra caution.

### ONE VARIABLE AT A TIME

If you have to troubleshoot a system, and you have already isolated the leading culprits, you will now need to make certain changes to prove and disprove your theories. One way is to simply make a whole bunch of adjustments and measure the system response. A much better way is to tweak a single parameter at a time. With the first method, if nothing happens, you are probably okay, and you can move on to the next set of values, but if you see a change in the behavior, you will not know which of the many components contributes to the response, in what degree, and if there is interaction between different pieces.

### PROBLEMS WITH LINEAR COMPLEXITY

Linear problems are fun. You change your input by a certain fraction, and the response changes proportionally. Linear problems are relatively easy to spot and troubleshoot. Unfortunately, they will be a minority of cases you encounter in the environment.

However, if you do see issues where the response is linearly related to the inputs, you should invest time in carefully studying and documenting them, as well as trying to create a mathematical formula that maps the problem and the solutions. It will help you in the long run, and maybe even allow you to establish a baseline that can serve, indirectly, to look for other, more complex problems.

### NONLINEAR PROBLEMS

Most of the time, you will struggle finding an easy correlation between a change in a system state and the expected outcome. For instance, how does latency affect the performance of an application? What is the correlation between CPU utilization and runtime? What is the correlation between memory usage and system failures? How does disk space usage affect the server response times?

The correlation may or may not exist. Even if it does, it might be difficult to reduce to numbers. Worse yet, you will not be able to easily establish acceptable work margins because the system might seemingly suddenly spin out of control.

Troubleshooting nonlinear problems will mostly involve understanding the triggers that lead to their manifestation rather than mitigating the symptoms. Nonlinear problems will also force you to think innovatively because they could come to bear in strange and seemingly indirect ways. Later on, we will learn a variety of methods that could help you control the situation.

## RESPONSE MAY BE DELAYED OR MASKED

In Chapter 1, we discussed about the manifestation of problems, wrong conclusions, and problems with reactive monitoring. We focused on one of the great shortcomings of monitoring, which is the fact that we do not always fully understand the systems, and therefore, we invest a lot of energy in trying to follow known patterns and alerting when system metrics deviate from normal thresholds, rather than resolving the problems at their source.

The issue is compounded by the fact that response may be delayed. A change today may only come to bear negatively only in large numbers, after a long time. The change might affect the system immediately, but it may not be apparent because the tools might be accurate enough, they might capture the wrong metrics, or there is some other, more acute problem taking all of the efforts.

Effectively, this means that you cannot really make changes in a system unless you know what the response ought to be – not necessarily its magnitude, but its type. Moreover, this also means that the usual approach of problem solving, from input to output, is not very good for complex environments such as data centers. There are better ways to achieve leads in the investigation, especially when dealing with nonlinear problems.

## Y TO X RATHER THAN X TO Y

The concept of focusing your investigation starting with the effect and then going back to the cause rather than the other way around is not the typical, well-accepted methodology in the industry, especially not in the information technology.

Normally, problem solving focuses on possible factors that may affect outcome, they are tweaked in some often arbitrary manner, and then the output is measured. However, because this can be quite complex, what most people do is make one change, run the test, write down the results, and repeat, with as many permutations as the system allows. This kind of process is slow and not very effective.

In contrast, statistical engineering offers a more reliable way of narrowing down the root cause by measuring the variance in response. The idea is to look for the one parameter that causes the greatest change, even if there are dozens of parameters involved, allowing you to simplify your understanding of complex systems.

Unfortunately, while it has shown great merit in the manufacturing sector, it is yet to gain significant traction in the data center. There are many justifications to this, the chief one being the assumption that software and its outputs cannot be as easily quantified as the variation in pressure in an oil pump or the width of a cutting tool in a factory somewhere.

However, the reality is more favorable. Software and hardware obey the same statistical laws as everything else, and you can apply statistical engineering to data center elements with the same basic principles as you do with metal bearings, stamping machines, or cinder blocks. We will discuss this at greater length in Chapter 7.

## COMPONENT SEARCH

Another method to help isolate your problem is through the use of component search. The general idea is to swap parts between the supposedly good and bad systems. Normally, this method applies to mechanical systems, with thousands of components, but it can also be used in the software and hardware world. Good and bad systems or parts can also be applied to application versions, configurations, or server setups. Again, we will discuss this subset of statistical engineering in more detail in Chapter 7.

## CONCLUSIONS

This chapter hones the basic art of problem solving and investigation by focusing on the common pitfalls that you may encounter in your investigation. Namely, we tried to address the concerns and challenges with problem isolation, containment and reproduction, how and when to rerun the test case with the least number of variables, a methodical approach to changes and measurement of the expected outcome, as well as how to cope with problems that do not have a clear, linear manifestation. Last, we introduced industry methods, which should greatly aid us later in this book.

# Basic investigation

## 3

## PROFILE THE SYSTEM STATUS

Previous chapters have taught us the necessary models when approaching what may appear to be a problem in our environment. The idea is to carefully isolate the problem, reduce it to a minimal set of variables, and then use industry-accepted methods to prove and disprove your theories. Now, we will learn about the tools that can help us in our quest.

## ENVIRONMENT MONITORS

Typically, data center hosts are configured to periodically report their health to a central console, using some kind of a client–server setup. Effectively, this means you do have an initial warning system to potential issues.

However, in Chapter 1, if you recall, we disclaimed the usefulness of existing monitors. We challenged you to always question the status quo and search for new, more useful, and accurate ways of watching and controlling the environment. At the moment though, at the very beginning of your problem-solving journey, your initial assumption should be that this mechanism provides valuable information, even though the monitoring facility may be old, ineffective, may not be as scalable as you would like, may be slow to react, and may suffer from many other failings. At the moment, it is your gateway to problems.

The first indication to a perturbation in the environment does not necessarily mean there is a problem, but someone in the support team should examine and acknowledge the exception raised by the monitoring system. The severity and classification of the alert will direct your problem solving. Regardless, it should always begin with simple, basic tools.

## MACHINE ACCESSIBILITY, RESPONSIVENESS, AND UPTIME

Data center servers are, after all, as their name implies, a service point, and they need to be accessible. Even if the initial alert does not indicate problems with accessibility, you should check that normal ways of connection work. This may be a certain process running and responding normally to queries, the ability to get metrics from a service, and more.

Timely response is also critical. If you expect to receive an answer to your command within a certain period of time – and this means it must be defined beforehand – then you should also check this parameter. Last, you may want to examine the server load and correlate its activity to expected results.

The simplest Linux command that achieves all these checks is the uptime (Uptime, n.d.) command. Executed remotely, often through SSH (M. Joseph, 2013), uptime will collect and report the system load, how long the system has been running, and the number of users currently logged on.

```
ssh myhost12 uptime

09:47am  up 60 days 21:00,  12 users,  load average: 0.06, 0.03, 0.05
```

Let us briefly examine the output of the command. The *up* value is useful if you need to correlate the system runtime with the expected environment availability. For instance, if you rebooted all your servers in the last week, and a host reports an uptime of 41 days, you may assume that this particular host – and probably others – may not have been included in the operation. For instance, this can be important if you installed security patches or a new kernel, and they required a reboot to take effect.

The number of logged-on users is valuable if you can correlate it to an expected threshold. For example, a VNC server that ought not to have more than 20 users utilizing its resources could suddenly be overloaded with more than 50 active logins, and it could be suffering from a degraded performance.

The system load (Wikipedia, n.d., the free encyclopedia) is a very interesting set of figures. Load is a measure of amount of computational work that a system performs, with average values for the last one, 5, and 15 minutes displayed in the output, from right to left. On their own, these numbers have no meaning whatsoever, except to show you a possible trend in the increase or decrease of workload in the last 15 minutes.

Analyzing load figures requires the system administrator to be familiar with several key concepts, namely the number of running processes on a host, as well as its hardware configuration.

A completely idle system has a load number of 0.00. Each process using or waiting for CPU increments the load number by 1. In other words, a load amount of 1.00 translates into full utilization of a single CPU core. Therefore, if a system has eight CPU cores, and the relevant average load value is 6.74, this means there is free computation capacity available. On the other hand, the same load value on a host with just two cores probably indicates an overload. But it gets more complicated.

High load values do not necessarily translate into actual workload. Instead, they indicate the average number of processes that waited for CPU, as well as processes in the uninterruptible sleep state (D state) (Rusling, 1999). In other words, processes waiting for I/O activity, usually disk or network, will also show in the load average numbers, even though there may be little to no actual CPU activity. Finally, the exact nature of the workload on the host will determine whether the load numbers should be a cause of concern.

For the first-level support team, the uptime command output is a good initial indicator whether the alert ought to be investigated in greater depth. If the SSH command takes a very long time to return or times out, or perhaps the number of users on a host is very high, and the load numbers do not match the expected work profile for the particular system, additional checks may be needed.

## LOCAL AND REMOTE LOGIN AND MANAGEMENT CONSOLE

At this point, you might want to log in to the server and run further checks. Connecting locally means you have physical access to the host, and you do not need an active network connection to do that. In data centers, this is pretty uncommon, and this method is mostly used by technicians working inside data center rooms.

A more typical way of system troubleshooting is to perform a remote login, often through SSH. Sometimes, virtual network computing (VNC) (Richardson, 2010) may also be used. Other protocols exist, and they may be in use in your environment.

```
ssh testhost04

**************************************************************************

*  Welcome to Data Center

*  Use of this system by UNAUTHORIZED persons or in an UNAUTHORIZED manner

*  is strictly prohibited.

**************************************************************************

INFO: your password will expire in 54 days.

testhost04>
```

If standard methods of connecting to a server do not work, you may want to use the server management console. Most modern enterprise hardware comes with a powerful management facility, with extensive capabilities. These systems allow power regulation, firmware updates, controlling entire racks of servers, and health and status monitoring. They often come with a virtual serial port console, a Web GUI, and a command-line interface.

This means you can effectively log in to a server from a remote location as if you were working locally, and you do not need to rely on network and directory service for a successful login attempt. The Web GUI runs through browsers and requires plugins such as Adobe Flash Player, Microsoft Silverlight, or Oracle Java to work properly. Moreover, you do need to have some kind of a local account credentials, often root, to be able to log in and work on the server.

## THE MONITOR THAT CRIED WOLF

While working on your problems, it is important to pause, step back, and evaluate your work. Sometimes, you may discover that you are on a wild-goose chase, and that your investigations are not bearing any fruit. This could indicate you may be doing all the wrong things. But, it may also point to a problem in your setup. Since your work begins with environment monitors, you should examine those also. As we have mentioned in the previous chapters, event thresholds need to reflect the reality and not define it. In complex scenarios, monitors can often become outdated, but they may remain in the environment and continue alerting, even long after the original problem for which the monitor was conceived in the first place, or the symptom thereof, has been eliminated. In this case, you will be trying to resolve a nonexistent problem by responding to false alarms. Therefore, whenever your investigation ends up in a dead end, you should ask yourself a couple of questions. Is your methodology correct? Is there a real problem at hand?

## READ THE SYSTEM MESSAGES AND LOGS

To help you answer these two questions, let us dig deeper into system analysis. A successful login indicates a noncatastrophic error, for the time being, and you may continue working for a while. It may quickly escalate into a system crash, a hardware failure, or some similar situation, which is why you should be decisive, collect information for an offline analysis if needed, copy all relevant logs and data files, record your activity, even as a side note in a text file, and make sure your work can be followed and reproduced by other people.

## USING PS AND TOP

Two very useful tools for analysis system behavior are the ps (ps(1), n.d.) and top (top(1), n.d.) commands. They may sound trivial, and experienced system administrators may disregard them as newbie tools, but they can offer a wealth of information if used properly. To illustrate, let us examine a typical system out for the top command.

```
top - 11:22:45 up 377 days,  1:15,  1 user,  load average: 40.58, 43.24, 47.23

Tasks: 643 total,  23 running, 620 sleeping,  0 stopped,  0 zombie

Cpu(s):  0.4%us,  1.5%sy, 47.8%ni, 44.5%id,  5.8%wa,  0.0%hi,  0.0%si,  0.0%st

Mem:   258313M total,   45281M used,   213032M free,    960M buffers

Swap:  457830M total,    1629M used,  456200M free,   21540M cached



  PID USER      PR  NI  VIRT  RES  SHR S  %CPU %MEM    TIME+  COMMAND

11209 igor      39  19 1354m 1.1g 102m R   142  0.4  5:28.40 dd_exit

33193 igor      39  19 1532m 1.1g 217m R    99  0.4 26:32.21 java

34818 david     39  19 1530m 1.1g 217m R    99  0.4 25:47.12 engine.bin
```

The top program provides a dynamic real-time view of a running system. The view is refreshed every 3 seconds by default, although users can control the parameter.

Moreover, the command can be executed in a batch mode, so the activity can be logged and parsed later on.

Top can display user-configurable system summary information, as well as a list of tasks currently being managed by the Linux kernel. Some of the output looks familiar, namely the uptime and load figures, which we have seen earlier.

Tasks – this field lists the total number of tasks (processes) on the system. Typically, most processes will be sleeping, and a certain percentage will be running (or runnable). The number may not necessarily reflect the load value. Processes that have been actively stopped or are being traced (like with strace or gdb, which we will see later) will show as the third field. The fourth file refers to zombie (Herber, 1995) processes, an interesting phenomenon in the UNIX/Linux world.

Zombies are defunct processes that have died (finished running) but still remain as an entry in the process table and will only be deleted when the parent process that has spawned them collects its exit status. Sometimes, though, malformed scripts and programs, often written by system administrators themselves, may leave zombies behind. Although not harmful in effect, they do indicate a problem with one of the tasks that has been executed on the system. In theory, a very large number of zombie processes could completely fill in the process table, but this is not a limitation on modern 64-bit systems. Nevertheless, if you are investigating a problem and encounter many zombies, you might want to inform your colleagues or check your own software, to make sure you are not creating a problem of your own.

CPU(s) – this line offers a wealth of useful indicators on the system behavior. The usage of the available cores is divided based on the type of CPU activity. Computation done in the user space is marked under %us. The percentage of system calls activity is listed under %sy.

A proportion of niced (nice(1), n.d.) processes, that is, processes with a modified scheduling priority, show under %ni. Users may decide that some of their tasks ought to run with adjustness niceness, which could affect the performance and runtime of the program.

I/O activity, both disk and network, is reflected in the %wa figure. The CPU wait time is an indication of storage and network throughput, and as we explained before, it may directly affect the load and responsiveness of a host even though actual CPU computation might be low.

Hardware and software interrupts are marked with %hi and %si. The importance of these two values is beyond the scope of this book, and for most part, users will rarely if ever have to handle problems related to these mechanisms. The last field, %st, refers to time stolen by the hypervisor from virtual machines, and as such, it is only relevant in virtualized environments.

As a rule of thumb, very high %sy values often indicate a problem in the kernel space. For instance, there may be significant memory thrashing, a driver may be misbehaving, or there may be a hardware problem with one of the components. Having a very high percentage of niced processes can also be an indicator of a problem, because there could be contention for resources due to user-skewed priority. If you encounter %wa values above %10, it is often an indication of a performance-related problem, which could be slow response from a remote file system, network congestion, much local disk activity due to large amounts of write requests or swapping, and similar issues.

Mem and Swap lines are pretty straightforward. They tell us the current usage of the memory subsystem. However, some of the values may be a little misleading.

- Free – free memory in the virtual memory.
- Buffers – pages used for in-memory block device I/O buffers.
- Cached – page cache, containing dirty pages that need to be written to disk and the pages used in recent read requests. Although the cache size may be very large, it will shrink if a running program requests additional memory. Therefore, for all practical purposes, users may treat cached memory as free memory.

An exercise that can emphasize this important distinction is to drop all caches (Hansen, 2009). This action may take some time to complete, as the system will be busy committing changes to disk. For instance:

```
echo 3 > /proc/sys/vm/drop_caches
```

An alternative way to emphasize the caching mechanism is to download, compile, and run the memhog (Reber, n.d.) program. This little tool will use an amount of memory specified on the command line and then subsequently free it. If you run the tool with a value very close to the actual size of the physical memory, after it completes running and exits, you will see that the size of the cache will have shrunk considerably.

```
./memhog 2048M

hogging 2048 MB: 20 40 60 80 100 120 140 160 180 200 220 240 260 280 300 320 340 360
380 400 420 440 460 480 500 520 540 560 580 600 620 640 660 680 700 720 740 760 780
800 820 840 860 880 900 920 940 960 980 1000 1020 1040 1060 1080 1100 1120 1140 1160
1180 1200 1220 1240 1260 1280 1300 1320 1340 1360 1380 1400 1420 1440 1460 1480 1500
1520 1540 1560 1580 1600 1620 1640 1660 1680 1700 1720 1740 1760 1780 1800 1820 1840
1860 1880 1900 1920 1940 1960 1980 2000 2020 2040 2048
```

Swap usage reflects the same idea, except it refers to the swap mechanism, if enabled on the system. Again, like all other fields, you must analyze the information within the context of your situation and/or problem. For instance, there might be a lot of free memory available on the host, and yet your system could be using swap, which might lead to a performance degradation, or at the very least, question regarding the system use.

This is because the swapping policy depends on the swappiness ratio, defined in the virtual memory subsystem, under the /proc pseudo-filesystem. Indeed, the top command gathers its information from the /proc tree. Earlier, we mentioned memory usage, which we can also obtain by printing the memory info to the standard out. We will discuss this in the subsequent chapters.

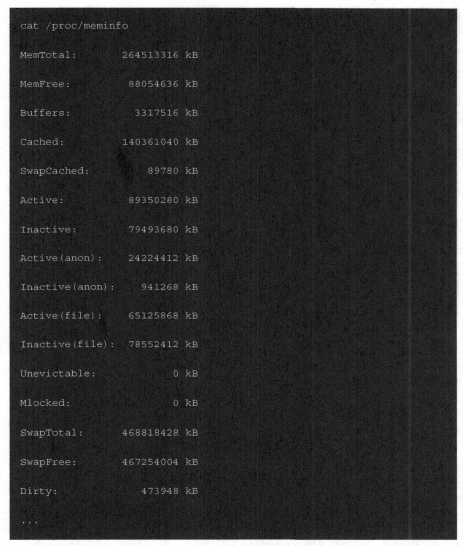

```
cat /proc/meminfo

MemTotal:         264513316 kB

MemFree:           88054636 kB

Buffers:            3317516 kB

Cached:           140361040 kB

SwapCached:           89780 kB

Active:            89350280 kB

Inactive:          79493680 kB

Active(anon):      24224412 kB

Inactive(anon):      941268 kB

Active(file):      65125868 kB

Inactive(file):    78552412 kB

Unevictable:              0 kB

Mlocked:                  0 kB

SwapTotal:        468818428 kB

SwapFree:         467254004 kB

Dirty:               473948 kB

...
```

The default display of top-hitting processes contains additional useful information, including the username under which the task runs, priority, nice value, the requested memory allocation, real usage, shared memory, process state, percentage of CPU, percentage of total available physical memory, CPU time, and a short command line. These fields can be changed using the –f switch while working in the interactive mode, as shown in Fig. 3.1.

At a glance, the displayed list can give an indication of potential issues or bottlenecks. You may see that certain processes may be using too much memory or CPU,

```
Current Fields: AEHIOQTWKNMbcdfgjplrsuvyz{|X  for window 1:Def
Toggle fields via field letter, type any other key to return

* A: PID       = Process Id             0x00000002  PF_STARTING
* E: USER      = User Name              0x00000004  PF_EXITING
* H: PR        = Priority               0x00000040  PF_FORKNOEXEC
* I: NI        = Nice value             0x00000100  PF_SUPERPRIV
* O: VIRT      = Virtual Image (kb)     0x00000200  PF_DUMPCORE
* Q: RES       = Resident size (kb)     0x00000400  PF_SIGNALED
* T: SHR       = Shared Mem size (kb)   0x00000800  PF_MEMALLOC
* W: S         = Process Status         0x00002000  PF_FREE_PAGES (2.5)
* K: %CPU      = CPU usage              0x00008000  debug flag (2.5)
* N: %MEM      = Memory usage (RES)     0x00024000  special threads (2.5)
* M: TIME+     = CPU Time, hundredths   0x001D0000  special states (2.5)
  b: PPID      = Parent Process Pid     0x00100000  PF_USEDFPU (thru 2.4)
  c: RUSER     = Real user name
  d: UID       = User Id
  f: GROUP     = Group Name
  g: TTY       = Controlling Tty
  j: P         = Last used cpu (SMP)
  p: SWAP      = Swapped size (kb)
  l: TIME      = CPU Time
  r: CODE      = Code size (kb)
  s: DATA      = Data+Stack size (kb)
  u: nFLT      = Page Fault count
  v: nDRT      = Dirty Pages count
  y: WCHAN     = Sleeping in Function
  z: Flags     = Task Flags <sched.h>
  {: Badness   = oom_score (badness)
  |: Adj       = oom_adjustment (2^X)
* X: COMMAND   = Command name/line

Flags field:
  0x00000001  PF_ALIGNWARN
```

**FIGURE 3.1  Top Command Fields**

find processes which seem to be stuck looping without any progress, abnormal run-times, and other anomalies, which could further direct your investigation. A cursory check of the top output can help you narrow down the issue, which you can then explore using the ps command.

The top command comes with several useful switchers and shortcuts:

- -b – Run top in batch mode.
- -d – Change the refresh delay (default is 3 seconds).
- -u – Display only processes that match the given UID or username.
- -p – Monitor a comma-delimited list of up to 20 processes; this can be very useful if you suspect certain processes to be culprits of a system issue.
- -r – Renice a process with a matching PID. Positively values will decrease the process priority. Certain negative values may only be used by the root process, and standard users cannot renice processes that belong to others.
- -k – Kill a process with a matching PID. By default, SIGTERM is used.
- -q – Quit.

Summary area commands are also quite useful. They affect the way the information is displayed and can help you filter or sort the data. For instance, "t" will display processes based on their task state, "m" will display them in a top-down fashion based on memory and swap usage, "1" will toggle CPU information to show a single line for all cores, or display them individually. Sometimes, depending on the number of the processes and the size of the console screen, it might not be possible to show individual cores (e.g., cpu0, cpu1, and so forth), and you will have to use the single view instead.

Unlike top, which refreshes its view every few seconds and limits the display to top hitters, based on the applied filter the ps command dumps a snapshot of all running processes on a system in a single view.

The ps command is very interesting in that it accepts options in several notations, including BSD, UNIX, and GNU, which are nonprefixed, prefixed by a single dash, and prefixed by two dashes, respectively. Ps usage is straightforward. For instance, just to display every process on the system:

```
ps -ef
```

Alternatively, the BSD syntax can be used:

```
ps aux
```

The notable options include the following:

- -e|-A – Display all processes (everything).
- -u|--user – Display only tasks that belong to the listed UID.
- -p|--pid – Select a specific process by its identifier (PID).
- --ppid – Select by parent process.
- -o – User-specified format with space- or comma-delimited values. The following command ps -eo pid,tid,class,rtprio,ni,pri,psr,pcpu,stat,wchan:14,comm will return:

```
ps -eo pid,tid,class,rtprio,ni,pri,psr,pcpu,stat,wchan:14,comm

PID    TID CLS RTPRIO  NI PRI PSR %CPU STAT WCHAN          COMMAND

  1      1 TS       -   0  19  23  0.0 Ss   ?              init

  2      2 TS       -   0  19  36  0.0 S    kthreadd       kthreadd

  3      3 TS       -   0  19   0  0.0 S    run_ksoftirqd  ksoftirqd/0

  5      5 TS       -   0  19   8  0.0 S    worker_thread  kworker/u:0
```

```
   6      6 FF     99    - 139    0  0.0 S    cpu_stopper_th migration/0

   7      7 FF     99    - 139    0  0.0 S    watchdog       watchdog/0

   8      8 FF     99    - 139    1  0.0 S    cpu_stopper_th migration/1

  10     10 TS      -    0  19    1  0.0 S    run_ksoftirqd  ksoftirqd/1

  12     12 FF     99    - 139    1  0.0 S    watchdog       watchdog/1

  13     13 FF     99    - 139    2  0.0 S    cpu_stopper_th migration/2

...
```

The output contains an ascending list of processes, sorted by PID. The second column contains the thread ID, also known as lightweight processes (LWP). Rtprio refers to realtime priority, in this case. NI columns tell the niceness of the process, whereas the PRI column reports the dynamic priority. PSR is the processor number to which the task is currently assigned. We also get the percentage of CPU usage and the task state. WCHAN refers to the last kernel function the process was waiting on (wait channel), with the output set to 14 characters. For instance, this can be useful when debugging processes that seem to be stuck or stalled. Finally, we have the task command.

The BSD syntax is also quite useful. The default view provides information that is very similar to the UNIX output, but there are some interesting differences. The columns VSZ and RSS report the virtual memory size and resident set size, similar to the top command. The STAT column shows a multicharacter process state for each displayed PID. The list of available states is quite extensive. For instance, "s" refers to section leaders, "N" is used for processes with lowered priority (N), "l" means the process is multithreaded, and so forth.

START shows the time the command was started, with only the year reported if the process was launched in the previous year. The COMMAND field shows the process command line, up to the maximum width of the print buffer, which is normally the standard output. Kernel threads are marked in square braces, and they will have zero values for memory and CPU usage.

```
ps aux

USER       PID %CPU %MEM   VSZ   RSS TTY      STAT START   TIME COMMAND

root         1  0.0  0.0 10540   112 ?        Ss   2014    6:51 init [3]

root         2  0.0  0.0     0     0 ?        S    2014    0:28 [kthreadd]
```

```
root          3  0.0  0.0      0     0 ?      S     2014 156:02 [ksoftirqd/0]

root          5  0.0  0.0      0     0 ?      S     2014   0:14 [kworker/u:0]

root          6  0.0  0.0      0     0 ?      S     2014 263:50 [migration/0]

...

root       2161  0.3  0.0      0     0 ?      S     01:01   1:44 [kworker/10:1]

igor       2368  0.0  0.0   4612  2396 ?      SN    09:04   0:00 /nfs/process.bin

igor       2787  0.0  0.0   4616  2400 ?      SN    09:25   0:00 /nfs/process.bin

root       5226  0.0  0.0      0     0 ?      S     2014  15:29 [kworker/28:1]

root       5289  0.0  0.0   4004   184 ?      Ss    2014   0:00 /sbin/acpid

100        5302  0.0  0.0  47944  6396 ?      Ss    2014   0:59 /bin/dbus-daemon

...
```

There is no hard and fast rule as to what the ps command ought to tell you about your system behavior. The information must always be taken within the context of the possible problem or symptom you are analyzing. Sometimes, very high memory usage might be acceptable, and other times, it will be the source of your problem. The same applies to CPU utilization, process state, and other parameters.

At the beginning of your investigation, you should consult the top and ps output for anomalies and then narrow down your search. Moreover, it is possible that these commands will not give you the clues you require, and you will have to extend your work.

## SYSTEM LOGS

The next logical step in troubleshooting is to check and read system logs. There are many available log types, formats, and filenames, some of which are system-wide and others are process-specific. The default location for log is under /var/log, and you may need root permissions to check some of these. Others may be world-readable. Some applications may store their own files in custom locations outside the /var partition, or may require logging to be enabled manually. The standard system log will typically be either /var/log/messages or /var/log/syslog.

Working with system logs is a double-edged sword. On one hand, you might find indicators to problems bugging your system. On the other hand, you may find instances of possible errors that are not related to the issue you are facing. Moreover, some of the entries may appear error-like, but they might be misleading, and they could detract you from the actual investigation.

It is important not to look in the log for the sake of looking. Often, there will be errors showing up in the messages, and their timestamps will sometimes almost too coincidentally correlate to environment issues. However, this does not necessarily mean the two are indeed linked, and you should avoid any hasty assumption just based on a cursory glance in the log.

The flow of your investigation should be evidence driven. You should postulate a theory based on initial data, expand the checks to create additional dimensions of understanding, propose a solution, and then test whether your idea is correct. This means that you should look in the logs only after you have a solid idea of what to look for. Let us examine two distinct log sections.

```
Sep  9 22:28:21 test01 automount[3619]: attempting to mount entry /nfs/disks/checks

Sep  9 22:28:21 test01 automount[3619]: attempting to mount entry /nfs/disks/sh

Sep  9 22:28:21 test01 automount[3619]: lookup(program): lookup for sh failed

Sep  9 22:28:21 test01 automount[3619]: failed to mount /nfs/disks/sh

Sep  9 22:28:21 test01 automount[3619]: mounted /nfs/disks/checks
```

The excerpt from the messages shows an automount lookup failure for an NFS disk. Let us say this issue occurred at about the same time one of your customers reported slow access to their shared worked area.

At this point, in a moment of haste, despair, and confusion, you might decide there is a problem with the automounter service, and that this is somehow related. After all, your environment is configured with NFS and autofs access. But remember, investigations should be data driven. Is the customer work area located on the same disk as the one that shows the error? More importantly, what does the lookup error mean? Can it be related to what your customer has reported? For instance, slow access implies a possible performance issue, network latency, or an internal problem with one of the customers' tools or utilities, whereas a lookup failure indicates there might not be an autofs map entry for the relevant path, which would result in no access at all, and the area would not be mounted. It might point to a completely different issue, but not the one you are initially trying to solve.

The second example is more meaningful. Let us say that you encounter it while going through the log, without any clear indication of a problem on the servicer side. You see this message on a virtual machine, which is located on SAN storage. The listed device (power2) corresponds to an SAN storage volume.

```
Dec 25 11:49:16 srv04 kernel: [664932.553083] EXT3-fs error (device power2):
ext3_lookup: deleted inode referenced: 147457

Dec 25 11:49:16 srv04 kernel: [664932.560319] EXT3-fs error (device power2):
ext3_lookup: deleted inode referenced: 147457
```

The message does not appear innocent, as it indicates a real problem with the filesystem, which could be a result of a serious hardware error. None of your monitors are alerting, and this means you should probably not invest any energy resolving this.

Half an hour later though, you get a call from the first-level support, informing you that one of the databases, running on that particular server and with the tables stored on the SAN device, has gone offline at about the same time the EXT3-fs error messages started showing up. All of a sudden, the entries are meaningful, and you know what to do, but then you might have been able to prevent damage or downtime if you had responded early enough.

This example goes against the basic principle of data-driven investigation, because there was no investigation when you encountered the data, and yet it is clearly related to a big system problem. The solution in this case is to improve the monitoring facility rather than change problem-solving methods. In fact, whenever you encounter a gap in the way you work, you should examine your situational awareness stack and make changes so that you get meaningful data earlier, and if possible, identify problems on lower levels than those currently monitored and checked.

If the default view does not provide any useful information, and you are certain there might be a problem with one of the running services, you might want to consider briefly increasing the verbosity of the output.

In general, you probably do not want to change the logging policy on the server. But, you can alter the way services report their information to the system log. Using NFS as an example, if you are troubleshooting an issue that seems to be related to network storage, you might increase the debug level of the NFS service or client for a while, collect additional information, and then restore the values to their original state. For instance:

```
echo 32767 > /proc/sys/sunrpc/nfs_debug

echo 32767 > /proc/sys/sunrpc/nfs_debug
```

Working under /proc and making immediate changes to the system behavior is a very useful way of trying to isolate problems, as well as test scenarios that can improve performance and stability. We will discuss that in the next chapter.

Another useful log is /var/log/kernellog. This file contains messages printed by the kernel since reboot, and it is equivalent to the data provided by the dmesg command, with one notable exception; you also get timestamps, which are extremely useful in correlating problems.

Kernel messages are even more cryptic and potentially misleading than the system log. Some of the printed information may not make much sense, and you should avoid trying to decipher it unless you are handling a problem.

```
Jun 22 14:26:17 appsrv5 kernel: ACPI: Power Button (FF) [PWRF]

Jun 22 14:26:17 appsrv5 kernel: No dock devices found.

Jun 22 14:26:17 appsrv5 kernel: bnx2x: eth0: using MSI-X  IRQs: sp 130  fp 138

Jun 22 14:26:17 appsrv5 kernel: JBD: barrier-based sync failed on /dev/sda5 -
disabling barriers
```

Likewise, programs may crash, and the instance might be registered in the kernel log. This can be useful when trying to analyze an application issue. We will examine this later.

```
Nov 27 16:41:04 appsrv5 kernel: tcsh[23566] trap divide error rip:424b4e
rsp:7fffffffcb160 error:0


...

Dec  7 14:06:32 appsrv5 kernel: node[17387] trap divide error rip:2aaaaaab382f
rsp:7fffffffdec0 error:0
```

Sometimes, the information will be valuable and highly relevant to environment-related alerts and problem reports. For example, a network outage is clearly evident in the kernel log, because the server is struggling trying to establish a connection with several servers. Later on, the problem is resolved. The actual manifestation of the issue may be customer complaints of unresponsive applications, slowness, and more.

```
Sep  7 05:09:27 vnc4 kernel: nfs: server nfs5b not responding, still trying

Sep  7 05:09:27 vnc4 kernel: nfs: server 10.184.132.151 not responding, still trying

Sep  7 05:09:27 vnc4 kernel: nfs: server 10.184.132.115 not responding, still trying

Sep  7 05:12:35 vnc4 kernel: nfs: server nfs44c OK

Sep  7 05:12:36 vnc4 kernel: nfs: server 10.184.132.151 OK

Sep  7 05:12:36 vnc4 kernel: nfs: server 10.184.132.115 OK
```

You might also be interested in data the system provided during its boot sequence, as well as those from the previous boot. In some distributions, the information will be contained in the boot.msg and boot.omsg, respectively.

Other useful logs include cron, cups, audits, mail, and samba. Some of these may not exist in your system, and others may have to be configured to work properly. Moreover, if your system is set up with the log rotation, several older logs will be retained as compressed files. They can be useful for comparing system behavior before and after major changes, and sometimes during a long investigation that can span several weeks.

# PROCESS ACCOUNTING

Troubleshooting Linux problems may not always be effective in real time, and you will want to analyze data at a later time. Process accounting is one of the methods that can narrow down the investigation. For instance, if a server is suddenly rebooted using the system reboot command, you will not have the opportunity to examine the issue while it is happening, but a post-reboot check will definitely be warranted.

If the kernel is built with the process accounting option enabled, it is possible to start process accounting. With the mechanism in place, the kernel will write a record to the accounting log file as each process on the system terminates. This record contains information about the terminated process, including user and system CPU time, average memory usage, user and group IDs, command name, and other data types.

By default, the accounting writes to /var/account/pacct. The path may differ, and the files might be located under /var/log or even /var/adm. If it is not enabled, it can be turned on with /usr/sbin/accton. Accounting files are binary, so you will need to use a dumping utility (dump-acct) to convert them into a human-readable format.

```
dump-acct /var/account/pacct > /tmp/human-readable-acct-log.log
```

It is also possible to display the output of the accounting file with lastcomm and sa commands. The service may also be started using init scripts (usually named acct or psacct). Default output includes the following data:

```
cut      |   0.0|   0.0|   0.0|    0|    0|2692.0|   0.0|Mon Feb  2 06:00:02 2015
sh       |   0.0|   0.0|   0.0|    0|    0|8040.0|   0.0|Mon Feb  2 06:00:02 2015
iostat   |   0.0|   0.0| 500.0|    0|    0|2696.0|   0.0|Mon Feb  2 05:59:57 2015
sh       |   0.0|   0.0| 500.0|    0|    0|8040.0|   0.0|Mon Feb  2 05:59:57 2015
pstree   |  21.0|  10.0|  31.0|    0|    0|5656.0|   0.0|Mon Feb  2 06:00:03 2015
grep     |   0.0|   0.0|  31.0|    0|    0|2804.0|   0.0|Mon Feb  2 06:00:03 2015
sh       |   0.0|   0.0|  31.0|    0|    0|8040.0|   0.0|Mon Feb  2 06:00:03 2015
status   |   7.0|   0.0| 987.0|10720| 2222|4680.0|   0.0|Mon Feb  2 05:59:54 2015
...
```

The first field is the command name. User time and system time are the second and third columns, respectively, followed by effective time. UID and GID are next, and you can see that some processes were executed by root, and others by an ordinary user. After that, examine the pattern of command execution.

## EXAMINE PATTERN OF COMMAND EXECUTION

We can now revisit out earlier reboot incidence. Imagine, or just recall, a case in which an important customer server was restarted without early coordination. You may want to learn how it was done, as well as who might have executed the command.

```
all      |  0.0|   0.0|   0.0|    0|   0|4288.0|   0.0|Tue Feb  3 11:16:50 2015
sleep    |  0.0|   0.0| 100.0|    0|   0|4292.0|   0.0|Tue Feb  3 11:16:50 2015
reboot   |  0.0|   0.0| 230.0|    0|   0|9592.0|   0.0|Tue Feb  3 11:16:49 2015
ps       |  1.0|   0.0|   1.0|    0|   0|4736.0|   0.0|Tue Feb  3 11:16:51 2015
grep     |  0.0|   0.0|   1.0|    0|   0|4540.0|   0.0|Tue Feb  3 11:16:51 2015
awk      |  0.0|   0.0|   1.0|    0|   0|9208.0|   0.0|Tue Feb  3 11:16:51 2015
kill     |  0.0|   0.0|   0.0|    0|   0|4292.0|   0.0|Tue Feb  3 11:16:51 2015
xargs    |  0.0|   0.0|   2.0|    0|   0|4572.0|   0.0|Tue Feb  3 11:16:51 2015
umount   |  0.0|   0.0|   0.0|    0|   0|7432.0|   0.0|Tue Feb  3 11:16:51 2015
ypwhich  |  0.0|   0.0|   0.0|    0|   0|9456.0|   0.0|Tue Feb  3 11:16:55 2015
sleep    |  0.0|   0.0|1000.0|    0|   0|4292.0|   0.0|Tue Feb  3 11:16:51 2015
shutdown |  0.0|   0.0|   0.0|    0|   0|4008.0|   0.0|Tue Feb  3 11:17:01 2015
```

## CORRELATE TO PROBLEM MANIFESTATION

Now that you have the exact time when the reboot command was issued, we can go back to analyzing system logs. At the time being, we do not know whether the reboot was an interactive command or a part of a scheduled cron job running a script. Indeed, looking through the server logs, we find a suspicious SSH login of a user capable of running sudo shortly before the restart. The combination of all the data we have then proves that the command was indeed executed interactively.

```
Feb 3 11:15:51 test003 sshd2[7216]: info category(Server.Auth)  Accepted gssapi-
with-mic for roger from 10.77.190.239 port 41870 ssh2
```

## AVOID QUICK CONCLUSIONS

The abundance of information available in system logs, as well as the presence of various warnings and errors, can easily mislead. It is all too easy to decide there is a problem just by looking at some of the messages, even if they are not strictly related to the issue at hand. Moreover, instinctively, we seek patterns and anomalies around us, and the unfamiliar wealth of hardware and software events in the logs can send us down the wrong path.

## STATISTICS TO YOUR AID

After preliminary analysis using ps and top, and initial examination of information in the system logs, we may need to expand our investigation. There are several very useful tools that can help us narrow down the scope of the problem. Let us examine them.

### VMSTAT

Vmstat (vmstat(8), n.d.) reports information about processes, memory, paging, block I/O activity, traps, and CPU usage. If executed without any parameters, the command will print a single line with average values for the collected parameters since the last reboot. The tool can also run for a specified number of iterations, with a delay between each iteration. For instance:

```
vmstat 1 10

procs-----------memory---------- ---swap-- -----io---- -system-- -----cpu------
 r  b   swpd     free    buff   cache   si   so    bi    bo    in   cs us sy id wa st
 8  2 15979116 135282296 968864 66456440 12    9    28   174     0    0 56  2 37  5  0
11  1 15979116 135256640 968868 66456488  0    0     0    40  5879 6093 22  1 74  3  0
 8  2 15979116 135368648 968868 66457004  0    0     0     0  6658 6718 23  1 73  3  0
 8  2 15979116 135306968 968868 66457368  0    0     0    56  4901 4706 20  0 76  4  0
10  2 15979116 135031876 968872 66458624  0    0     0   608  5784 5842 23  1 73  4  0
10  2 15979116 134842708 968884 66471248  0    0     0   704  6263 5818 27  1 68  4  0
10  2 15979116 134891684 968884 66460372  0    0     0    41  5730 6135 23  1 71  5  0
12  1 15979116 135298052 968936 66463540  0    0     0     0  6253 6721 24  1 72  3  0
 9  1 15979116 135262432 969036 66464244 32    0    32    60  6096 6156 23  0 74  3  0
10  1 15979116 135172072 969144 66465208  0    0     0     8  5613 6283 24  1 72  2  0
```

The first two columns in the output report the number of processes in the running and uninterruptible sleep (blocked) states, respectively. This information is very useful in trying to understand if there is a bottleneck on the system. Ideally, there will be few blocked processes. A high number may indicate network or storage latency, but it should be correlated to other metrics and tools.

Memory output includes the amount of virtual memory used, idle memory, buffers, and cache. Using the –a switch will also display the amount of active and inactive memory. The two swap columns show the amount of bytes being currently swapped in and out from the disk, per second. These values are useful when troubleshooting memory usage problems as well as responsiveness of systems with interactive usage.

I/O activity reports blocks sent and received to all block devices attached to the system. It shows the total amount and does not differentiate between different devices, so if you want additional granularity, you will need to use the –d switch.

System activity includes the number of interrupts (in) and context switches (cs) per second. These two values can be highly useful when troubleshooting performance and responsiveness problems, but they do require a decent understanding of the nature and behavior of running tasks.

CPU columns report information that is very similar to the metrics we saw when running the top command. By now, you should start piecing together different vectors of information. For example, a high number of blocked processes correlate to an increase in the %wa values. Likewise, a high number of interrupts often indicates disk activity, and you may see a drop in user CPU and an increase in %sy and %wa figures. This can be helpful when trying to debug system problems.

```
vmstat 1 10

procs-----------memory---------- ---swap-- -----io---- -system-- -----cpu------
 r  b    swpd    free    buff   cache    si   so    bi     bo    in    cs us sy id wa st
 9  2 15976360 144705656 978816 66545680 12    9    28    173     0     0 56  2 37  5  0
10  2 15976360 144776532 978816 66546536  0    0     0     16  4507  4157 24  1 73  3  0
 8  4 15976360 144537052 978816 66548160  0    0     0 293083  9000  7473 24  4 64  8  0
 9  3 15976360 145010676 978816 66548916  0    0     0  54892  6116  5732 20  1 73  7  0
 8  2 15976360 144890588 978816 66548944  0    0     0     32  4950  4003 21  0 76  3  0
...
```

Usually, you will not be able to point any single metric in the vmstat output as the key indicator to a problem, but the overall behavior trend in the collection information will often narrow down the search.

## IOSTAT

A tool very similar to vmstat is iostat (iostat(1), n.d.), which is used to monitor system I/O device loading. Much like vmstat, it can be executed without any switches, or you may use optional flags to extend the output, as well as change the number of runs and the delay between them. Despite its name, iostat also reports CPU statistics in a header above the listed block devices, in a manner very similar to the top command. CPU statistics are averaged for all processors.

The two most useful switches for iostat are –n for NFS filesystems and –x, which allow extended information to be shown. Other options include –c and –d for CPU and device utilization report, respectively, –h for human-readable output when the –n flag is used, and –z can reduce the verbosity of the printed data by omitting idle devices with no activity during the current sample.

```
iostat -x 1 2

Linux 3.0.51-default (bhost442)   02/05/2015      _x86_64_


avg-cpu:   %user    %nice  %system %iowait   %steal    %idle

           0.65    55.16     1.81    5.30     0.00    37.07


Device:   rrqm/s   wrqm/s     r/s     w/s   rsec/s    wsec/s avgrq-sz avgqu-sz

          await    svctm    %util

sda        3.23  1608.65   10.78   43.39  1288.41  13200.29   267.47     1.84

          33.86     1.13     6.10

sdb        1.08    21.26  118.73   63.33   958.49    690.47     9.06     0.16

           0.86     0.04     0.72


avg-cpu:   %user    %nice  %system %iowait   %steal    %idle

           0.38    12.62     0.55    4.95     0.00    81.50


Device:   rrqm/s   wrqm/s     r/s     w/s   rsec/s    wsec/s avgrq-sz avgqu-sz

          await    svctm    %util
```

```
sda          0.00      0.00      0.00      0.00      0.00      0.00      0.00      0.00

             0.00      0.00      0.00

sdb          0.00      0.00      0.00      0.00      0.00      0.00      0.00      0.00

             0.00      0.00      0.00
```

There is much information available in the output. Let us briefly describe the displayed columns and what they mean:

- rrqm/s – The number of read requests per second that were queued to the device.
- wrqm/s – The number of write requests per second that were queued to the device.
- r/s – The number of read requests that were issued to the device per second.
- w/s – The number of write requests that were issued to the device per second.
- rsec/s – The number of sectors read from the device per second.
- wsec/s – The number of sectors written to the device per second.
- avgrq-sz – The average size (in sectors) of the requests that were issued to the device.
- avgqu-sz – The average queue length of the requests that were issued to the device.
- await – The average time (in milliseconds) for I/O requests issued to the device to be served. This includes the time spent by the requests in queue and the time spent servicing them.
- svctm – The average service time (in milliseconds) for I/O requests that were issued to the device. This metric is considered deprecated and may not show in the output on your system. Overall, the average wait time is good enough to consider when trying to assess the workload against a block device.
- %util – This metric reports the percentage of CPU time during which I/O requests were issued to the device. In a way, it is bandwidth utilization for the device, and higher values may indicate device saturation.

In the provided example above, we can see that the current disk utilization for both sda and sdb is nil, whereas there has been some use of both resources since the last boot, as shown in the first reported summary. Now, let us examine a different kind of report.

One of your customers complains that a system normally used for interactive work is slow and that programs are somewhat sluggish. Indeed, even during the SSH login into the server, you observe a noticeable delay in the time it takes for the login prompt to return. The top command does not return an unequivocal result. The %wa values are low, but the %sy figure is somewhat high. The 1-minute load has also gone up. Still, the information is not conclusive. However, it does point to a potential responsiveness issue that the customer mentioned.

```
top - 11:52:12 up 5 days, 32 min,  2 users,  load average: 4.12, 0.99, 0.36

Tasks: 193 total,   4 running, 189 sleeping,   0 stopped,   0 zombie

Cpu(s):  0.3%us, 15.4%sy,  0.0%ni, 84.2%id,  0.0%wa,  0.0%hi,  0.0%si,  0.0%st

Mem:     64393M total,     5174M used,    59219M free,      506M buffers

Swap:    65538M total,        0M used,    65538M free,     3801M cached


  PID USER      PR  NI  VIRT  RES  SHR S  %CPU %MEM    TIME+  COMMAND

27391 igor      20   0  8604  632  524 R   34  0.0  0:09.73 dd

27397 igor      20   0  8604  632  524 D   25  0.0  0:05.30 dd

27401 igor      20   0  8604  632  524 D   24  0.0  0:05.29 dd

27400 igor      20   0  8604  632  524 D   24  0.0  0:04.98 dd

27394 igor      20   0  8604  632  524 D   23  0.0  0:06.18 dd

27403 igor      20   0  8604  632  524 R   22  0.0  0:04.77 dd

27396 igor      20   0  8604  632  524 D   22  0.0  0:05.39 dd

27399 igor      20   0  8604  632  524 D   22  0.0  0:05.15 dd

27402 igor      20   0  8604  632  524 D   21  0.0  0:05.20 dd

27393 igor      20   0  8604  632  524 R   19  0.0  0:06.20 dd

27395 igor      20   0  8604  632  524 R   17  0.0  0:05.47 dd

27398 igor      20   0  8604  632  524 D   17  0.0  0:05.23 dd

  153 root      20   0     0    0    0 S    1  0.0  0:30.74 kworker/2:1

  162 root      20   0     0    0    0 S    1  0.0  0:32.79 kworker/3:1

...
```

Now, if you are an experienced system administrator, you may immediately point your finger at the 12 running dd command instances, but let us assume that these are just user-compiled programs. In fact, if these 12 processes were called igor.bin, you might not be immediately able to decide whether they are legitimate tasks that should run on the interactive system.

In this case, the preliminary checks and system logs are not helpful in narrowing down the search. However, if you run the iostat command, you may find some interesting pointers. Although the two data snapshots do not correlate to the exact same moment, the overall behavior over a period of several seconds is quite indicative.

```
avg-cpu:  %user   %nice %system %iowait  %steal   %idle
           0.32    0.00   17.85    8.09    0.00   73.74


Device:   rrqm/s  wrqm/s     r/s     w/s  rsec/s   wsec/s avgrq-sz avgqu-sz
           await   svctm   %util
sdb         0.00    0.00    0.00    0.00    0.00     0.00     0.00     0.00
            0.00    0.00    0.00
sdc         0.00    0.00    0.00    0.00    0.00     0.00     0.00     0.00
            0.00    0.00    0.00
sda         0.00 23559.00    0.00  248.00    0.00 91728.00   974.71   150.08
          620.50    4.03  100.00


avg-cpu:  %user   %nice %system %iowait  %steal   %idle
           0.32    0.00   17.49    8.20    0.00   73.99


Device:   rrqm/s  wrqm/s     r/s     w/s  rsec/s   wsec/s avgrq-sz avgqu-sz
           await   svctm   %util
sdb         0.00    0.00    0.00    0.00    0.00     0.00     0.00     0.00
            0.00    0.00    0.00
sdc         0.00    0.00    0.00    0.00    0.00     0.00     0.00     0.00
            0.00    0.00    0.00
sda         0.00 25865.00    0.00  423.00    0.00 93872.00   529.25   154.43
          418.95    2.36  100.00
```

System CPU usage is very high. Iowait values are not negligible, but they are also not atypical for network- or disk-related activity on a busy machine. However, if we look at some of the other metrics in the iostat report, we can see that we are indeed facing a severe slowness due to disk access. The sda device experiences an average of 500 ms average wait time for requests to be processed. Normally, disk operations should be in low single-digit values at most, so either we have a very slow hard disk that cannot cope with the workload, or the workload is extremely heavy. Moreover, the wait time limit for an action for which most users will experience degradation in user responsiveness, the so-called Doherty threshold, is about 400 ms (Doherty, 1982), and it applies here, explaining the user's report. Moreover, the sda device utilization is 100%, which means the disk has reached its maximum throughput, and it will not gracefully handle other requests. All of the combined align well with the reported issue.

Still, this does not fully help you isolate the problem, although you can correlate the I/O activity with the processes in the top command. We will now study another system utility that can aid us in our troubleshooting.

## SYSTEM ACTIVITY REPORT (SAR)

SAR (sar(1), n.d.), also commonly spelled sar, is a highly versatile system monitoring tool that can collect, analyze, and report a whole range of system loads, including CPU, memory paging, network and storage utilization, filesystem usage, and more. The tool comes with several utilities:

- sar collects and displays system activities statistics. The command runs from the command line in a manner very similar to vmstat and iostat. The output can be redirected to a file, or it can be written to a binary file. The advantage of the latter method is that all metrics will be recorded, and users and system administrators can then check and correlate all of them, whereas simple redirection will only capture the current collection view.
- sadc (sadc(8), n.d.) stands for system activity data collector, and it is the backend tool used by SAR.
- sa1 is a utility that runs from cron. It stores system activities collected by sadc into a binary log.
- sa2 is also a tool that runs in a scheduled manner, and it creates daily summaries of collected statistics. It is useful for generating trends in the environment and for monitoring the behavior of various servers over longer periods of time, usually after problems have been resolved, or in a preventive manner, to avoid possible bottlenecks, resources contention and starvation, and similar issues.
- sadf is a helper tool that can be used to convert the binary data reports to human-readable files in CSV, XML, and other formats, which can then be parsed in various ways, used to generate graphs, and more.

In general, it is possible to gather all the required data just by using the sar command, but you will need to adjust the logging and numbering to create the necessary history for statistics. For instance, the sa1 utility writes to /var/log/sa/saXX files, with daily rotation. If you want to use sa2 to create the necessary reports, you may need to manually create and enumerate the logs.

SAR has many collection modes, which can be used to filter only specific subsets of information. The flags can be invoked against a binary log or interactively on the command line, for instance, with the –u flag (CPU activity, all processors):

```
sar -u 1 5

Linux 2.6.18-smp (vncserver22)        02/08/2015


12:49:04 PM     CPU     %user     %nice   %system   %iowait    %steal     %idle

12:49:05 PM     all      9.54      0.00      7.88      0.17      0.00     82.41

12:49:06 PM     all     12.03      0.00      8.38      0.00      0.00     79.59

12:49:07 PM     all     12.37      0.00      5.48      0.41      0.00     81.74

12:49:08 PM     all     12.57      0.00      6.74      1.58      0.00     79.10

12:49:09 PM     all     11.17      0.00      7.67      0.08      0.00     81.08

Average:        all     11.54      0.00      7.23      0.45      0.00     80.78
```

The same data can be retrieved from a log (written with –o flag beforehand):

```
sar -u /var/log/sa/mysar.log
```

Some of the most useful and common options include the following:

- -A – Report everything. This option is equivalent to -bBdqrRSuvwWy -I SUM -I XALL –n ALL -u ALL -P ALL.
- -b – Report I/O transfer rate statistics.
- -d – Report activity for each block device. Effectively, the information shown here is identical to metrics reported by iostat.
- -i – Set interval for data collection.
- -n – Report network statistics.
- -P { cpu I ALL } – Report per-processor statistics for the specified processor or processors. Specifying the ALL keyword reports statistics for each individual processor, and globally for all processors. Processors are enumerated from 0.
- -q – Report queue length and load averages.

- -r – Report memory utilization statistics. This is different from the –R option, which shows the number of memory pages being freed, buffered, or cached per second. Negative values are also allowed, and this mode is normally useful for someone looking for a very specific behavior pattern in the operating system.
- -S – Report swap statistics. Optionally, -W will show swapping data per second.
- -u – Report CPU utilization.
- -w – Report task creation and system switching activity.
- -v – Report status of inode, file, and other kernel tables.

Let us take a look at our earlier example, in which a user reported perceptible slowness in the responsiveness of their work environment on an interactive-use service. If we analyze and collect the data with sar, we will be able to check multiple vectors of the same behavior at a given time.

```
Linux 3.0.51-default (test44)  02/08/2015    _x86_64_


03:30:03 PM   CPU   %user   %nice   %system   %iowait   %steal   %idle
03:30:04 PM   all   0.00    0.00    0.00      0.06      0.00     99.94

...

03:30:55 PM   all   0.19    0.00    13.80     0.00      0.00     86.01
03:30:56 PM   all   0.32    0.00    14.13     0.00      0.00     85.55
03:30:57 PM   all   0.26    0.00    13.62     0.00      0.00     86.13
03:30:58 PM   all   0.32    0.00    15.86     3.26      0.00     80.56
03:31:01 PM   all   0.19    0.00    8.37      6.22      0.00     85.22
03:31:02 PM   all   1.01    0.00    11.09     9.95      0.00     77.95
```

CPU utilization for the system goes up once the dd activity begins. I/O wait values also go up, once all the pages start being written to the disk. This is indeed correlative to the device utilization. For brevity, I removed the rd_sec/s column in the output:

```
Linux 3.0.51-default (test44)  02/08/2015    _x86_64_


03:30:03 PM DEV   tps   wr_sec/s  avgrq-sz  avgqu-sz  await  svctm  %util
03:30:04 PM sda   3.03  202.02    66.67     0.01      4.00   4.00   1.21
```

```
...
03:30:55 PM  sda     3.09    379.38   122.67   0.00     0.00     0.00     0.00
03:30:56 PM  sda     3.06    277.55    90.67   0.00     0.00     0.00     0.00
03:30:57 PM  sda     5.26    412.63    78.40   0.00     0.00     0.00     0.00
03:30:58 PM  sda 12181.05 720614.74   141.25 113.13     6.64     0.08   102.74
03:31:01 PM  sda   385.98 237654.55   615.71 148.27   378.76     2.65   102.42
03:31:02 PM  sda  1456.04 246874.73   169.55 158.40   117.43     0.75   109.89
```

You might also be interested in memory activity (-r) and swapping (-S). Combined information from these different views can tell much about a possible system problem. The really useful thing about this method of logging is the atomicity of data, as well as the ability to correlate, which may not always be easy when using multiple utilities. Sar can also be used when running performance benchmarks and optimization, because it allows a very fine granularity of investigation due to changes, enabling you to fine-tune your system behavior.

## CONCLUSIONS

First-level troubleshooting of system and environment problems is about establishing the link between reported symptoms and actual behavior of hardware and software resources. To that end, we learned how to perform preliminary checks and investigation using system tools and utilities such as ps, top, vmstat, iostat, and others, as well as how to read system logs and correlate events and errors messages to monitoring alerts. Moreover, we also discussed the details of what various programs give us, and where and how the information may be useful in our case. We wrap up the initial work with a highly versatile tool such as sar, which allows us to bring our knowledge and insight together.

## REFERENCES

Doherty, W.J., 1982. The economic value of rapid time. Retrieved from: <http://www.vm.ibm.com/devpages/jelliott/evrrt.html> (accessed Feb 2015).

Hansen, D., 2009. Drop caches. Retrieved from: <http://linux-mm.org/Drop_Caches> (accessed Feb 2015).

Herber, R.J., 1995. UNIX system V (concepts). Retrieved from: <http://www-cdf.fnal.gov/offline/UNIX_Concepts/concepts.zombies.txt> (accessed Feb 2015).

iostat(1), n.d. Retrieved from: <http://linux.die.net/man/1/iostat> (accessed Feb 2015).

M. Joseph, J.S., 2013. P6R's secure shell public key subsystem. Retrieved from: <http://www. rfc-editor.org/rfc/rfc7076.txt> (accessed Feb 2015).

nice(1), n.d. Retrieved from: <http://linux.die.net/man/1/nice> (accessed Feb 2015).

ps(1), n.d. Retrieved from: <http://linux.die.net/man/1/ps> (accessed Feb 2015).

Reber, A., n.d. *memhog.c*. Retrieved from: <http://lisas.de/~adrian/memhog.c> (accessed Feb 2015).

Richardson, T., 2010. The RFB protocol. Retrieved from: <http://www.realvnc.com/docs/rfb-proto.pdf> (accessed Feb 2015).

Rusling, D.A., 1999. The Linux documentation project. Retrieved from: <http://www.tldp.org/ LDP/tlk/kernel/processes.html> (accessed Feb 2015).

sadc(8), n.d. Retrieved from: <http://linux.die.net/man/8/sadc> (accessed Feb 2015).

sar(1), n.d. Retrieved from: <http://linux.die.net/man/1/sar> (accessed Feb 2015).

top(1), n.d. Retrieved from: <http://linux.die.net/man/1/top> (accessed Feb 2015).

Uptime, n.d. Retrieved from: <http://linux.die.net/man/1/uptime> (accessed Feb 2015).

vmstat(8), n.d. Retrieved from: <http://linux.die.net/man/8/vmstat> (accessed Feb 2015).

Wikipedia, n.d. The free encyclopedia. Retrieved from: <http://en.wikipedia.org/wiki/ Load_%28computing%29> (accessed Feb 2015).

# A deeper look into the system

4

By now, you have seen the /proc string mentioned in the text several times, and if you have worked with Linux to some extent in the past, you are familiar with what it means. Proc is a special filesystem in UNIX-like operating systems (/proc, n.d.) that presents the information about processes in a human-readable hierarchal tree-like structure. Mounted under /proc, this filesystem acts as an interface to the internal structures in the kernel, and therefore it is a highly useful and important element of any troubleshooting.

There are many advantages to this method of abstraction. For instance, the ps command reads data directly from under the /proc tree, without having to execute system calls to obtain information. However, despite being labeled as a filesystem, /proc does not allow working with its files in the same manner that you would with regular block devices, which is why it is sometimes referred to as a pseudo-filesystem. Most of the values are read-only, but some kernel variables can be changed.

## WORKING WITH /PROC

Direct access to the kernel internals gives skilled administrators, developers, and engineers a great degree of power and freedom. It allows them to make changes to the system on the fly, without having to reboot and disrupt the normal work. This makes it an ideal way of testing new configurations and settings. For instance, if you are working on optimizing system performance, you can instantly alter the way some of the subsystems behave or respond.

On the other hand, direct access to the kernel also has its drawbacks and perils. You have the ability to drastically affect the way the operating system behaves, for better or worse. As a crude example, you can reboot a host or even cause the kernel to crash, just by echoing a "wrong" value into an object under the /proc filesystem.

Proc has importance in troubleshooting system issues. During your investigation, if and when you decide that there might be a problem related to how the system itself behaves, you can make changes under /proc to prove or disprove your theories.

It is important to make this distinction compared to other tools we have seen so far, as well as methods for troubleshooting. Proc values do not directly indicate if there is a problem or not, so you will have to measure their effect through symptoms exhibited by the system and the applications. Moreover, working with /proc often means leaving the rest of the environment unchanged. You do not manipulate running tasks; you change the reality in which these tasks run and observe the change.

## HIERARCHY

Before we start making changes, we need to acquaint ourselves with the /proc file-system tree. There are a large number of variables, some of which can be changed (tunables), and it is important to understand what they do and how they might affect the system. Wrong changes not only can adversely influence the performance of the programs, but also might affect the stability of the host, or even cause a kernel crash. Sometimes, the effect may be beneficial for a particular workload, but it could negatively affect a different service or application that is not currently running. Later on, you might not be able to correlate the two events.

## PER-PROCESS VARIABLES

For each process, there are a large number of variables stored under /proc. The information is useful in troubleshooting application-specific problems, and they allow engineers and technical personnel to better understand the behavior of programs and services.

- /proc/PID – Numerical subdirectories for each process, making the process ID. The subdirectories contain a range of useful pseudo-files and directories. Some of the objects and their values can be highly useful when debugging system issues. For brevity, we will omit the listing of all the available fields and only focus on the more important ones. The full list is available as part of the operating system documentation, or online (Seinbold, 2009).
- /proc/PID/cmdline – This variable contains the complete command line for the process, unless it is a zombie, in which case the variable is empty. The field is useful if you need to know all the flags, switchers, and optional strings in a process command line, and such information may not be available in the top or ps commands.
- /proc/PID/cwd – Symbolic link to the current working directory of a process.
- /proc/PID/environ – The listing of all the environment variables for the process. Again, this is very useful for trying to understand the circumstances under which the task runs, or for comparing two sets to see whether something may have changed in the environment that is affecting the process performance or behavior.
- /proc/PID/exe – Symbolic link to the pathname of the executed command.
- /proc/PID/fd – This subdirectory contains one entry for each file handle held open by the process. The default set will include 0 (standard input), 1 (standard output), and 2 (standard error). There may be other file descriptors.

```
cd /proc/self/fd/



11



total 5
```

```
dr-x------ 2 igor igor  0 2015-01-08 14:35 .

dr-xr-xr-x 5 igor igor  0 2015-01-08 14:35 ..

lrwx------ 1 igor igor 64 2015-01-08 15:34 15 -> /dev/pts/635

lrwx------ 1 igor igor 64 2015-02-05 09:31 16 -> /dev/pts/635

lrwx------ 1 igor igor 64 2015-01-08 15:34 17 -> /dev/pts/635

lrwx------ 1 igor igor 64 2015-01-08 15:34 18 -> /dev/pts/635

lrwx------ 1 igor igor 64 2015-01-08 15:34 19 -> /dev/pts/635
```

The symbolic links point to devices and objects. In some cases, the links may be broken, or you might not be able to easily interpret device names.

```
total 7

dr-x------ 2 root root  0 Jan 13 09:50 ./

dr-xr-xr-x 5 root root  0 Jan 13 09:50 ../

lrwx------ 1 root root 64 Jan 13 09:50 0 -> /dev/null

lrwx------ 1 root root 64 Jan 13 12:24 1 -> /dev/null

lrwx------ 1 root root 64 Jan 13 12:24 2 -> /dev/null

lrwx------ 1 root root 64 Jan 13 12:24 3 -> socket:[1717302238]

lrwx------ 1 root root 64 Jan 13 12:24 4 -> /dev/ptmx

lrwx------ 1 root root 64 Jan 13 12:24 5 -> socket:[1717302238]

lrwx------ 1 root root 64 Jan 13 12:24 6 -> socket:[1717302414]
```

- Proc/PID/io – In newer kernels, this file displays the I/O statistics for each running process. The metrics include the number of bytes read and written from any storage (including pagecache) in the form of rchar and wchar, respectively, as well as the number of bytes read from block storage (read_bytes, write_ bytes). The file also shows the number of read and write system calls, and a less trivial cancelled_write_bytes parameter. This set of variables is very useful in debugging I/O-related problems, as well as in accounting process behavior in profiling and performance tweaking. For instance, in the example below, we can see that PID 6301 did a large amount of reads, but none of these were read from physical storage.

```
cat /proc/6301/io

rchar: 33760661089

wchar: 2697716789

syscr: 27856351

syscw: 1774843

read_bytes: 0

write_bytes: 97828864

cancelled_write_bytes: 0
```

- /proc/PID/limits – This file displays the soft and hard limits for process resources, such as the maximum number of file locks, stack size, priority, open files, and more. For instance, this can be useful to debug scenarios in which a process exhausts its resource space.

```
cat /proc/9654/limits

Limit                 Soft Limit       Hard Limit       Units

Max cpu time          unlimited        unlimited        ms

Max file size         unlimited        unlimited        bytes

Max data size         unlimited        unlimited        bytes

Max stack size        8388608          unlimited        bytes

Max core file size    0                unlimited        bytes

Max resident set      unlimited        unlimited        bytes
```

| Max processes | 500 | 500 | processes |
|---|---|---|---|
| Max open files | 4096 | 8192 | files |
| Max locked memory | 32768 | 32768 | bytes |
| Max address space | unlimited | unlimited | bytes |
| Max file locks | unlimited | unlimited | locks |
| Max pending signals | 385318 | 385318 | signals |
| Max msgqueue size | 819200 | 819200 | bytes |
| Max nice priority | 0 | 0 | |
| Max realtime priority | 0 | 0 | |

- /proc/PID/maps – A list of mapped memory regions and their permissions currently used by the process. We will discuss this a little later on.
- /proc/PID/mem – The process memory space, in binary format. The file is not human-readable, but it can be accessed using open, read, and seek system calls.
- /proc/PID/mounts – List of all mount points held by the process. This information is available from kernel 2.6.26 onward, and the exact syntax of this field is beyond the scope of this chapter.
- /proc/PID/oom_adjust – This file can be used to change the score used to select which process should be killed in an out-of-memory (OOM) situation. When the server runs out of memory, the kernel will try to kill processes with the highest memory score to prevent a system lockup. The score is reflected in the /proc/PID/oom_score (badness) variable, and is calculated using a range of parameters, such as the process time, priority, number of children, hardware access, and more. Normally, the variable is best left alone. The badness score can be useful in determining system behavior and identifying "rogue" processes. This can useful on systems in which processes may suddenly spin out of control, taking lots of memory and spawning children. Analyzing OOM situations can also help system administrators determine the best usage model for their systems.
- /proc/PID/stat – Status information about the process, including PID, PPID, executable filename, the number of minor and major page faults, priority, virtual memory size, resident set size, and more.
- /proc/PID/status – This file provides output that is similar to the stat file, in a format that is easier for humans to read. The output is mostly useful when you know what you are looking for and need to compare very specific pieces of information between two states, often before and after a system change, a code change, or similar situations.

```
cat status

Name:   perl

State:  S (sleeping)

Tgid:   2983

Pid:    2983

PPid:   1

TracerPid:      0

Uid:    0       0       0       0

Gid:    0       0       0       0

FDSize: 64

Groups:

VmPeak:     50268  kB

VmSize:     50264  kB

VmLck:          0  kB

VmHWM:      12860  kB

VmRSS:      12860  kB

VmData:     10684  kB

VmStk:        136  kB
```

## KERNEL DATA

Much like the process entries, these files offer information about the kernel itself. Some of the objects may not be present on all systems, and will depend on how the kernel was configured, and whether all the required modules are loaded into memory.

- /proc/cmdline – This file shows the arguments (Kernel Parameters, n.d.) passed to the Linux kernel at boot done. The information can be useful when comparing system states and different configurations between platforms with the same hardware and workloads that might be exhibiting different performance or application behavior. It is also useful to verify that certain boot time parameters have been correctly passed to the kernel.

- /proc/config.gz – This file contains the kernel configuration in a compressed archive. The contents can be viewed using commands such as zcat or zgrep and dumped into a regular text file with redirection. The usefulness of the file is in that it contains all the configurations used to compile the running kernel, and they may not necessarily match the .config file under /usr/src/Linux. Again, this is very useful when comparing system behavior.
- /proc/cpuinfo – This variable is a collection of CPU information, including model, CPU clock frequency, the number of physical and logical cores and threads. System administrators may want to consult the data if they need to debug issues related to CPU speed, hyperthreading, comparison between processor models, and more. The file also shows all the CPU flags and supported architecture-dependent extensions. For instance, if you need to use hardware-assisted virtualization (such as Intel VT-x), you can check whether the system supports this. Some of the flags may be masked by the BIOS/UEFI.

```
...

processor       : 15

vendor_id       : GenuineIntel

cpu family      : 6

model           : 45

model name      : Intel(R) Xeon(R) CPU E5-2670 0 @ 2.60GHz

stepping        : 7

cpu MHz         : 1200.000

cache size      : 20480 KB

physical id     : 1

siblings        : 8

core id         : 7

cpu cores       : 8

apicid          : 46

initial apicid  : 46

fpu             : yes
```

```
fpu_exception    : yes

cpuid level      : 13

wp               : yes

flags            : fpu vme de pse tsc msr pae mce cx8 apic sep mtrr pge mca cmov pat
pse36 clflush dts acpi mmx fxsr sse sse2 ss ht tm pbe syscall nx pdpe1gb rdtscp lm
pclmulqdq dtes64 monitor ds_cpl vmx smx est tm2 ssse3 cx16 xtpr pdcm dca sse4_1
sse4_2 x2apic popcnt aes xsave avx lahf_lm ida arat epb xsaveopt pln pts dtherm
tpr_shadow vnmi flexpriority ept vpid

bogomips         : 5187.41

clflush size     : 64

cache_alignment  : 64

address sizes    : 46 bits physical, 48 bits virtual

power management:

...
```

- /proc/interrupts – The file records the number of interrupts per CPU, for each registered I/O device, as well as interrupts such as nonmaskable interrupts (NMI), TLB flush interrupts (TLB), and others. You should consult these data if you suspect one of the hardware resources may be malfunctioning, and to examine the performance of specific subsystems, such as network cards or the ATA interface, for instance. On systems with a very large number of processor cores, the output may be difficult to read, as it will almost inevitably overflow the console buffer. Sample output (shortened, for brevity):

```
            CPU0        CPU1        CPU2   ...   CPU15                           timer
  94:          2           0           0             0     IR-PCI-MSI-edge      eth0
  95:    9430734           0           0             0     IR-PCI-MSI-edge      eth1
 NMI:      17771       11683        2761           950     Non-maskable interrupts
```

- /proc/kcore – This file represents the physical memory of the system (in ELF format). Using a debugger and unstrapped kernel binary, it is possible to read and examine the current state of kernel structures.

- /proc/meminfo – Reports statistics about memory usage of the system, as we have briefly mentioned in the previous chapter. A large number of fields is reported (Documentation for /proc/sys/vm/*, n.d.), including totally usable RAM, free memory, buffers, caches, cached swap, amount of memory pages in different states, and more. The full listing is beyond the scope of this chapter, but some portions thereof can be useful when troubleshooting system issues.

```
cat /proc/meminfo

MemTotal:        65939324 kB

MemFree:         59294976 kB

Buffers:           434716 kB

Cached:           5079052 kB

SwapCached:             0 kB

Active:           5125192 kB

Inactive:          502832 kB

Active(anon):      114372 kB

Inactive(anon):        64 kB

Active(file):     5010820 kB

Inactive(file):    502768 kB

Unevictable:            0 kB

Mlocked:                0 kB

SwapTotal:       67111420 kB

SwapFree:        67111420 kB

Dirty:                120 kB

Writeback:              0 kB

AnonPages:         114284 kB
```

```
Mapped:              24368 kB

Shmem:                 180 kB

. . .
```

Consider the following example. One of your users complains that they observe a degradation in responsiveness after a prolonged heavy I/O activity on one of their systems. You can confirm the symptoms on the affected single host, but you cannot immediately decide why it only comes to bear on that particular system and not the others, even though the engineers run the same kind of workload and I/O activity patterns.

Analyzing this kind of problem might not be easy, and a deep understanding of the system memory management facility is required, but if you know where to look, you could narrow down the investigation to a more manageable set of unknowns.

We will discuss some of the concepts later on, but let us very briefly deviate into the space of memory management. The Linux virtual memory (VM) subsystem is accessible under /proc/sys/vm. The tunables under this subtree govern the behavior of the memory when certain thresholds are reached. For example, the "dirty" parameters define when the write cache should be flushed to disk. The policies include a ratio of total memory, size, and expiration time.

An experienced system administrator may immediately see a possible source for the problem. Since some of the dirty parameters are expressed as a percentage of total memory, systems with different values – or even different physical memory size – will not react in the same way even when subject to seemingly the same workloads. The same policies apply to huge pages, caches, swap behavior, and more.

If you compare the system experiencing degradation under sustained I/O load to other systems that do not exhibit the same issue, you may discover different values under the vm tree, which could possibly explain the behavior.

Again, on their own, the values are not as useful as when *compared* to other systems, because they provide insights into how seemingly identical platforms are configured. This is a valuable tool for troubleshooting complex problems without a simple root cause. Moreover, if you make changes to the vm subsystem, you might want to observe and measure the results through the meminfo file.

- /proc/modules – A list of all kernel modules currently loaded into memory. The same information is provided by the lsmod command.
- /proc/mounts – The list of all mounted filesystems. The information can be correlated to the /etc/mtab file. On some systems, the latter may actually be a symbolic link to this pseudo-filesystem. The list is useful when troubleshooting issues related to network locations, mount and umount problems, stale mount points or hanging filesystems, and more.

- /proc/slabinfo – This file provides information about kernel caches. Although the total size of slab pools is available in the meminfo variable, a higher level of details is available here. However, the contents are best parsed using a command such as slabtop or slabinfo.

## PROCESS SPACE

Let us go back to the process maps. We have briefly discussed the /proc/PID/maps set of variables, but they are far more useful than a precursory glance. They allow for a deeper understanding of the process behavior, especially if you know what a particular application is supposed to be doing. Here is a sample process:

```
#cat /proc/2971/maps

00400000-0041b000 r-xp 00000000 08:06 24525        /usr/sbin/avahi-daemon

0061a000-0061b000 r--p 0001a000 08:06 24525        /usr/sbin/avahi-daemon

0061b000-0061c000 rw-p 0001b000 08:06 24525        /usr/sbin/avahi-daemon

0061c000-0063d000 rw-p 00000000 00:00 0            [heap]

0063d000-0069f000 rw-p 00000000 00:00 0            [heap]

7fd281dde000-7fd281df3000 r-xp 00000000 08:02 37   /lib64/libnsl-2.11.3.so

7fd281df3000-7fd281ff2000 ---p 00015000 08:02 37   /lib64/libnsl-2.11.3.so

...

7fd28240e000-7fd28257d000 r-xp 00000000 08:02 26   /lib64/libc-2.11.3.so

7fd28257d000-7fd28277d000 ---p 0016f000 08:02 26   /lib64/libc-2.11.3.so

7fd28277d000-7fd282781000 r--p 0016f000 08:02 26   /lib64/libc-2.11.3.so

7fd282781000-7fd282782000 rw-p 00173000 08:02 26   /lib64/libc-2.11.3.so

7fd282782000-7fd282787000 rw-p 00000000 00:00 0

7fd282787000-7fd28279e000 r-xp 00000000 08:02 52   /lib64/libpthread-2.11.3.so

...

7fd283878000-7fd283879000 rw-p 00000000 00:00 0

7fff11268000-7fff11289000 rw-p 00000000 00:00 0    [stack]

7fff11370000-7fff11371000 r-xp 00000000 00:00 0    [vdso]

ffffffffff600000-ffffffffff601000 r-xp 00000000 00:00 0 [vsyscall]
```

For each line, in the first column, we get the start and end address in memory. The second column specifies the permissions of the particular region in memory. There are four permissions available, including read, write, execute, and shared. Private regions are marked with p, and they cannot be accessed by other processes. Such attempts will result in a violation and a segmentation fault.

If a file was read from a disk and loaded into memory using the mmap (mmap(2), n.d.) system call, then in the third column we will see the offset from the beginning of the file. The fourth column specifies the major and minor numbers of the corresponding device for regions that were mapped from a file. The full listing of major and minor numbers can be found in the Documentation/devices.txt file in the kernel source tree.

```
...

7 char      Virtual console capture devices

            0 = /dev/vcs          Current vc text contents

            1 = /dev/vcs1         tty1 text contents

                ...

            63 = /dev/vcs63       tty63 text contents

            128 = /dev/vcsa       Current vc text/attribute contents

            129 = /dev/vcsa1      tty1 text/attribute contents

            ...

            191 = /dev/vcsa63     tty63 text/attribute contents


            NOTE: These devices permit both read and write access.


7 block     Loopback devices

            0 = /dev/loop0        First loop device

            1 = /dev/loop1        Second loop device

            ...


            The loop devices are used to mount filesystems not
```

```
        associated with block devices.  The binding to the

        loop devices is handled by mount(8) or losetup(8).


 8 block       SCSI disk devices (0-15)

         0 = /dev/sda          First SCSI disk whole disk

        16 = /dev/sdb          Second SCSI disk whole disk

        32 = /dev/sdc          Third SCSI disk whole disk

...
```

For instance, for the libc-211.3.so library, we can see it was read from a 08:02 device, which means the file was read from the second partition of the first SCSI/SATA disk device, in other words sda2, which is indeed the / on the specific host.

The fifth column is the inode number, and the sixth the actual name of the loaded object. The field is blank for regions that were anonymously mapped. Now, we also need to pay attention to the different rows in the /proc/PID/maps output.

The first entry corresponds to the code (text) of the binary in question. Naturally, this region is marked as executable. The second line shows the binary data, which also includes all initialized global variables. The third line corresponds to heap, for dynamically allocated memory, using system calls such as malloc. It may also include additional segments of the binary code, such as the .bss segment, with statically linked and uninitialized global variables. If the .bss segment is small, it may be stored in the data segment.

Shared libraries are listed next, and the list can be very long. At the end of the output, there are three special lines, also marked in square brackets. There is the stack, followed by vdso and vsyscall.

```
7fff11268000-7fff11289000 rw-p 00000000 00:00 0              [stack]

7fff11370000-7fff11371000 r-xp 00000000 00:00 0              [vdso]

ffffffffff600000-ffffffffff601000 r-xp 00000000 00:00 0 [vsyscall]
```

We will begin with the last. Vsyscall was introduced to replace the slower int $0 \times 80$ interrupt used for system calls on older architectures (Bar, 2000). However, it comes with certain restrictions, such as the size of the memory allocation and possible security implications. Vsyscall is mapped in the kernel (notice the address region), and it depends on the particular kernel configuration.

Vdso (vDSO) (object, vDSO – overview of the virtual ELF dynamic shared, n.d.), which stands for virtual dynamic shared object, is a small library map shared automatically by the kernel into the address space of all applications. This object is used to improve performance by providing faster access to some commonly used system calls, and it overcomes the limitations of the vsyscall (Corbet, 2011). This method is preferred over vsyscall whenever possible. On some systems, vDSO may also be known as linux-gate.so (Petersson, 2005).

Understanding the process space is very important for debugging and trouble-shooting. In most cases, system administrators will not manually manipulate the memory space, but when additional tools are used to trace the execution of a process, the insight can be useful, and it might shed new light on the issue at hand.

## EXAMINE KERNEL TUNABLES

So far, we have mostly discussed the information that can be gathered from a running host and used to aid us in our investigations. More importantly, once we have the initial direction, we will want to create changes to prove and disprove our hypotheses. To this end, we will now focus on the /proc/sys tree.

### SYS SUBSYSTEM

The most important part of the /proc filesystem is tunables directly related to the kernel. Found under /proc/sys, their variables can affect different aspects of the system behavior, including kernel itself, memory management, network, and others. Values can be changed simply by echoing new ones into the relevant file, with all the great responsibility and risk that such actions entail.

There are several important subdirectories under the sys directory. For the purpose of our work, we will focus on the filesystem, memory, network, and kernel-related tunables.

```
total 0

dr-xr-xr-x    1 root  root  0 Feb  8 14:22 .

dr-xr-xr-x  191 root  root  0 Feb  8 16:22 ..

dr-xr-xr-x    0 root  root  0 Feb  8 14:24 abi

dr-xr-xr-x    0 root  root  0 Feb  8 14:23 crypto

dr-xr-xr-x    0 root  root  0 Feb  8 14:24 debug
```

```
dr-xr-xr-x    0 root root 0 Feb  8 14:24 dev

dr-xr-xr-x    0 root root 0 Feb  8 14:22 fs

dr-xr-xr-x    0 root root 0 Feb  8 14:24 fscache

dr-xr-xr-x    0 root root 0 Feb  8 14:22 kernel

dr-xr-xr-x    0 root root 0 Feb  8 14:22 net

dr-xr-xr-x    0 root root 0 Feb  8 14:23 sunrpc

dr-xr-xr-x    0 root root 0 Feb  8 14:22 vm
```

## MEMORY MANAGEMENT

Memory management is one of the more complex parts of system troubleshooting, as it involves a certain degree of guesswork and estimation. Still, you can achieve good results by monitoring the tunables and adjusting them to match your scenario. This means being familiar with the meaning of available parameters and their associated values.

- Dirty_background_bytes – Contains the amount of dirty memory threshold value at which the kernel will start writing dirty pages to the permanent storage. This will be done by background kernel threads (known as pdflush). Why is this useful? For instance, you may see pdflush processes using a very high percentage of CPU, hogging the resources. This could be an indicator of a wider problem. In some situations, you may have the freedom to change the dirty parameters and check whether the issue temporarily goes away.
- Dirty_background_ratio – This parameter is the percentage of total available memory at which the kernel will start writing dirty data. On high-memory machines, this could translate into tens of gigabytes of pages.
- Dirty_bytes – To complicate things a little, this tunable contains the amount of dirty memory at which the flushing will be triggered. It is mutually exclusive of dirty_ratio, and one or the other will be zero (unused).
- Dirty_expire_centisecs – This tunable defines the age of dirty data that can be flushed in hundredths of a second. Pages that have been stored in the memory for longer than the specified interval will be written to disk.
- Dirty_ratio – The percentage threshold at which the process generating disk writes will start writing out dirty data. Again, on systems with large memory, the percentage can translate into a significant amount.
- Dirty_writeback_centisecs – This tunable specifies the interval for the kernel flusher threads to wake and write dirty data to disk.

It becomes apparent that the disk writing policy is a nontrivial mask combining different values set in these variables. However, being aware of their power can help, especially when troubleshooting performance or optimizing systems.

- Drop_caches – When set, this tunable tells the kernel to begin dropping caches. It can accept a limited set of integers, namely, 1 (pagecache), 2 (slab objects), or 3 (both). The operation is nondestructive, and no data will be lost by running it. However, the purpose of this tunable may seem questionable. Why would anyone want to interfere with the normal way the kernel manages its memory?

Again, we go back to the question of performance troubleshooting and optimization. It may be useful to drop caches to time system operations by making sure no object is retrieved from memory, which is essentially a fast operation, but rather from the intended storage, like a network file system or local disk. Furthermore, if the host is exhibiting abnormal operation (possibly due to a bug) with very large caches, dropping them and observing the behavior may confirm the suspicion. However, do note that dropping caches can take a very long time, because it might essentially mean tens or hundreds of megabytes (or even gigabytes) worth of data being written to disk, causing a temporary I/O and CPU load.

- Swappiness – This is another useful tunable, which defines how aggressively the kernel swaps memory pages to swap devices (if present). The values range from 0 to 100, with 100 being the most aggressive routine. The default value will vary between distributions and kernel versions. It is important in that it can affect interactive responsiveness and performance, and the number may have to be tweaked to match the hardware, including the size of physical memory, as well as the usage model.

## FILESYSTEM MANAGEMENT

Changing tunables under this subdirectory will affect the way filesystems behave. Most often, the values will not affect system performance, but they will define the envelope of operations in which the server can work without encountering problems. Working with the fs parameters is useful for servers with high I/O and network loads, such as Web servers, SQL servers, Rsync servers, and more.

- /proc/sys/fs – Indeed, this directory contains objects related to file systems. It is possible to read the existing values and limits, as well as to set new ones. For instance, /proc/sys/fs/file-max defines a system-wide limit on the number of open files for all processes. In some cases, you might encounter a server that has exhausted the available number of open files, and there might be a kernel log message indicating that.

```
[582258.937432] VFS: file-max limit 4926328 reached
```

Echoing a new value can help alleviate the problem – or confirm it – although a permanent solution might be required to address the issue. On its own, such a change is not sufficient and cannot be treated as a plug-n-play fix. First, dynamic changes to the kernel will not be preserved on reboot (unless saved using sysctl). Second, there are often delicate dependences between several tunables, and adjusting just one might cause more harm, or complicate things further.

In this particular case, you may not exceed the maximum number of open files than the limit set during the kernel compilation. Furthermore, another tunable, /proc/sys/fs/file-nr, will also be affected by the change. This other variable shows the number of allocated file handles, free handles, and the maximum number, and the last figure will change if you echo a new value into the file-max field. Moreover, one should also consider the number of available in-memory inodes, to prevent moving the bottleneck from one tunable to another.

## NETWORK MANAGEMENT

The networking part of the /proc/sys subsystem is one of the more complex pieces and requires deeper understanding of networking protocols to use and work effectively. It will also invariable directly affect the performance of the host related to any remote operation. Although you may gain significant benefits tuning the network stack, you can also severely affect the system speed and throughput of services running on the system.

There are a very large number of parameters available, and most of them are beyond the scope of this book. However, some of them are quite important and should be consulted if you encounter network-related issues.

- Rmem_default, rmem_max – These tunables define the default and maximum size of the receive socket buffer (in bytes). They are located under /proc/sys/net/core.
- Wmem_default, wmem_max – As above, except related to the send socket buffer.
- Tcp_rmem, tcp_wmem – Under the ipv4 subdirectory, increasing the values of read and write TCP buffers can allow for larger window sizes, especially on systems with high-speed network and low latency.
- Tcp_fin_timeout – This tunable defines the default time the sockets will remain in the wait state before closing. Lowering this value can free sockets, especially on servers with many inbound connections.
- Tcp_tw_reuse – Accordingly, this parameter tells the kernel to reuse sockets in the TIME_WAIT state, if it runs out of free sockets.

The big problem with all of the above is that fine-tuning the parameters almost takes the form of black magic and takes much work and experience, as well as the most adequate use cases to configure properly. It is also somewhat difficult to affect changes on production systems, and replicating the exact work conditions on isolated test boxes in a contained laboratory environment might not always be possible.

## SUNRPC

Tunables located in this tree relate to the Sun Remote Procedure Call (RPC) protocol, as well as NFS. These parameters are often overlooked by system administrators, but they can be very useful in debugging problems associated with the NFS performance. For example, you may want to increase the verbosity (debug) level of the RPC/NFS stack so that every operation is written to the messages. In combination with a network sniffer such as tcpdump (tcpdump(8), n.d.), it might be possible to obtain useful insights into fileserver congestion and responsiveness, packet errors, and more.

- Nfs_debug – Determines verbosity of debug. The default value is 0, and it can be increased to 32767. The values are bitmask flags, corresponding to the definition under /usr/include/Linux/nfs.h (NFS Debugging, n.d.).

```
/*

 * NFS debug flags

 */

#define NFSDBG_VFS          0x0001

#define NFSDBG_DIRCACHE     0x0002

#define NFSDBG_LOOKUPCACHE  0x0004

#define NFSDBG_PAGECACHE    0x0008

#define NFSDBG_PROC         0x0010

#define NFSDBG_XDR          0x0020

#define NFSDBG_FILE         0x0040

#define NFSDBG_ROOT         0x0080

#define NFSDBG_CALLBACK     0x0100

#define NFSDBG_CLIENT       0x0200

#define NFSDBG_MOUNT        0x0400

#define NFSDBG_FSCACHE      0x0800

#define NFSDBG_PNFS         0x1000
```

```
#define NFSDBG_PNFS_LD        0x2000

#define NFSDBG_STATE          0x4000

#define NFSDBG_ALL            0xFFFF
```

Similarly, nfsd_debug, rpc_debug, and nlm_debug are available with the same kind of behavior and definitions. A very good knowledge of the RPC and NFS stack is required to be able to derive meaningful conclusions from the data.

- Min_resport, max_resport – These two tunables define the minimum and maximum numbers of reserved ports for NFS traffic. The values can be useful on servers with a very high level of NFS traffic to avoid port exhaustion.

## KERNEL

Tunables under this tree affect the kernel behavior directly, and therefore they are among the most delicate and dangerous ones, but also with highest benefit for engineers during troubleshooting sessions.

- Core_pattern – When an application crashes, in some conditions, a dump of its memory contents may be stored on disk, in the form of a "core" file, this in reference to the magnetic core memory, used between 1950 and 1975 (Cruz, 2001). When no pattern is specified, the core will only use the bareword string core. If you want a more meaningful format, you can set it here.
- Core_uses_pid – This parameter will attach PID to a process core, when defined.
- Kexec_load_disabled – This tunable defines whether the kexec_load system call can be used. In the later chapters, we will learn why this tunable is highly important and usable.
- Panic_on_oops – If the kernel encounters an unrecoverable bug, it may try to continue operation or crash immediately, which will freeze the system and make it effectively unusable until the next reboot. Again, we will focus more on kernel oopses and panic later on.
- Panic_on_unrecoverable_nmi – If the system encounters an interrupt that cannot be handled properly, you may want to crash the system rather than resume operation with a possible logical error in the computation. This can be important in a scenario in which device drivers are used, such as kernel profilers, and it may also expose conflicts with the platform settings, including BIOS/UEFI parameters and even faulty hardware components.
- Tainted – This parameter specified if the kernel has been "tainted" with the loading of an unsigned module into memory. For instance, modules that use no license or use a non-GPL license will be classified in this manner, even if they are perfectly sane. A variety of hardware check errors, kernel warnings, firmware errors, and bad pages will also be reflected under this variable,

and therefore, it is highly useful when troubleshooting system crashes or freezes.

```
   1 - A module with a non-GPL license has been loaded, this

       includes modules with no license.

       Set by modutils >= 2.4.9 and module-init-tools.

   2 - A module was force loaded by insmod -f.

       Set by modutils >= 2.4.9 and module-init-tools.

   4 - Unsafe SMP processors: SMP with CPUs not designed for SMP.

   8 - A module was forcibly unloaded from the system by rmmod -f.

  16 - A hardware machine check error occurred on the system.

  32 - A bad page was discovered on the system.

  64 - The user has asked that the system be marked "tainted".  This

       could be because they are running software that directly modifies

       the hardware, or for other reasons.

 128 - The system has died.

 256 - The ACPI DSDT has been overridden with one supplied by the user

        instead of using the one provided by the hardware.

 512 - A kernel warning has occurred.

1024 - A module from drivers/staging was loaded.

2048 - The system is working around a severe firmware bug.

4096 - An out-of-tree module has been loaded.

8192 - An unsigned module has been loaded in a kernel supporting module

       signature.

16384 - A soft lockup has previously occurred on the system.

32768 - The kernel has been live patched.
```

## SYSCTL

Before we delve any deeper, an important question arises. Assuming that we did some testing and changed certain parameters, how can we make sure that they are preserved between reboots?

This can be achieved using the sysctl (sysctl(8), n.d.) tool, which can modify kernel parameters at runtime. The static configuration for sysctl is stored under /etc/sysctl.conf, and it may contain some or all parameters that override system defaults. The snippet below shows a sample configuration from a configuration file. Comments are optional, but highly useful, especially if less common options are used.

```
# Disable response to broadcasts.

# You don't want yourself becoming a Smurf amplifier.

net.ipv4.icmp_echo_ignore_broadcasts = 1

# enable route verification on all interfaces

net.ipv4.conf.all.rp_filter = 1

# enable ipV6 forwarding

#net.ipv6.conf.all.forwarding = 1

# increase the number of possible inotify(7) watches

fs.inotify.max_user_watches = 65536
```

Additionally, the tool can be used from the command line to perform changes to specific values. There are several useful flags available.

- -A – Print all values. When stored to a file, they can be used to compare system configurations, even if the hardware and kernel are supposedly identical. This is an excellent way of driving standardization in the environment, as well as of testing changes and trying to understand why two or more hosts with supposedly the same setup exhibit different results or behavior.
- -w – Set a change to a sysctl setting.
- -p – Load changes from a configuration file (usually sysctl.conf).

The command line use is also very convenient, namely:

```
/sbin/sysctl -a

/sbin/sysctl -w sunrpc.min_resvport = 200
```

## CONCLUSIONS

Initial problem solving revolves around the use of some common applications and utilities. The next step in the process takes us into the process space and into the kernel, and in order to use tools that expose the structure of tasks and the operating system itself, we need deeper knowledge of the underlying building blocks.

The simple way of working with the Linux internals is through the /proc pseudo-filesystem, which offers a wealth of information, as well as great freedom in making changing to the way the system behaves. Difficult, complex environment issues will inevitably lead to this domain, and engineers and administrators will find themselves dabbling in kernel tunables to eliminate erroneous investigation leads and clues and isolate the problem. On top of that, /proc offers immense advantages in profiling and performance optimization, both of which are of critical importance in large, mission-critical data centers.

The familiarity with the process space and the kernel now allows us to take the next step and intervene directly into the system and its tasks. We will now learn how to trace and debug programs and even the kernel itself in the next chapters.

## REFERENCES

/proc, n.d. Retrieved from: <http://www.tldp.org/LDP/Linux-Filesystem-Hierarchy/html/proc.html> (accessed May 2015)

Bar, M., 2000. Linux system calls. Retrieved from: <http://www.linuxjournal.com/article/4048> (accessed May 2015)

Corbet, J., 2011. On vsyscalls and the vDSO. Retrieved from: <http://lwn.net/Articles/446528/> (accessed May 2015)

Cruz, F. d., 2001, Jan. Magnenetic-core memory. Retrieved from: <http://www.columbia.edu/cu/computinghistory/core.html> (accessed May 2015)

Documentation for /proc/sys/vm/*, n.d. Retrieved from: <https://www.kernel.org/doc/Documentation/sysctl/vm.txt> (accessed May 2015)

Kernel Parameters, n.d. Retrieved from: <https://www.kernel.org/doc/Documentation/kernel-parameters.txt> (accessed May 2015)

mmap(2), n.d. Retrieved from: <http://linux.die.net/man/2/mmap> (accessed May 2015)

NFS Debugging, n.d. Retrieved from: <http://initrd.org/wiki/NFS_Debugging> (accessed May 2015)

object, vDSO – overview of the virtual ELF dynamic shared, n.d. Retrieved from: <http://man7.org/linux/man-pages/man7/vdso.7.html> (accessed May 2015)

Petersson, J., 2005. What is linux-gate.so.1? Retrieved from: <http://www.trilithium.com/johan/2005/08/linux-gate/> (accessed May 2015)

Seinbold, S., 2009. The /proc filesystem. Retrieved from: <https://www.kernel.org/doc/Documentation/filesystems/proc.txt> (accessed May 2015)

sysctl(8), n.d. Retrieved from: <http://linux.die.net/man/8/sysctl> (accessed May 2015)

tcpdump(8), n.d. Retrieved from: <http://linux.die.net/man/8/tcpdump> (accessed May 2015)

# Getting geeky – tracing and debugging applications

## 5

## WORKING WITH STRACE AND LTRACE

Sometimes, the process of investigating problems by reading logs and examining the overall behavior of the system will not yield fruitful results. The root cause of the issue affecting your customer base or your applications will remain a mystery. At this stage, you will need to dig in deeper, and this means analyzing what affected processes do.

### STRACE

Strace (strace(1) – Linux man page, n.d.) is a utility that can trace system calls and signals. If you are wondering what system calls are, they are a translation mechanism that provides interface between a process and the operating system (kernel) (The GNU C Library, n.d.). These calls can be intercepted and read, allowing for a better understanding of what a process is trying to do at a given runtime.

By hooking these calls, we can get a better understanding of how a process behaves, especially if it is misbehaving. The operating system functionality that allows tracing is called ptrace (ptrace(2) – Linux man page, n.d.). Strace calls on ptrace and reads the process behavior, reporting back.

In the simplest case, strace runs the specified command until it exits. It intercepts and records the system calls that are called by a process and the signals that are received by a process. The name of each system call, its arguments, and its return value are printed on a standard error or to a log file.

Each line in the trace contains the system call name, followed by its arguments in parentheses and its return value. Let us examine a trivial test case, in which we will run and trace the dd command, namely dd <input file> <output file> <options>. When executed with strace, the command will look as follows:

```
strace /bin/dd if=/dev/zero of=/tmp/file bs=1024K count=5
```

Now, let us take a look at the output of the strace command and digest it:

```
execve("/bin/dd", ["dd", "if=/dev/zero", "of=/tmp/file", "bs=1024K", "count=5"], [/*
62 vars */]) = 0

brk(0)                                  = 0x60d000

mmap(NULL, 4096, PROT_READ|PROT_WRITE, MAP_PRIVATE|MAP_ANONYMOUS,-1, 0) =
0x7ffff7ffa000

access("/etc/ld.so.preload", R_OK)      = -1 ENOENT (No such file or directory)

open("/etc/ld.so.cache", O_RDONLY)      = 3

fstat(3, {st_mode=S_IFREG|0644, st_size=127604, ...}) = 0

mmap(NULL, 127604, PROT_READ, MAP_PRIVATE, 3, 0) = 0x7ffff7fda000

close(3)                                = 0

open("/lib64/librt.so.1", O_RDONLY)     = 3
```

The first line of the code is execve, which executes the desired program. The command completes successfully, as indicated by the exit status (= 0).

```
execve("/bin/dd", ["dd", "if=/dev/zero", "of=/tmp/file", "bs=1024K", "count=5"], [/*
62 vars */]) = 0
```

Conversely, errors (typically a return value of −1) have the errno symbol and error string appended, for instance:

```
open("/foo/bar", O_RDONLY) = -1 ENOENT (No such file or directory)
```

In the same manner, signals are printed as a signal symbol and a signal string.

```
sigsuspend([] <unfinished ...>

--- SIGINT (Interrupt) ---

+++ killed by SIGINT +++
```

Let us get back to our example. The second line is a brk(0). It changes the data segment size.

```
brk(0)                                  = 0x60d000
```

On the third line, we create a new mapping in the virtual address space of the calling process.

```
mmap(NULL, 4096, PROT_READ|PROT_WRITE, MAP_PRIVATE|MAP_ANONYMOUS, -1, 0) =
0x7ffff7ffa000
```

The fourth system call to be logged is an attempt to access the ld.so.preload file under /etc. Since the file does not exist, we get a failed call, marked with −1 exit status, plus the error string ENOENT.

```
access("/etc/ld.so.preload", R_OK)      = -1 ENOENT (No such file or directory)
```

The fifth line is also interesting. Here, we can see a successful open of the /etc/ld.so.cache file, as a read-only object. We can also see that the file was mapped to file descriptor 3. Indeed, later in the log, there is a closing of the file descriptor with close(3) = 0.

```
open("/etc/ld.so.cache", O_RDONLY)      = 3
```

And so forth. Now, what if you want to know additional information about the executed system calls or signals? To that end, you may want to use the man pages, specifically sections 2 and 7, respectively. For example, if you want to know what the access system call does, then man 2 access will reveal additional information.

In the SYNOPSIS part of the man page, you will find the system call signature, namely how to declare it in your code, as well as the input arguments. The access system call is fairly simple, taking only the path name and the mode. You also get a detailed description of the behavior of the system call.

```
NAME

       access - check real user's permissions for a file

SYNOPSIS

       #include <unistd.h>

       int access(const char *pathname, int mode);

DESCRIPTION

       access() checks whether the calling process can access the file pathname.  If
pathname is a symbolic link, it is dereferenced.

       The mode specifies the accessibility check(s) to be performed, and is either
the value  F_OK,  or a mask  consisting of the bitwise OR of one or more of R_OK,
W_OK, and X_OK.  F_OK tests for the existence of the file.  R_OK, W_OK, and X_OK test
whether the file exists and grants  read,  write,  and execute permissions,
respectively.

       The  check is done using the calling process's real UID and GID, rather than
the effective IDs as is done when actually attempting an operation (e.g., open(2)) on
the  file.   This  allows  set-user-ID programs to easily determine the invoking
user's authority.

       If  the calling process is privileged (i.e., its real UID is zero), then an
X_OK check is successful for a regular file if execute permission is enabled for any
of the file owner, group, or other.


RETURN VALUE

       On success (all requested permissions granted), zero is returned.  On error
(at  least  one  bit  in mode asked for a permission that is denied, or some other
error occurred), -1 is returned, and errno is set appropriately.
```

If a system call is being executed and meanwhile another one is being called from a different thread/process, then strace will try to preserve the order of those events and mark the ongoing call as being unfinished. When the call returns it will be marked as resumed.

```
[pid 28772] select(4, [3], NULL, NULL, NULL <unfinished ...>

[pid 28779] clock_gettime(CLOCK_REALTIME, {1130322148, 939977000}) = 0

[pid 28772] <... select resumed> )       = 1 (in [3])
```

Interruption of a (restartable) system call by a signal delivery is processed differently as kernel terminates the system call and also arranges its immediate re-execution after the signal handler completes.

```
read(0, 0x7ffff72cf5cf, 1)              = ? ERESTARTSYS (To be restarted)

--- SIGALRM (Alarm clock) @ 0 (0) ---

rt_sigreturn(0xe)                       = 0

read(0, ""..., 1)                       = 0
```

Arguments are printed in a symbolic form. This example shows the shell performing ">>file" output redirection:

```
open("file", O_WRONLY|O_APPEND|O_CREAT, 0666) = 3
```

Here, the three-argument form of open is decoded by breaking down the flag argument into its three bitwise-OR constituents and by printing the mode value in octal by tradition. Where traditional or native usage differs from ANSI or POSIX, the latter forms are preferred. In some cases, strace output has proven to be more readable than the source.

Structure pointers are dereferenced and the members are displayed as appropriate. In all cases arguments are formatted in the most C-like fashion possible. For example, the essence of the command "ls -l /dev/null" is captured as

```
lstat("/dev/null", {st_mode=S_IFCHR|0666, st_rdev=makedev(1, 3), ...}) = 0
```

Notice how the "struct stat" argument is dereferenced and how each member is displayed symbolically. In particular, observe how the st_mode member is carefully decoded into a bitwise-OR of symbolic and numeric values. Also notice in this example that the first argument to lstat is an input to the system call and the second argument is an output. Since output arguments are not modified if the system call fails, arguments may not always be dereferenced. For example, retrying the "ls -l" example with a nonexistent file produces the following line:

```
lstat("/foo/bar", 0xb004) = -1 ENOENT (No such file or directory)
```

Character pointers are dereferenced and printed as C strings. Nonprinting characters in strings are normally represented by ordinary C escape codes. Only the first strsize (32 by default) bytes of strings are printed; longer strings have an ellipsis appended following the closing quote. Here is a line from "ls -l" where the getpwuid library routine is reading the password file:

```
read(3, "root::0:0:System Administrator:/"..., 1024) = 422
```

Although structures are annotated using curly braces, simple pointers and arrays are printed using square brackets with commas separating elements. Here is an example from the command "id" on a system with supplementary group ids:

```
getgroups(32, [100, 0]) = 2
```

On the other hand, bit-sets are also shown using square brackets but set elements are separated only by a space. Here is the shell preparing to execute an external command:

```
sigprocmask(SIG_BLOCK, [CHLD TTOU], []) = 0
```

Here, the second argument is a bit-set of two signals, SIGCHLD and SIGTTOU. In some cases, the bit-set is so full that printing out the unset elements is more valuable. In that case, the bit-set is prefixed by a tilde like this:

```
sigprocmask(SIG_UNBLOCK, ~[], NULL) = 0
```

Here, the second argument represents the full set of all signals.

### Options
There are several useful options you should consider when tracing processes.

- -c – Count time, calls, and errors for each system call and report a summary on program exit. On Linux, this attempts to show system time (CPU time spent running in the kernel) independent of wall clock time. If -c is used with -f or -F (below), only aggregate totals for all traced processes are kept.

- -f – Trace child processes as they are created by currently traced processes as a result of the fork(2) system call. On non-Linux platforms the new process is attached to as soon as its pid is known (through the return value of fork(2) in the parent process). This means that such children may run uncontrolled for a while (especially in the case of a vfork(2)), until the parent is scheduled again to complete its (v)fork(2) call. On Linux the child is traced from its first instruction with no delay. If the parent process decides to wait(2) for a child that is currently being traced, it is suspended until an appropriate child process either terminates or incurs a signal that would cause it to terminate (as determined from the child's current signal disposition).
- -ff – If the -o filename option is in effect, each processes trace is written to filename.pid where pid is the numeric process id of each process. This is incompatible with -c, since no per-process counts are kept.
- -t – Prefix each line of the trace with the time of day.
- -tt – If given twice, the time printed will include the microseconds.
- -ttt – If given thrice, the time printed will include the microseconds and the leading portion will be printed as the number of seconds since the epoch.
- -T – Show the time spent in system calls. This records the time difference between the beginning and the end of each system call.
- -e expr – A qualifying expression which modifies which events to trace or how to trace them. The format of the expression is [qualifier = ][!]value1[,value2]..., where qualifier is one of trace, abbrev, verbose, raw, signal, read, or write and value is a qualifier-dependent symbol or number. The default qualifier is trace. Using an exclamation mark negates the set of values. For example, -eopen means literally -e trace = open, which in turn means trace only the open system call. By contrast, -etrace = !open means to trace every system call except open. In addition, the special values all and none have the obvious meanings. Note that some shells use the exclamation point for history expansion even inside quoted arguments. If so, you must escape the exclamation point with a backslash.
- -e trace = set – Trace only the specified set of system calls. The -c option is useful for determining which system calls might be useful to trace. For example, trace = open,close,read,write means to only trace those four system calls.
- -o filename – Write the trace output to the file filename rather than to stderr. Use filename.pid if -ff is used. If the argument begins with 'I' or with '!' then the rest of the argument is treated as a command and all output is piped to it. This is convenient for piping the debugging output to a program without affecting the redirections of executed programs.
- -p pid – Attach to the process with the process ID pid and begin tracing. The trace may be terminated at any time by a keyboard interrupt signal (CTRL -C). Strace will respond by detaching itself from the traced process(es) leaving it (them) to continue running. Multiple -p options can be used to attach to up to 32 processes in addition to command (which is optional if at least one -p option is given).

- -s strsize – Specify the maximum string size to print (the default is 32). Note that filenames are not considered strings and are always printed in full.

## *What you need to know before using strace*

Strace is a useful diagnostic, instructional, and debugging tool. System administrators, diagnosticians, and troubleshooters will find it invaluable for solving problems with programs for which the source is not readily available as they do not need to be recompiled to trace them. Students, hackers, and the overly curious will find that a great deal can be learned about a system and its system calls by tracing even ordinary programs. And programmers will find that since system calls and signals are events that happen at the user/kernel interface, a close examination of this boundary is very useful for bug isolation, sanity checking, and attempting to capture race conditions.

There are a few things we would like to emphasize before we start exploring the power of this great tool:

- Strace is not a magic bullet. It will only provide some limited information about the running process. To get the full picture, you will have to use ltrace, as well as a debugger. You may also need to have your applications, or the kernel, compiled with debugging symbols, or you may use a profiling framework to examine the runtime of an affected process.
- Strace is only the beginning. But it is a very good beginning. It will point you in the right direction. It will let you know whether to leave things be or to power up the full debugging process. Better yet, it may provide you with a solution to your problem.
- Strace should be used when you encounter *reproducible* issues with your programs without an obvious sign for problems. We will soon see a few examples that demonstrate this in crystal-clear detail.
- Strace hooks processes and basically forces them to repeat every system call twice, once for the trace and once for the actual execution. This introduces a time penalty into the run. Furthermore, this means that delicate problems dependent on exact timing of execution, such as various race condition bugs[1], may not manifest when traced.
- Strace may crash your applications.
- Strace 64-bit may not work well with 32-bit programs.

Not all programs can be traced and they may crash, either because of bugs or the way they have been coded, including purposefully trying to prevent tracing to keep the process execution as secret as possible. This is often the case with proprietary software.

---

[1]A race condition is the behavior of an electronic, software, or other system where the output is dependent on the sequence or timing of other uncontrollable events. It becomes a bug when events do not happen in the order the programmer intended. The term originates with the idea of two signals racing each other to influence the output first.

### Strace from the standpoint of a system administrator

Using strace requires some basic hacking instinct. It is not for everyone. Most home users will probably never need or want to use strace, but they just might. Likewise, most system administrators doing level I or II maintenance or helpdesk will probably not be tempted to put strace to good use.

However, if you have a curious nature or would like to understand better what your system is doing, or perhaps your job requires that you dabble with the internals, then strace is a good place to start and then spend some time. Now, when and how to use strace – and most importantly – what kind of information to pay attention to, this takes a form of black art, but with some discipline and an inkling to code, you will be able to master strace and use it successfully.

### Strace has friends

Strace is not the only utility that can trace system calls. There is another utility called ltrace (ltrace(1) – Linux man page, n.d.), which can trace both system calls and library calls. Then, there is also the famous GNU Debugger (gdb) (GDB: The GNU Project Debugger, n.d.), which is a fully featured code debugger. We will talk about these soon.

Furthermore, it is important to remember that although strace is less powerful than its two aforementioned friends, it is much easier and safer to use. ltrace is more prone to crashing traced processes. Gdb is much more complex, requires a deeper knowledge of code, and works best if you have the source code available, which may not always be the case.

### Basic usage

We will begin with the basics and then we will show you two test cases that simulate real problems with program execution that cannot be solved by using the programs or looking for visual clues for the errors, but which are easily deciphered when strace is brought into play.

Strace can be invoked at the command line, which can be a binary or a script, or it can be attached to an already running process. Output can be shown on the screen, but this is usually of limited value unless the runs are really short and simple, or redirected into a file, which is the preferred way of doing things.

Special flags can be used. For example, you may measure system call timing, both the timing within individual calls and the timing between system calls. Child processes forked off the parent can also be traced, and environment variables can also be shown. There is the string length for the output, and you have the ability to filter only specific system calls and create a useful summary for the entire run. Here is the most basic form:

```
strace <command-line>
```

Here is an example, with the dd command we mentioned earlier:

```
strace dd if=/dev/zero of=/tmp/file bs=1024K count=5
```

This will produce the following output:

```
#strace dd if=/dev/zero of=/tmp/file bs=1024K count=5

execve("/bin/dd", ["dd", "if=/dev/zero", "of=/tmp/file", "bs=1024K", "count=5"], [/*
62 vars */]) = 0

brk(0)                                        = 0x60d000

mmap(NULL, 4096, PROT_READ|PROT_WRITE, MAP_PRIVATE|MAP_ANONYMOUS, -1, 0) =
0x7ffff7ffa000

access("/etc/ld.so.preload", R_OK)            = -1 ENOENT (No such file or directory)

open("/etc/ld.so.cache", O_RDONLY)      = 3

fstat(3, {st_mode=S_IFREG|0644, st_size=127604, ...}) = 0

mmap(NULL, 127604, PROT_READ, MAP_PRIVATE, 3, 0) = 0x7ffff7fda000

close(3)                                      = 0

open("/lib64/librt.so.1", O_RDONLY)     = 3

...
```

The output looks cluttered and messy and not easy to follow. Indeed, this is not how you should be using strace unless you can read really, really fast.

```
Extra flags
```

You should invoke strace with extra flags:

```
strace -o /tmp/strace-file -s 512 dd if=/dev/zero of=/tmp/file bs=1024k count=5
```

We used the following flags:

- -o output file, this is where the output goes now and can be read at leisure.
- -s 512 increases the string length to 512 bytes; the default is 32.

Now it looks cleaner:

```
#strace -o /tmp/strace-file -s 512 dd if=/dev/zero of=/tmp/file bs=1024k count=5

5+0 records in

5+0 records out

5242880 bytes (5.2 MB) copied, 0.00680734 s, 770 MB/s
```

And the file content:

```
execve("/bin/dd", ["dd", "if=/dev/zero", "of=/tmp/file", "bs=1024k", "count=5"], [/*
62 vars */]) = 0

brk(0)                                    = 0x60d000

mmap(NULL, 4096, PROT_READ|PROT_WRITE, MAP_PRIVATE|MAP_ANONYMOUS, -1, 0) =
0x7ffff7ffa000

access("/etc/ld.so.preload", R_OK)        = -1 ENOENT (No such file or directory)

open("/etc/ld.so.cache", O_RDONLY)        = 3

fstat(3, {st_mode=S_IFREG|0644, st_size=127604, ...}) = 0

mmap(NULL, 127604, PROT_READ, MAP_PRIVATE, 3, 0) = 0x7ffff7fda000

close(3)                                  = 0

open("/lib64/librt.so.1", O_RDONLY)       = 3

read(3,
"\177ELF\2\1\1\0\0\0\0\0\0\0\0\0\3\0>\0\1\0\0\0\340\"\0\0\0\0\0\0\0@\0\0\0\0\0\0\0\20
4\0\0\0\0\0\0\0\0

\0\0@\0\0008\0\t\0@\0%\0"\0\6\0\0\0\5\0\0\0@\0\0\0\0\0\0\0@\0\0\0\0\0\0\0@\0\0\0\0\0\0
\0\370\1\0\0\0\0\0\0\370\

1\0\0\0\0\0\0\10\0\0\0\0\0\0\0\3\0\0\0\4\0\0\0000b\0\0\0\0\0\0\0000b\0\0\0\0\0\0\0000b\0\
0\0\0\0\0\34\0\0\0\0\0\0\0

0\34\0\0\0\0\0\0\0\20\0\0\0\0\0\0\0\1\0\0\0\5\0\0\0\0\0\0\0\0\0\0\0\0\0\0\0\0\0\0\0\0\0
\0\0\0\0\0\0\0\274r\0\0\0

\0\0\0\274r\0\0\0\0\0\0\0\0 \0\0\0\0\0\1\0\0\0\6\0\0\0x}\0\0\0\0\0\0\0x} \0\0\0\0\0\0x}
\0\0\0\0\0\0\364\4\0\0\0\0\0

\0x\16\0\0\0\0\0\0\0\0 \0\0\0\0\0\2\0\0\0\6\0\0\0\260}\0\0\0\0\0\0\260}
\0\0\0\0\0\0\260} \0\0\0\0\0\360\1\0\0\0
```

```
\0\0\0\360\1\0\0\0\0\0\0\10\0\0\0\0\0\0\0\4\0\0\0\4\0\0\0008\2\0\0\0\0\0\0008\2\0\0\0
\0\0\0008\2\0\0\0\0\0\0\\

\0\0\0\0\0\0\0\0\\\0\0\0\0\0\0\0\0\4\0\0\0\0\0\0\0\0\0P\345td\4\0\0\0Lb\0\0\0\0\0\0Lb\0\0\0\0
\0\0Lb\0\0\0\0\0\0T\2\0\0

\0\0\0\0T\2\0\0\0\0\0\0\0\4\0\0\0\0\0\0\0\0Q\345td\6\0\0\0\0\0\0\0\0\0\0\0\0\0\0\0\0\0\0\0\0\
0\0\0\0\0\0\0\0\0\0\0\0\0

\0\0\0\0\0\0\0\0\0\0\0\0\10\0\0\0\0\0\0\0\0"..., 832) = 832
```

But we can enhance the tracing process even more. For example, you may not only be interested in the gory details, you may also want to see a summary table of all system calls used by the process, including errors. This can be quite useful when comparing a healthy system with a bad one, allowing you to spot notable differences instantly.

```
strace -c <command>
```

And our example:

```
#strace -c -s 512 dd if=/dev/zero of=/tmp/file bs=1024k count=5
5+0 records in
5+0 records out
5242880 bytes (5.2 MB) copied, 0.00557598 s, 940 MB/s
% time     seconds  usecs/call     calls    errors syscall
------ ----------- ----------- --------- --------- ----------------
100.00    0.001924         241         8           write
  0.00    0.000000           0        10           read
  0.00    0.000000           0        11         2 open
  0.00    0.000000           0        12           close
  0.00    0.000000           0         7           fstat
```

```
   0.00    0.000000            0        1           lseek

   ...

  ------  ----------  ----------  ---------  ---------  ----------------

 100.00    0.001924                    100          4 total
```

For example, we had 11 open calls, including two errors. One hundred percent of the process time was spent writing, which is expected from the dd command. But we also had quite a few reads.

Other useful flags include -f (fork) and -Tt (time inside/between system calls). To trace an already running process, you need the -p flag for the process ID (PID), which you can find by running ps and looking for your process name.

```
strace -p PID
```

Now that we know how to use strace, let us see what it can do.

### Test case 1

We will copy a file. Very simple. Except that we will make sure the source file does not exist and redirect error output to /dev/null, so the command line user will not know what happens when the copy command is executed.

```
#ls -l

total 8

-rw-r--r-- 1 root root  714 Dec  8 10:48 file1

-rw-r--r-- 1 root root 1780 Dec  8 10:48 file2
```

Now, if we rename the source and try to copy, we will hit an error:

```
#mv file1 file1.old

#cp file1 file3

cp: cannot stat `file1': No such file or directory
```

But what if you could not see the cp: cannot stat error message on your screen? How would you know when something went wrong and what it was that went wrong with the execution of your program? To demonstrate this, we will redirect all output to /dev/null, so no messages are displayed to the user:

```
<command> > /dev/null 2>&1
```

The last bit, 2>&1, tells the system to redirect STDERR (FD 2) to the same location as STDOUT (FD 1), in this case, /dev/null, so you will not see any errors. Next, we will check the exit status with echo $?. If the exit status is 0, then it is good; anything else and we have a problem.

```
#cp file1 file3 > /dev/null 2>&1

#echo $?

1
```

The copy command has completed with no visible errors. Now, checking the exit status, it is 1, so something went wrong. When it is a simple copy, then investigating is easy, but what if you have a complex script that goes through tens of directories and copies hundreds of files? Enter strace. We will now trace the unsuccessfully copy command and then analyze the strace log.

```
strace -o /tmp/cp-fail -s 512 cp file1 file3 > /dev/null 2>&1
```

We have the log file, called cp-fail. We will open it in a text editor and look at it. The big question is, what are we looking for? Well, in our case, we have a copy, which requires source and destination. Either we have a problem with the existence of the source/destination, the permissions, or maybe disk space. Any one of these is a possibility. So we will look for the name of source file in the log and see if there are any errors there.

```
munmap(0x7ffff7ff2000, 4096)            = 0

geteuid()                               = 0
```

```
stat("file3", 0x7fffffffe130)          = -1 ENOENT (No such file or directory)

stat("file1", 0x7fffffffdf20)          = -1 ENOENT (No such file or directory)

write(2, "cp: ", 4)                    = 4

write(2, "cannot stat `file1'", 19)    = 19

write(2, ": No such file or directory", 27) = 27
```

Indeed, it is there! The stat system call fails. It exits with ENOENT (no such file or directory). There is the problem right there. We do not have the source file! Now, we could have enhanced and simplified our search. Instead of tracing everything, we could have limited our investigation only to specific system calls. That is what the -e flag does. The -e flag allows you to trace only specific system calls. For example:

```
strace -e trace=stat <command>
```

This means we are only interested in the stat system call and no other. Indeed, the output is now much shorter and easier to sort, since we only have two files that need to be accessed.

```
stat("file3", 0x7fffffffe130)          = -1 ENOENT (No such file or directory)

stat("file1", 0x7fffffffdf20)          = -1 ENOENT (No such file or directory
```

Let us see our second example.

## Test case 2

In this example, we will show you how to debug network problems. We will try to ping the gateway of our LAN. First, we will see a successful example, and then we will stop the network and see an error. Next, we will redirect all errors to /dev/null, as we did with the copy example, so we do not know what is happening. Strace will help us pinpoint the root cause. Here is a healthy ping:

```
#ping -c 3 10.184.201.254

PING 10.184.201.254 (10.184.201.254) 56(84) bytes of data.

64 bytes from 10.184.201.254: icmp_seq=1 ttl=64 time=0.524 ms
```

```
64 bytes from 10.184.201.254: icmp_seq=2 ttl=64 time=0.698 ms

64 bytes from 10.184.201.254: icmp_seq=3 ttl=64 time=1.83 ms



--- 10.184.201.254 ping statistics ---

3 packets transmitted, 3 received, 0% packet loss, time 1998ms

rtt min/avg/max/mdev = 0.524/1.019/1.837/0.583 ms
```

Now, we shut down the network

```
/etc/init.d/network stop
```

and the ping fails with network unreachable error

```
#ping -c 3 10.184.201.254

Connect: Network is unreachable
```

However, if we redirect the output and errors to /dev/null, we will not see the message and will not know what is wrong. Imagine this is some application that pings its server for license or tries to retrieve updates.

```
ping -c 3 10.184.201.254 >/dev/null 2>&1

echo $?

2
```

As you can see, the exit status is 2, which is no good. But we do not know why. It is time to put strace to work and find out the root cause.

```
strace -o /tmp/ping -s 512 ping -c 3 10.184.201.254 > /dev/null 2>&1
```

Now, let us take a look at the log file. Since we do not know what to expect, we will browse and look for errors related to 10.184.201.254.

```
rt_sigaction(SIGINT, {0x555555556990, [], SA_RESTORER|SA_INTERRUPT, 0x7ffff7882bd0},
NULL, 8) = 0

socket(PF_INET, SOCK_DGRAM, IPPROTO_IP) = 4

connect(4, {sa_family=AF_INET, sin_port=htons(1025),
sin_addr=inet_addr("10.184.201.254")}, 16) = -1 ENETUNREACH (Network is unreachable)

dup(2)
```

And there it is. We open a socket and try to connect. But then, we get the ENETUNREACH error, which is "Network is unreachable." The root cause is found. Of course, we now need to understand why the network is down, but we can focus on a solution to the problem instead of wondering idly what might have gone wrong.

### Summary
Strace is a mighty tool. It is so simple to use, yet it offers rewards almost instantly. It is not for everyone, definitely not the majority of home users, but with some patience, basic investigative instinct combined with a curious soul and desire to learn, you can put strace to effective use.

## LTRACE
For all practical purposes, ltrace usage is identical to strace. The tool flags and options are almost identical. If you are familiar with strace, you will have no problem using ltrace.

Ltrace simply runs specified commands until it exits. It intercepts and records the dynamic library calls that are called by the executed process and the signals that are received by that process. It can also intercept and print the system calls executed by the program. Due to its more intrusive nature, ltrace may crash applications when used. A typical usage is shown below:

```
32613 __libc_start_main(0x407ee0, 3, 0x7fffffffe058, 0x411da0, 0x411d90 <unfinished
...>

32613 strrchr("ls", '/')                                        = NULL

32613 setlocale(6, "")                                          =
"LC_CTYPE=en_US.UTF-8;LC_NUMERIC="...
```

```
32613 bindtextdomain("coreutils", "/usr/share/locale")          =
"/usr/share/locale"

32613 textdomain("coreutils")                                   = "coreutils"

32613 __cxa_atexit(0x40b8e0, 0, 0, 0x736c6974756572, 0x413f61)  = 0

32613 isatty(1)                                                 = 1

32613 getenv("QUOTING_STYLE")                                   = NULL

32613 getenv("LS_BLOCK_SIZE")                                   = NULL

...
```

We will not be demonstrating any extensive usage with ltrace on its own. Instead, we will show you how you can use ltrace together with strace to achieve a full understanding of problems you face.

## COMBINE BOTH TOOLS FOR BEST RESULTS

Now, we will learn how to use both strace and ltrace at the same time.

### *The problem we have*

All right, let us assume that the startup of customer applications is slow. You wait 5–10 seconds for application windows to launch. Sometimes, it works fast, but you are not really sure why. Usually, the problems occur after you log out of your session or following a reboot. The most annoying thing is that if you try to fire up those same programs with sudo or as root, there are no startup delays, and all seems to run fine. So how do you debug a problem such as this one? Remember, your customers are displeased.

### *Rules of engagement*

Let us briefly recap what we have learned in the previous chapters. If you want to be an awesome system debugger, then there are several would-be rules you must follow whenever you are trying to resolve a difficult problem. If it is something trivial you can fix in 2 minutes, fine, but if this is a brand new issue that has stumped you and your colleagues for more than an hour, then you should pause, rethink, and be methodical about it.

### *Be methodical*

Having a formulaic approach may make you appear to be a noob – or a very efficient person. You choose. You should have a strategy that is uniform, generic, and all-encompassing for every problem that may come up. This means that you will be able to handle the situation whether you are fixing airplanes or hacking the kernel.

### Always begin with simple tools

In theory, you can try to fix any problem with gdb right away, but that is not a smart use of either the tools at hand or your intellect and time. You should always begin with simple things. Check the system logs for weird errors. Check top to assess the basic system health. Make sure you are not out of memory. Examine the disk and CPU load.

### Comparison to a healthy system

We have mentioned this approach in Chapter 2, and indeed, this may not always be applicable, but if you have a machine with an identical hardware and software configuration that does not exhibit the same problems, or two workload scenarios that produce different results, then you should compare between them to try to find what might be causing the bad system or the component to misbehave. This may not always be easy, but component search is the most powerful tool in statistical engineering and it applies well for mechanical parts as well as software. Now, we are ready to dig in.

### Symptoms

Our healthy system fires up xclock, our sample graphical tool, in less than a second. The bad system does the same, except it takes 10 times longer. So we know something is slowed down but not necessarily broken.

### Strace

At this stage, running strace seems like a good idea. Rather than tracing every system call through endless logs, we will only do the summary run, specified with -c flag. We want to see if there is anything significant in the tool's run.

### Strace log, good system

Let us see what an strace run gives us. The output is shown in Fig. 5.1.

### Strace log, bad system

The same thing for the misbehaving case, as shown in Fig. 5.2.

### Strace comparison

Looking at the two logs side by side, we can see that there is a significant difference in the behavior of the two cases. On the good system, the top four system calls are read, mprotect, open, and fstat. We get system calls in the range of several tens to several hundreds, with some errors probably stemming from seeking files in the $PATH. Another important element is the execution time, which takes about 1–2 milliseconds for each of the four system calls.

On the bad system, the top hitters are open, munmap, mmap, and stat. Moreover, we have system calls in the range of thousands, approximately 10–20 times more than previously. We also have a huge number of open errors. The execution time is in the range of 8–12 milliseconds, which is approximately 10 times longer than before. So we know something is wrong, but we do not know what exactly.

```
roger@linux-aif3:~> strace -c xclock
% time     seconds  usecs/call     calls    errors syscall
------ ----------- ----------- --------- --------- ----------------
 23.05    0.001397           4       375       151 read
 22.52    0.001365          28        48           mprotect
 17.35    0.001052           9       116        27 open
 11.86    0.000719          11        64           fstat
  7.64    0.000463           3       169           poll
  6.94    0.000421           5        92           mmap
  5.25    0.000318           3        91           close
  2.95    0.000179           4        48        19 access
  2.18    0.000132          12        11           munmap
  0.26    0.000016           0        66           writev
  0.00    0.000000           0         7           write
  0.00    0.000000           0        48         6 stat
  0.00    0.000000           0         2           lseek
  0.00    0.000000           0         8           brk
  0.00    0.000000           0         1           getpid
  0.00    0.000000           0         2           socket
  0.00    0.000000           0         2           connect
  0.00    0.000000           0         1           getsockname
  0.00    0.000000           0         1           getpeername
  0.00    0.000000           0         1           execve
  0.00    0.000000           0         4           uname
  0.00    0.000000           0         6           fcntl
  0.00    0.000000           0         2           getdents
  0.00    0.000000           0        19           gettimeofday
  0.00    0.000000           0         1           arch_prctl
------ ----------- ----------- --------- --------- ----------------
100.00    0.006062                  1185       203 total
roger@linux-aif3:~> 
```

**FIGURE 5.1  Output of an strace -c Run on a "Good" System**

### Ltrace

We will now use ltrace and perhaps discover something else. System calls shows a marked difference in the behavior, but we do not know what is causing the problem. Maybe, we will be able to determine the issue by looking at libraries, which is exactly what ltrace does. Again, we will execute the tool with -c flag, to see the summary.

### Ltrace log, good system

This gives us a whole new plate of information. The most significant library function is the creation of the xclock widget, which takes 20 milliseconds and almost 40% of the total execution time. Second on the list is XftFontOpenName. This is shown in Fig. 5.3.

### Ltrace log, bad system

Here, we see something else. XftFontOpenName is the leading function with a total of 18 seconds of execution time. Then, we have the creation of the widget, with no less impressive 16 seconds. After that, nothing else matters. Figure 5.4 clearly demonstrates this.

```
roger@linux-aif3:~> strace -c xclock
% time     seconds  usecs/call     calls    errors syscall
------ ----------- ----------- --------- --------- ----------------
 21.27    0.012636           2      6407      1524 open
 15.03    0.008928           2      4794           munmap
 13.47    0.008001           2      4868           mmap
 12.60    0.007482           2      4846         6 stat
 10.16    0.006033           1      4885           close
 10.03    0.005956           1      4787           fcntl
  9.62    0.005714           1      4832           fstat
  1.95    0.001158           3       369       153 read
  1.25    0.000743          23        32           getdents
  1.05    0.000624           4       170           poll
  1.03    0.000614          13        48           mprotect
  0.76    0.000453          14        33           write
  0.42    0.000247           5        47           brk
  0.35    0.000205           2        87        32 access
  0.31    0.000185           3        66           writev
  0.27    0.000160          12        13           link
  0.23    0.000134          10        13        13 chmod
  0.20    0.000121           3        39        13 unlink
  0.00    0.000000           0        15           lseek
  0.00    0.000000           0         1           getpid
  0.00    0.000000           0         2           socket
  0.00    0.000000           0         2           connect
  0.00    0.000000           0         1           getsockname
  0.00    0.000000           0         1           getpeername
  0.00    0.000000           0         1           execve
  0.00    0.000000           0         4           uname
  0.00    0.000000           0        13           rename
  0.00    0.000000           0        21           gettimeofday
  0.00    0.000000           0         1           arch_prctl
------ ----------- ----------- --------- --------- ----------------
100.00    0.059394                 36398      1741 total
roger@linux-aif3:~> █
```

**FIGURE 5.2  Output of an strace -c Run on a "Bad" System**

```
roger@linux-aif3:~> ltrace -c xclock
% time     seconds  usecs/call     calls      function
------ ----------- ----------- --------- --------------------
 47.25    0.200116      200116         1 XtCreateManagedWidget
 18.92    0.080115       80115         1 XftFontOpenName
 13.52    0.057246       57246         1 XtOpenApplication
  6.03    0.025551       25551         1 XSetWMProtocols
  5.27    0.022306       22306         1 setlocale
  2.00    0.008469        4234         2 XCreateBitmapFromData
  1.31    0.005536          44       124 XRenderCompositeDoublePoly
  1.19    0.005034        5034         1 XtRealizeWidget
  1.02    0.004310          34       124 XftDrawSrcPicture
  0.67    0.002832        2832         1 XCloseDisplay
  0.47    0.001978         989         2 XInternAtom
  0.34    0.001447         361         4 XtGetGC
```

**FIGURE 5.3  Ltrace Output on a "Good" System**

```
roger@linux-aif3:~> ltrace -c xclock
% time     seconds  usecs/call     calls      function
------ ----------- ----------- --------- --------------------
 52.56   17.908641    17908641         1 XftFontOpenName
 47.01   16.019731    16019731         1 XtCreateManagedWidget
  0.18    0.059982       59982         1 XtOpenApplication
  0.07    0.023112       23112         1 setlocale
  0.06    0.021342       21342         1 XSetWMProtocols
  0.03    0.008574        4287         2 XCreateBitmapFromData
  0.02    0.007340          59       124 XRenderCompositeDoublePoly
  0.02    0.005701        5701         1 XtRealizeWidget
  0.01    0.005058          40       124 XftDrawSrcPicture
  0.01    0.002659        1329         2 XInternAtom
  0.00    0.001059         176         6 XtDisplay
  0.00    0.000915         228         4 XtGetGC
```

**FIGURE 5.4 Ltrace Output on a "Bad" System**

### Ltrace comparison

We can clearly see that there is something wrong with fonts. On the good system, the relevant library call took a fraction of the time, while on the bad system, it lasted almost 20 seconds. Now, if we cross-reference the strace logs with these two, we start to get a clearer picture. The long duration of the function responsible for creating the widget definitely explains the slowness we experience. Moreover, it aligns nicely with the huge number of system calls and errors on the bad system. We now have a clue.

## ADDITIONAL TOOLS

Our initial investigation with strace and ltrace has provided us with a great lead into what the underlying problem is. But we need to familiarize ourselves with additional software, because sometimes we may not be able – or allowed – to use tracing tools, the performance penalty might be too high, we could eliminate the delicate timing issue that affects the customer runs, and there might be a risk of crashing the production applications. Moreover, the exposure to new tools will help us gain better, more comprehensive understanding of our systems, as well as any problems we might face.

### Combined approach with several tools

Now, we will see an example in which we cross-reference the knowledge and findings we accumulated by using a number of different tools to create a complete picture of the problem we are facing and find a solution to our issue.

### Additional analysis with vmstat

Some people could decide they already have enough information – something seems to be wrong with fonts. But, let us say you are still not 100% convinced and you want to learn more. Let us try using vmstat, which we have introduced in Chapter 3.

## Good system

The vmstat tool provides useful information on the memory and CPU usage. Right now, the fields of interest are CPU metrics in the last five columns, specifically the two labeled us and sy, as well as the cs and in fields under system.

The us and sy labels indicate the percentage of CPU usage by user and system, respectively. The cs and in labels refer to context switches and interrupts. The first metric tells us roughly how often the running process had to relinquish its place in the runqueue in favor of another waiting process. In other words, there was a context switch from one process to another. Interrupts indicates the number of times the running process had to access the underlying hardware, for example how many times the process accessed the disk to read data from the filesystem, poll the screen or the keyboard, and so on.

Let us see what happens when we launch the xclock program. Ignore the first line because it displays the average values since the last uptime. We can see that there is a brief spike of user CPU, also reflected in the high number of interrupts and context switches. Xclock is launched by the time the fourth line is displayed, as illustrated in Fig. 5.5.

## Bad system

Here, the situation is a little different. We can see a significant increase in user CPU for almost 5–7 seconds. However, there are fewer context switches than before and many more interrupts. What does this mean? We can see that the launching of xclock, which is an interactive application and should be therefore treated as an interactive process, is behaving like a computational (batch) process.

For interactive processes, we want as much responsiveness as possible, which means lots of context switches and little CPU activity so that we get dynamic priority from the scheduler and spend as little time thinking, giving control to the user. However, in our case, the process does fewer context switches than before and uses a lot more CPU, which is typical behavior for batch processes. This means there is some thinking going on. What is happening is that our system is reading fonts and creating the cache while we are waiting for xclock. This also explains the increase in IO activity and some wa CPU values, as we have to perform this operation on the local filesystem. This is shown in Fig. 5.6.

```
roger@linux-aif3:~> vmstat 1 10
procs ------------memory---------- ---swap-- -----io---- -system-- -----cpu-----
 r  b   swpd   free  buff  cache   si   so    bi    bo   in    cs us sy id wa st
 1  0  18508 225440    28 783740    3    5   411   103  479   636  4  6 87  3  0
 0  0  18508 225432    28 783740    0    0     0     0 1410  1705 11  9 81  0  0
 3  0  18508 223920    28 784236    0    0   480     0 1319  1791  5  8 86  0  0
 0  0  18508 223904    28 784220    0    0     0     0  452   459  1  4 95  0  0
 0  0  18508 223904    28 784220    0    0     0     0 1330  1646  2  6 93  0  0
 0  0  18508 224772    28 784220    0    0     0     0 1962  2492  6 10 84  0  0
 0  0  18508 224772    28 784220    0    0     0     0  959  1081  1  5 94  0  0
 0  0  18508 224772    28 784220    0    0     0     0  923  1108 10  8 82  0  0
 0  0  18508 224772    28 784220    0    0     0     0  324   300  1  4 96  0  0
 0  0  18508 224772    28 784220    0    0     0     0  360   284  0  3 96  0  0
roger@linux-aif3:~> ▮
```

**FIGURE 5.5 Vmstat Output on a "Good" System, Showing the CPU Activity at the Time the xclock Program Was Launched**

```
roger@linux-aif3:~> vmstat 1 30
procs ----------memory---------- ---swap-- -----io---- -system-- -----cpu------
 r  b   swpd   free   buff  cache   si   so    bi    bo   in   cs us sy id wa st
 0  0  18140 228704    28 783132    3    5   403   101  479  634  4  6 87  3  0
 0  0  18140 228704    28 783132    0    0     0     0 1522 1847 13 10 78  0  0
 3  0  18140 228580    28 783132    0    0     0     0  393  352  0  4 96  0  0
 1  0  18140 224844    28 783412    0    0   152     0 1319  851 34  6 60  1  0
 2  0  18140 222860    28 783416    0    0     8  3200 2056 1001 50  8 41  3  0
 1  0  18140 223488    28 783672    0    0     0     0 1463 1062 48  8 43  0  0
 1  0  18140 223116    28 784052    0    0     0     0 1303  501 47  7 47  0  0
 0  0  18140 222248    28 784752    0    0   248     0 1530 1747 19  9 71  1  0
 0  0  18140 222256    28 784752    0    0     0     0 1144 1266  1  6 93  0  0
 0  0  18140 225596    28 784752    0    0     0     0 2226 2789  7 15 78  0  0
 1  0  18140 225596    28 784752    0    0     0     0 1669 2110  7  8 86  0  0
 0  0  18140 225596    28 784752    0    0     0     0  826  860  6  6 88  0  0
```

**FIGURE 5.6 Vmstat Output on a "Bad" System, Showing the CPU Activity at the Time the xclock Program Was Launched; Notice the Difference in Interrupts, Context Switches, and User Space CPU Activity Compared to the Healthy System**

Now, it is important to emphasize that this kind of analysis is meaningless if you do not know how your process is supposed to behave and what it is supposed to do. However, if you have an inkling of an idea, then even a boring list of numbers as output by vmstat could provide you with a wealth of information.

### Problem resolution

We believe we have sufficient information to solve this. Something is wrong with fonts. The fact that applications take so long to start probably indicates the font cache is being rebuilt every time, which in turn indicates the programs started by the user cannot read the system font cache. This would also explain why sudo and root are not affected.

Going back to our problem, customer applications are slow to load. Strace logs indicate open errors. We could now run a full strace session and learn the exact paths of these errors. We would use -e flag on an open system call to reduce verbosity, and we would increase the string length using -s flag so we could see all of the information about failing paths. We would learn about fonts not being readable by the user.

But we do not need to do that. We cross-reference our information with ltrace, which points out the problem to be in the opening of fonts. This library call blocks the creation of the widget, which is why the applications appear to be slow in launching. Vmstat runs provide additional information, which help narrow down the issue further.

And if we check the system font cache, located under /var/cache/fontconfig, we learn that fonts are created with 600 permissions, that is, they are only readable by root. If we change the values to 644, we resolve the problem and all our applications start quickly. We also save disk space, because we do not require all users to create their own copy of fonts in their own home directory.

### Lsof comes to rescue

Now we will briefly demonstrate another problem. This one is completely different from the previous example. Moreover, in this case, strace and ltrace are completely useless because the process is stuck in a D state. We do not really know what might be wrong, but all of the tools above are of no help. Enter lsof (lsof(8), n.d.), a tool capable of reporting a list of all open files for running processes and a handy tool for what we have in mind.

OK, let us assume you have some Java process that seems "stuck" and not responding. Now, Java is always ugly and comes with hideous exception traces, but we must debug the issue and the conventional tools do not provide any useful information. In fact, this is what you see with strace:

```
futex(0x562d0be8, FUTEX_WAIT, 18119, NULL
```

But if you check the same process with lsof, you get something like this:

```
java   11511   user   32u   ipv4   1920022313   TCP   rogerbox:44332->rogerbox:22122
(SYN_SENT)
```

Voila. We can see our Java is using two IPv4 ports to communicate internally. It has sent a packet from one port to another, initiating a TCP connection. This is indicated by the SYN_SENT state, the first sequence in the three-point TCP handshake. For some reason, the server, listening on port 22122, is not responding.

At this stage, you may want to check why the packet is not being rejected or accepted by the server. Do we have a routing problem? On a local machine, this probably does not apply, but maybe the destination is somewhere else? Do we have a firewall problem? Can you connect to the relevant machine and port using telnet? At this point, you still do not have all the tools to fix the issue, but you are fully aware of what is causing Java to misbehave. For all practical purposes, the problem is solved.

## WORKING WITH PERF

The analysis of system issues may not be limited to the user space. Problems affecting your install base may have a deeper root cause. In such scenarios, the use of tools such as strace, ltrace, and others will not be effective enough. At this stage, it is prudent to explore additional software, such as process debuggers and profiling tools.

Profiling is a way of dynamic program analysis that measures various metrics of a program, like memory or time complexity, the usage of particular instructions, or frequency and duration of function calls. The most common use of profiling information is to aid program optimization. Profiling is achieved by instrumenting either the program source code or its binary executable form using a tool called a profiler (or code profiler). A number of different techniques may be used by profilers, such as event-based, statistical, instrumented, and simulation methods.

There are many commercial products available on the market. For example, you may be interested in Intel® Vtune™ Amplifier (Intel(R) VTune(TM) Amplifier XE 2013, n.d.), a performance analysis tool for 32- and 64-bit x86-based machines. Although basic features work on both Intel and AMD hardware, advanced hardware-based sampling requires an Intel-manufactured CPU. The VTune Amplifier assists in various kinds of code profiling including stack sampling, thread profiling, and hardware event sampling. The profiler result consists of details such as time spent in each subroutine, which can be drilled down to the instruction level. The time taken by the instructions is indicative of any stalls in the pipeline during instruction execution. The tool can be also used to analyze thread performance.

Then, you may also want to explore and use Valgrind (Valgrind, n.d.), a programming tool for memory debugging, memory leak detection, and profiling. Valgrind is in essence a virtual machine using just-in-time (JIT) compilation techniques, including dynamic recompilation.

Both these tools, as well as others, require their own drivers to be installed and used on the target host to perform the collection and analysis. In this section, we will not be focusing on commercial implementations of profiling. Instead, we will examine a built-in kernel functionality called perf, available in the mainline release since version 2.6.31 (Perfcounters added to the mainline, n.d.).

## INTRODUCTION

Perf (Linux kernel profiling with perf, n.d.) is a performance analyzing tool in Linux. The user-space controlling utility called perf has git-like interface with subcommands. It is capable of statistical profiling of entire system (both kernel and user code), single CPU, or several threads.

The interface between the utility and the kernel consists of a single syscall (sys_perf_event_open) and is done via a file descriptor and a mmaped memory region. Perf also uses special purpose registers on the CPU to count events. Additional system calls are available for those who want to set up performance monitoring in their code. However, this topic is beyond the scope of this section.

Since most of the functionality is integrated into the kernel, perf does not require a system deamon and introduces a very low overhead, which makes it suitable for most tasks. Furthermore, perf works on a large variety of architecture platforms with hardware counters, including x86, PowerPC64, UltraSPARC III and IV, ARM v5, v6, v7, Cortex-A8 and A9, Alpha EV56, and SH.

## WHY NOT OPROFILE?

Another performance tool, very closely related to perf, is Oprofile (Oprofile, n.d.). OProfile is a system-wide statistical profiling tool for Linux, originally written for the Linux kernel version 2.4. It consists of a kernel module, a user-space daemon, and several user-space tools. The basic usage model is very similar to perf. In fact, one may claim that perf is the successor to OProfile, with the notable distinction of having been added to the mainline kernel.

OProfile is capable of profiling an entire system or its parts, from interrupt routines or drivers, to user-space processes. It has a low overhead. The most portable mode of OProfile uses a system timer to generate sampling interrupts (events). A less portable mode allows hardware performance counters to be used for sampling events generation on several processor architectures. In the Linux 2.6 family and above, there is wide support for several processor architectures, including x86 (32 and 64 bit), DEC Alpha, MIPS, ARM, sparc64, ppc64, and AVR32.

Because of the similarity between the usage models of the two tools, and the fact perf is a part of the mainline kernel, we will focus on perf rather than OProfile, which remains beyond the scope of this book. However, several online references (Smashing performance with OProfile, n.d.) (Tuning Performance with OProfile, n.d.) (Linux super-duper admin tools: OProfile, n.d.) provide a good starting point to testing and using OProfile.

## PREREQUISITES

The use of performance analysis tools is far from trivial. In most cases, it requires a very good understanding of the system and expected behavior to yield meaningful results. Moreover, you should be fairly proficient in the Linux core concepts and have some programming knowledge to be able to utilize the tools to the best effect.

## BASIC USAGE

The perf utility userspace package consists of several commands. Sometimes, these commands may be available as standalone wrapper scripts or binaries. The most basic syntax is

```
perf <command> <optional arguments>
```

Available commands include the following:

- stat: measure total event count for single program or for system for some time
- top: top-like dynamic view of hottest functions
- record: measure and save sampling data for single program
- report: analyze file generated by perf record; can generate flat, or graph profile.
- annotate: annotate sources or assembly
- sched: tracing/measuring of scheduler actions and latencies
- list: list available events

As we have mentioned above, any one command may be executed as a combination of the perf binary and the command, or through wrapper tools, such as perf-stat, perf-sched, and others.

## Events

The perf tool is capable of measuring events coming from different sources, including software events, such as pure kernel counters (context switchers, minor faults, and the like), as well as hardware events. Perf can measure microarchitectural events reported by the performance monitoring unit (PMU) in the processor, including the number of cycles, cache misses, and others. The collectable events depend on the processor type and model. The available list of supported events can be obtained by running the perf list command:

```
List of pre-defined events (to be used in -e):

  cpu-cycles OR cycles                                    [Hardware event]

  stalled-cycles-frontend OR idle-cycles-frontend         [Hardware event]

  stalled-cycles-backend OR idle-cycles-backend           [Hardware event]

  instructions                                            [Hardware event]

  cache-references                                        [Hardware event]

  cache-misses                                            [Hardware event]

  cpu-clock                                               [Software event]

  task-clock                                              [Software event]

  page-faults OR faults                                   [Software event]

  minor-faults                                            [Software event]

  major-faults                                            [Software event]

  ...
```

## Performance statistics

For any of the supported events, perf can keep a running count during process execution. In a way, this mode of work is similar to the use of the –e flag with strace, which outputs the summary of executed system calls, errors, and total time spent for each entry. Similarly, the perf stat command will display an output of aggregated events at the end of the application run. For instance, the output of the ls command:

```
Performance counter stats for 'ls /tmp/':


        0.771803 task-clock            #    0.612 CPUs utilized

              16 context-switches      #    0.021 M/sec

               0 CPU-migrations        #    0.000 M/sec

             276 page-faults           #    0.358 M/sec

         2475134 cycles                #    3.207 GHz

         1540889 stalled-cycles-frontend  #   62.25% frontend cycles idle

         1189255 stalled-cycles-backend   #   48.05% backend  cycles idle

         1840092 instructions          #    0.74  insns per cycle

                                       #    0.84  stalled cycles per insn

          385139 branches              #  499.012 M/sec

           16921 branch-misses         #    4.39% of all branches


      0.001261224 seconds time elapsed
```

It is also possible to narrow down the performance statistics counting by specifying one or more events of interest (similar to the -e flag used by strace and ltrace). The event selection is available using the rather obvious -e switch, with optional modifiers. For example:

- -e events – will measure events at both the user and kernel levels.
- -e events:u will only measure at the user level.
- -e events:k will count only kernel events.

Additional flags are available, for use with hypervisors and measuring events on the host or guest operating systems in a virtualized environment. Please consult the official documentation for more details.

The collection of hardware events is probably more interesting, but it also requires the use of hardware vendor documentation, as well as a deeper understanding of what these events do. For hardware events, you need to use the hexadecimal parameter code. Additional care is required when the number of events exceeds the number of counters, in which case multiplexing and scaling will be applied. This is beyond the scope of this book.

Perf can also be used to run repeated measurements to estimate the variation of a process execution. This can be useful if you expect your software to behave in a very predictable manner, and you need to understand the level of system noise or other environmental impacts that may alter the execution results. In turn, this may point to a problem with your setup or the software code. This kind of measurement is possible by using the -r switch, similar to the iostat and vmstat flags, as we have seen earlier.

Similarly, the granularity of event measurement can be restricted to individual threads, processes and processors (cores), or it can be applied to the whole system. Perf also supports attaching to running processes, which can be useful if you suspect a certain program is misbehaving, and you wish to examine its execution in real time.

## Sampling

Sampling differs from event counting in that it records a sample when the relevant sampling counter overflows. Data are collected using the corerd command, and the generated output is then analyzed using the report and annotate commands. As we have mentioned earlier, this mode of work is very similar to that of OProfile.

The default sampling event used with the perf record command is the cycles event. Depending on the actual processor architecture, the cycles event will map to a hardware-specific event, such as, for instance, UNHALTED_CORE_CYCLES on Intel architecture, or CPU_CLK_UNHALTD on AMD processors. Cycle counting will not report when the processor is idle. Let us explore an example:

What we did was execute a typical memory hog process, which took 1GG of memory, and then released it. The sampling data is saved in a file named perf.data in the home directory of the user running the perf record command.

```
#perf record /tmp/memhog 1024M

hogging 1024 MB: 20 40 60 80 100 120 140 160 180 200 220 240 260 280 300 320 340 360
380 400 420 440 460 480 500 520 540 560 580 600 620 640 660 680 700 720 740 760 780
800 820 840 860 880 900 920 940 960 980 1000 1020 1024

[ perf record: Woken up 1 times to write data ]

[ perf record: Captured and wrote 0.114 MB perf.data (~5000 samples) ]
```

An interesting metric is that the perf tool collected roughly 5000 samples. The default sampling rate is 1000 Hz, which indicates the tool run for about 5 seconds. This can be used to estimate the expected event rate for running processes in the respective environments, especially when comparing good (healthy) and bad systems.

If you time the execution of the memhog 1 GB allocation, you should see a total time that is roughly similar to the number of collected samples divided by the collection frequency.

```
#/usr/bin/time /tmp/memhog 1024M

hogging 1024 MB: 20 40 60 80 100 120 140 160 180 200 220 240 260 280 300 320 340 360
380 400 420 440 460 480 500 520 540 560 580 600 620 640 660 680 700 720 740 760 780
800 820 840 860 880 900 920 940 960 980 1000 1020 1024

2.33user 0.44system 0:04.38elapsed 63%CPU (0avgtext+0avgdata 4015936maxresident)k

0inputs+0outputs (0major+251032minor)pagefaults 0swaps
```

To analyze the data, simply run the perf report command. A sample run is shown in Fig. 5.7.

Before we discuss the actual results, let us briefly describe the report format. The first column indicates the percentage of the overall samples collected in the corresponding function. The second column reports the process from which the samples were collected. In the per-thread/per-process mode, this will always be the name of the monitored command. In the CPU-wide mode, the command name can vary.

The third column shows the name of the ELF image where the samples came from. If a program is dynamically linked, then this may show the name of a shared library. When the samples come from the kernel, then the pseudo ELF image name [kernel.kallsyms] is used. The fourth column indicates the privilege level at which the sample was taken, that is, the level at which the program was running when it

```
Events: 2K cycles
  88.22%  memhog  memhog               [.] main
   5.13%  memhog  [kernel.kallsyms]    [k] clear_page_c
   1.32%  memhog  [kernel.kallsyms]    [k] page_fault
   1.19%  memhog  [kernel.kallsyms]    [k] mem_cgroup_charge_common
   0.55%  memhog  [kernel.kallsyms]    [k] __mem_cgroup_commit_charge
   0.39%  memhog  ld-2.11.3.so         [.] dl_main
   0.33%  memhog  [kernel.kallsyms]    [k] __rmqueue
   0.29%  memhog  [kernel.kallsyms]    [k] page_add_new_anon_rmap
   0.22%  memhog  [kernel.kallsyms]    [k] mem_cgroup_add_lru_list
   0.18%  memhog  [kernel.kallsyms]    [k] get_page_from_freelist
   0.18%  memhog  [kernel.kallsyms]    [k] __alloc_pages_nodemask
   0.18%  memhog  [kernel.kallsyms]    [k] prep_new_page
   0.15%  memhog  [kernel.kallsyms]    [k] do_page_fault
   0.15%  memhog  [kernel.kallsyms]    [k] ____pagevec_lru_add_fn
   0.11%  memhog  [kernel.kallsyms]    [k] handle_mm_fault
   0.11%  memhog  [kernel.kallsyms]    [k] do_anonymous_page
   0.07%  memhog  [kernel.kallsyms]    [k] mem_cgroup_count_vm_event
   0.07%  memhog  [kernel.kallsyms]    [k] down_read_trylock
   0.07%  memhog  [kernel.kallsyms]    [k] _raw_spin_lock
   0.07%  memhog  [kernel.kallsyms]    [k] __inc_zone_page_state
   0.07%  memhog  [kernel.kallsyms]    [k] mem_cgroup_charge_statistics
```

**FIGURE 5.7  A Sample Run of Perf Report**

was interrupted. The following levels exist, and they correspond to the modifiers we mentioned earlier:

- [.]: user level
- [k]: kernel level
- [g]: guest kernel level (virtualization)
- [u]: guest OS user space
- [H]: hypervisor

The final column shows the symbol name. If you are interested in learning more about what the specific symbol name does, you can consult The Linux Cross Reference site (The Linux Cross Reference, n.d.) and search for the specific string entry, or if you have the kernel sources available for your distribution, normally under /usr/src/linux, consult them.

Going back to our example, we learn that our process, memhog, spent over 88% of time in the main function. But then, we also had a number of clear_page_c and page_fault events. On its own, the report might not be meaningful, but it can be a powerful indicator for comparisons between systems or applications with different performance or behavior patterns. Various output formatting options are available. Please consult the official documentation and man pages for additional details.

### Annotation

The use of the annotate commands allows you to drill down to the instruction level for profiled applications. In this mode, all the functions with samples will be disassembled and each instruction will have its relative percentage of samples reported. Interpreting this information is beyond the scope of this book due to its sensitive nature and the high level of understanding required of the profiled process.

### Perf top command

The perf tool can also operate in a mode that is very similar to the Linux top command, printing sampled functions in real time. By default, the top command will show a top down list of sampled functions, based on the time spent, working in the processor-wide mode. A variety of keyboard shortcuts are available to filter the displayed information in different ways. We can see this in Fig. 5.8.

## BASIC EXAMPLE

Now, we will perform the analysis of a system problem, where the performance hit cannot be perceived or analyzed using the more conventional tools including trace programs, and system information utilities are not very helpful either.

The problem is as follows. In a large data center, one of your customers is running compilations of their software tools, with multiple threads of execution and parallel jobs on several hosts. On a specific cluster of hosts, the customer reports results

```
  122 irqs/sec  kernel:73.0%  exact:   0.0% [1000Hz cycles],  (all, 16 CPUs)

samples  pcnt function                             DSO

455.00  19.4% intel_idle                           [kernel.kallsyms]
136.00   5.8% Perl_hv_common                       /usr/bin/perl
 77.00   3.3% find_busiest_group                   [kernel.kallsyms]
 63.00   2.7% __pthread_getspecific_internal       /lib64/libpthread-2.11.3.so
 56.00   2.4% Perl_sv_setsv_flags                  /usr/bin/perl
 56.00   2.4% Perl_re_compile                      /usr/bin/perl
 56.00   2.4% _int_malloc                          /lib64/libc-2.11.3.so
 45.00   1.9% Perl_leave_scope                     /usr/bin/perl
 43.00   1.8% Perl_pp_padsv                        /usr/bin/perl
 41.         1.7% rcu_needs_cpu                     [kernel.kallsyms]
 39.         1.7% Perl_pp_rv2av                     /usr/bin/perl
 37.00   1.6% Perl_re_intuit_start                 /usr/bin/perl
 34.00   1.4% Perl_pp_helem                        /usr/bin/perl
 34.00   1.4% _int_free                            /lib64/libc-2.11.3.so
 33.00   1.4% memcpy                               /lib64/libc-2.11.3.so
```

**FIGURE 5.8  Perf Top Output**

within the expected envelope, similar to their synthetic tests. However, a different batch of servers reports reduced performance.

At a first glance, the servers all appear to be identical on all levels of the hardware and software stack. They are all identical enterprise-grade systems, with the same specifications and even the same BIOS version and configuration. The network connectivity is identical, and so are the kernel as well as all the applications installed on these systems. Running the basic checks with the first- and second-level system administration tools reveals no difference.

Initially, you suspect there is a network component involved, but the network administration teams report seeing no performance degradation in their monitors. The problem is further compounded by the fact that multiple tasks are running on each host, so you cannot easily isolate problematic processes.

This kind of scenario is not that much different from what you will encounter in a large number of companies. However, politics and modus operandi aside, you wish to resolve the problem so that your customer may resume their normal work.

We will now utilize the perf tool, and will perform a methodical comparison between the so-called good and bad systems. We have already concluded basic analysis with the other tools, which is why we now resort to using perf.

First, let us take a look at the "good" run:

```
[ perf record: Woken up 773 times to write data ]

[ perf record: Captured and wrote 195.106 MB perf.data (~8524291 samples) ]
```

The statistics are as follows:

```
Performance counter stats for 'make 8':


    3798653.532225 task-clock                 #      8.051 CPUs utilized

           1390973 context-switches           #      0.000 M/sec

            190877 CPU-migrations             #      0.000 M/sec

         206911500 page-faults                #      0.054 M/sec

    11702909085060 cycles                     #      3.081 GHz

     6184300130309 stalled-cycles-frontend    #     52.84% frontend cycles idle

     4662835577081 stalled-cycles-backend     #     39.84% backend  cycles idle

    12026471058401 instructions               #      1.03  insns per cycle

                                              #      0.51  stalled cycles per insn

     2635513137580 branches                   #    693.802 M/sec

       79976854111 branch-misses              #      3.03% of all branches


      471.846130001 seconds time elapsed
```

Likewise, the drilldown for the perf report shows the following results:

```
74.21%       cc1  cc1                    [.] 0x2e4b80

 3.62%        as  as                     [.] 0x10665

 2.15%       cc1  libc-2.11.3.so         [.] _int_malloc

 1.45%       cc1  [kernel.kallsyms]      [k] clear_page_c

 1.37%       cc1  libc-2.11.3.so         [.] __GI_memset

 0.70%       cc1  libc-2.11.3.so         [.] vfprintf

 0.69%  genksyms  genksyms               [.] yylex
```

```
0.62%      cc1   libc-2.11.3.so        [.] _int_free

0.60%      cc1   [kernel.kallsyms]     [k] page_fault

0.59%      cc1   libc-2.11.3.so        [.] memcpy

0.45%      cc1   libc-2.11.3.so        [.] __GI___libc_free

0.41%      cc1   libc-2.11.3.so        [.] __GI___libc_malloc

0.41%      cc1   libc-2.11.3.so        [.] malloc_consolidate

0.38%      cc1   libc-2.11.3.so        [.] __calloc

0.35%  genksyms  genksyms              [.] find_symbol

0.31%      cc1   libc-2.11.3.so        [.] __strlen_sse42
```

The "bad" system behavior is very interesting because the difference from the "good" system is not immediately evident from the report. We can see a small difference in the total size of the captured data and the number of collected samples.

```
[ perf record: Woken up 850 times to write data ]

[ perf record: Captured and wrote 212.391 MB perf.data (~9279511 samples) ]
```

Moreover, the actual report is almost identical. Some 70% of time is spent compiling, followed by approximately 4% spent in the GNU Assembler. The figures closely correspond to the "good" system.

```
70.28%          cc1  cc1              [.] 0x4893b0

4.24%            as  as               [.] 0xfe40

1.97%           cc1  libc-2.11.3.so   [.] _int_malloc

1.49%           cc1  [kernel.kallsyms] [k] clear_page_c

1.28%           cc1  libc-2.11.3.so   [.] __GI_memset
```

```
 0.79%          genksyms   genksyms              [.] yylex

 0.70%                ccl   libc-2.11.3.so        [.] vfprintf

 0.61%                ccl   [kernel.kallsyms]     [k] page_fault

 0.57%                ccl   libc-2.11.3.so        [.] memcpy

 0.57%                ccl   libc-2.11.3.so        [.] _int_free

 0.41%                ccl   libc-2.11.3.so        [.] __GI___libc_free

 0.38%             fixdep   fixdep                [.] parse_dep_file
```

Collecting perf statistics (with perf stat) ought to shed more light on the problem. Indeed, we can observe a marked difference in the behavior of the two types of systems. On a typical bad host, the sampling took almost one hour. During this time, we can see that the average CPU utilization was only 0.995 cores, despite the parallelism in the make command.

```
   Performance counter stats for 'make -j 8':


3506718.545209 task-clock                    #     0.995 CPUs utilized

      2892157 context-switches               #     0.001 M/sec

         2100 CPU-migrations                 #     0.000 M/sec

    206912750 page-faults                    #     0.059 M/sec

11557036224689 cycles                        #     3.296 GHz

 6096210637867 stalled-cycles-frontend       #    52.75% frontend cycles idle

 4642587676357 stalled-cycles-backend        #    40.17% backend  cycles idle

11987904817934 instructions                  #     1.04  insns per cycle

                                             #     0.51  stalled cycles per insn

 2622512483595 branches                      #   747.854 M/sec

   81167564946 branch-misses                 #     3.10% of all branches

3524.728435564 seconds time elapsed
```

On a good system, the execution is significantly shorter, at only about 15 minutes. While the number of instructions per cycle and the overall branching speed are pretty much the same, the CPU utilization is different, at 8.051 cores, close to the expected throughput when running the make command with the -j 8 flag.

```
Performance counter stats for 'make -j 8':


    3798653.532225 task-clock                #    8.051 CPUs utilized

           1390973 context-switches          #    0.000 M/sec

            190877 CPU-migrations            #    0.000 M/sec

         206911500 page-faults               #    0.054 M/sec

    11702909085060 cycles                    #    3.081 GHz

     6184300130309 stalled-cycles-frontend   #   52.84% frontend cycles idle

     4662835577081 stalled-cycles-backend    #   39.84% backend  cycles idle

    12026471058401 instructions              #    1.03  insns per cycle

                                             #    0.51  stalled cycles per insn

     2635513137580 branches                  #  693.802 M/sec

       79976854111 branch-misses             #    3.03% of all branches



      471.846130001 seconds time elapsed

Performance counter stats for 'make -j 8':
```

What do we learn here? We see that, for some reason, the bad batch of hosts is underperforming when running multithreaded compilations. Since we do not observe any issue with the hardware configuration, BIOS settings or kernel tunables, we focus on the application stack. Indeed, digging into the actual application code reveals a faulty NUMA logic (based on network topography that assumed a specific hardware set) hardcoded in the application source files.

Once the customer was made aware of the issue, they adjusted their own software and regained the performance, as well as consistent behavior from their tasks. This was made possible by using the perf tool, whereas other system administration utilities failed to reveal any great clues to the root cause of the problem.

## ADVANCED EXAMPLE

Say you have a Linux system with multiple users working on it, running on an NFS filesystem. One of the users reports a certain performance degradation in accessing the network objects, such as files and directories. Other users have no such woes. You begin the investigation by using strace.

You execute a summary run with the -c flag; however, in both cases the quantity of system calls and errors, as well as their order, is identical. The only difference is that a specific system call for one user takes longer than for the others. You narrow down your tests using the -e flag, which lets you trace individual calls. With the so-called problematic user, you get a consistently slow result for the stat system call:

```
strace -tt -T -e lstat /usr/bin/stat /nfs/object.txt

14:04:28.659680 lstat("/nfs/object.txt", {st_mode=S_IFREG|0755,

st_size=291, ...}) = 0 <0.011364>
```

On the other hand, the so-called healthy user has no such worries:

```
strace -tt -T -e lstat /usr/bin/stat /nfs/object.txt

14:04:54.032616 lstat("/nfs/object.txt", {st_mode=S_IFREG|0755,

st_size=291, ...}) = 0 <0.000069>
```

There is no difference in the environment settings of the two users. They both use identical shells. Everything is perfect except that one small difference in the system call time for stat. With the usual set of your tools, you have just reached a dead end.

### Call the cavalry

Now, let us see what perf can do for us. Let us run the test wrapped around the stat command. It is a very good way to start your investigation, because you will get a neat summary of what happens in the kernel, which can then help point out the next lead in your troubleshooting. Indeed, for the healthy system, we get

```
Performance counter stats for '/usr/bin/stat /nfs/object.txt':

      3.333125  task-clock-msecs        #      0.455 CPUs

             6  context-switches        #      0.002 M/sec

             0  CPU-migrations          #      0.000 M/sec
```

```
        326   page-faults              #      0.098 M/sec

    3947536   cycles                   #   1184.335 M/sec

    2201811   instructions             #      0.558 IPC

      45294   cache-references         #     13.589 M/sec

      11828   cache-misses             #      3.549 M/sec


 0.007327727   seconds time elapsed
```

For the misbehaving user:

```
 Performance counter stats for '/usr/bin/stat /nfs/object.txt':


    14.167143   task-clock-msecs        #      0.737 CPUs

            7   context-switches        #      0.000 M/sec

            0   CPU-migrations          #      0.000 M/sec

          326   page-faults             #      0.023 M/sec

     17699949   cycles                  #   1249.366 M/sec

      4424158   instructions            #      0.250 IPC

       304109   cache-references        #     21.466 M/sec

        60553   cache-misses            #      4.274 M/sec


  0.019216707   seconds time elapsed
```

There is a marked difference between the two. While the CPU speed is the same, and the number of migrations, context switches, and page faults are identical, the bad user spins approximately five times longer, using more cycles and instructions, resulting in more total time needed for the command to complete. This already shows us there is something wrong.

Let us explore a little deeper. Let us now record the run and then analyze the data using the report command. This will give us a far more detailed understanding of what really happened. Here is the report for the good user:

```
# Samples: 56

#

# Overhead   Command      Shared Object    Symbol

# ........   .......      ...............   ......

#

    5.36%     stat   [kernel]              [k] page_fault

    5.36%     perf   /usr/bin/perf         [.] 0x0000000000d099

    3.57%     stat   [kernel]              [k] flush_tlb_others_ipi

    3.57%     stat   [kernel]              [k] handle_mm_fault

    3.57%     stat   [kernel]              [k] find_vma

    3.57%     stat   /lib64/libc-2...      [.] __GI_strcmp

    3.57%     stat   /lib64/ld-2.11...     [.] _dl_lookup_symbol_x

    3.57%     perf   [kernel]              [k] _spin_lock

    1.79%     stat   [kernel]              [k] flush_tlb_mm

    1.79%     stat   [kernel]              [k] finish_task_switch

    1.79%     stat   [kernel]              [k] ktime_get_ts
```

For the bad user, we see a different report:

```
# Samples: 143

#

# Overhead   Command    Shared Object   Symbol

# ........   .......    .............   ......

#

   57.34%      stat    [kernel]        [k] rpcauth_lookup_credcache [sunrpc]

    2.80%      stat    [kernel]        [k] generic_match [sunrpc]

    2.10%      stat    [kernel]        [k] clear_page_c

    1.40%      stat    [kernel]        [k] flush_tlb_others_ipi

    1.40%      stat    [kernel]        [k] __do_fault

    1.40%      stat    [kernel]        [k] zap_pte_range

    1.40%      stat    [kernel]        [k] handle_mm_fault

    1.40%      stat    [kernel]        [k] __link_path_walk

    1.40%      stat    [kernel]        [k] page_fault

    1.40%      stat    /lib64/libc-2...  [.] __GI_strcmp

    1.40%      stat    /lib64/ld-2.11... [.] _dl_load_cache_lookup
```

### Understanding the report

Thanks to perf, we can see the difference immediately. The bad user wastes much time using the rpcauth_lookup_credcache symbol, which is linked inside the sunrpc kernel module. At this point, you have all the information you need to go to the Internet to do a very narrow and intelligent search. Just by punching the name of the symbol, you will find several mailing list references, pointing to this phenomenon, which in turn points to a real bug. Our problem is *not* immediately solved, but the problem has an upstream owner, which can now handle the issue, with solid information gained by using the kernel profiler.

## SUMMARY

Perf is a powerful, advanced tool for detecting bottlenecks in the system CPU, memory, and bus stack. On one hand, it requires a deeper understanding of the

Linux system, and the results cannot be interpreted without context and some basic awareness of what the system is supposed to be doing when analyzed. On the other hand, it provides useful information that cannot be obtained using the more traditional system administration tools.

## WORKING WITH GDB

In this chapter, we first learned about analyzing applications by tracing their system calls and functions. After that, we dug much deeper and looked at the kernel events. Now, we will step up and into the application space, trying to understand how we can troubleshoot problems by examining the behavior of binaries through a step-by-step debugging process.

In a nutshell, it comes down to this: You wrote a piece of code, and you want to compile it and run it. Or you have a binary and you just run it. The only problem is, the execution fails with a segmentation fault. For all practical purposes, you call it a day. To make things worse, your customer is screaming for help because their critical piece of software is failing and they are clueless as to what might be the root cause.

To this end, we will now discuss the use of process debuggers. Namely, we will focus on the widely popular GNU Debugger, the standard process debugger for UNIX-like systems. We will learn how to handle misbehaving binary code, how to examine its execution step by step, how to interpret errors and problems, and we will even step into the assembly code and hunt for problems there.

### INTRODUCTION

Gdb allows you to see what is going on inside another program while it executes – or what another program was doing at the moment it crashed. Gdb can do four main kinds of tasks that can help you find and catch bugs in the act:

- Start your program, specifying anything that might affect its behavior.
- Make your program stop on specified conditions.
- Examine what has happened when your program has stopped.
- Change things in your program, so you can experiment with correcting the effects of one bug and go on to learn about another.

The program being debugged can be written in Ada, C, C + +, Objective-C, Pascal, as well as many other languages. Those programs might be executing on the same machine as the debugger (native) or on another machine (remote). Gdb can run on most popular UNIXm UNIX-like and Microsoft Windows variants.

### PREREQUISITES

We would like to emphasize that this will not be easy. Working with gdb is not something anyone can do at their leisure. There are many requirements you must meet before you can have a successful session.

### Source files

You can debug code without having access to source files. However, your task will be more difficult, because you will not be able to refer to the actual code and try to understand if there is any kind of logical fallacy in the execution. You will only be able to follow symptoms and try to figure out where things might be wrong, but not why.

### Sources code compiled with symbols

On top of that, you will want source code with symbols, so you can map instructions in the binary program to their corresponding functions and lines in the source code. Otherwise, you will be groping in the dark.

### Understanding of the Linux system

This is probably the most important element. First, you will need some core knowledge of the memory management in Linux, and then, the fundamental concepts such as code, data, heap, stack, and so on. You should also be able to navigate /proc with some degree of comfort. You should also be familiar with the AT&T Assembly syntax, which is the syntax used in Linux, as opposed to Intel syntax, for example.

## SIMPLE EXAMPLE

We will begin with a simple example: a null pointer. In layman's terms, a null pointer is a pointer to an address in the memory space that does not have a meaningful value and cannot be referenced by the calling program, for whatever reason. This will normally lead to an unhandled error, resulting in a segmentation fault. Here is our source code:

```
#include <stdio.h>

int main (int argc, char* argv[])
{
    int* boom=0;
    printf("hello %d",*boom);
}
```

Now, let us compile it, with symbols. This is done by using the -g flag when running gcc.

```
gcc -g source.c -o binary.bin
```

And then we run it and get a nasty segmentation fault:

```
#./binary.bin

Segmentation fault
```

Now, you may want to try to debug this problem using standard tools, such as perhaps strace, ltrace, maybe lsof, and a few others. Normally, you would do this, because having a methodical approach to problem solving is always good, and you should start with simple things first. However, we will purposefully not do that right now to simplify things. As we advance in the chapter, we will see more complex examples and the use of other tools, too.

All right, so now we need to start using the GNU Debugger. We will invoke the program once again, this time through gdb. The syntax is simple:

```
#gdb binary.bin

GNU gdb (GDB) SUSE (7.3-0.6.1)

Copyright (C) 2011 Free Software Foundation, Inc.

License GPLv3+: GNU GPL version 3 or later <http://gnu.org/licenses/gpl.html>

This is free software: you are free to change and redistribute it.

There is NO WARRANTY, to the extent permitted by law.  Type "show copying"

and "show warranty" for details.

This GDB was configured as "x86_64-suse-linux".

For bug reporting instructions, please see:

<http://www.gnu.org/software/gdb/bugs/>...

Reading symbols from /tmp/binary.bin...done.

(gdb)
```

For the time being, nothing happens. The important thing is that gdb has read symbols from our binary. The next step is to run the program and reproduce the segmentation fault. To do this, simply use the command run inside gdb.

```
(gdb) run

Starting program: /tmp/binary.bin



Program received signal SIGSEGV, Segmentation fault.

0x0000000000400557 in main (argc=1, argv=0x7fffffffe458) at file.c:6

6           printf("hello %d",*boom);

(gdb)
```

We see several important details. First, we see that our program crashes. The problem is in the sixth line of source code, as shown in the image, our printf line. Does this mean there is a problem with printf? Probably not, but something in the variable that printf is trying to use, most likely. The plot thickens.

Second, you may also see a message that separate debuginfo (symbols) for third-party libraries, which are not part of our own code, are missing. This means that we can hook into their execution, but we will not see any symbols. We will see an example soon.

What we learn here is that we have symbols that gdb will not run automatically and that we have a meaningful way of reproducing the problem. This is very important to remember, but we will recap this when we discuss when to run or not to run gdb.

### Breakpoint

Running through the program does not yield enough meaningful information. We need to halt the execution just before the printf line. Enter breakpoints, just like when working with a compiler. We will break into the main function and then advance step by step until the problem occurs again, then rerun and break, and then execute commands one at a time just short of the segmentation fault.

To this end, we need the break command, which lets you specify breakpoints either at functions, your own or third-party loaded by external libraries or specific lines of code in your sources – an example is on the way. Then, we will use the info command to examine our breakpoints. We will place the breakpoint in the main() function. As a rule of thumb, it is always a good place to start.

```
(gdb) break main

Breakpoint 1 at 0x40054b: file file.c, line 5.

(gdb) info breakpoint

Num     Type           Disp Enb Address            What

1       breakpoint     keep y   0x000000000040054b in main at file.c:5
```

Now we run the code again. The execution halts when we reach main().

```
(gdb) run

The program being debugged has been started already.

Start it from the beginning? (y or n) y

Starting program: /tmp/binary.bin



Breakpoint 1, main (argc=1, argv=0x7fffffffe458) at file.c:5

5               int* boom=0;

(gdb)
```

### Step by step

Now that we have stopped at the entry to main, we will step through code line by line, using the next command. Luckily for us, there is not that much code to walk through. After just two steps, we encounter a segmentation fault. Good.

```
(gdb) next

6               printf("hello %d",*boom);

(gdb) next
```

```
Program received signal SIGSEGV, Segmentation fault.

0x0000000000400557 in main (argc=1, argv=0x7fffffffe458) at file.c:6

6           printf("hello %d",*boom);

(gdb)
```

We will now rerun the code, break in the main(), do a single next that will lead us to printf, and then we will halt and examine the assembly code, no less!

```
(gdb) run

The program being debugged has been started already.

Start it from the beginning? (y or n) y

Starting program: /tmp/binary.bin


Breakpoint 1, main (argc=1, argv=0x7fffffffe458) at file.c:5

5           int* boom=0;

(gdb) next

6           printf("hello %d",*boom);

(gdb)
```

### Disassembly

Indeed, at this stage, there is nothing else the code can tell us. We have exhausted our understanding of what happens in the code. Seemingly, there does not seem to be any great problem, or rather, we cannot see it yet.

So we will use the disassemble command, which will dump the assembly code. Just type disassemble inside gdb and this will dump the assembly instructions that your code uses.

```
(gdb) disassemble

Dump of assembler code for function main:

   0x000000000040053c <+0>:     push   %rbp

   0x000000000040053d <+1>:     mov    %rsp,%rbp

   0x0000000000400540 <+4>:     sub    $0x30,%rsp

   0x0000000000400544 <+8>:     mov    %edi,-0x14(%rbp)

   0x0000000000400547 <+11>:    mov    %rsi,-0x20(%rbp)

   0x000000000040054b <+15>:    movq   $0x0,-0x8(%rbp)

=> 0x0000000000400553 <+23>:    mov    -0x8(%rbp),%rax

   0x0000000000400557 <+27>:    mov    (%rax),%esi

   0x0000000000400559 <+29>:    mov    $0x400664,%edi

   0x000000000040055e <+34>:    mov    $0x0,%eax

   0x0000000000400563 <+39>:    callq  0x400430 <printf@plt>

   0x0000000000400568 <+44>:    leaveq

   0x0000000000400569 <+45>:    retq

End of assembler dump.
```

This is probably the most difficult part of the tutorial yet. Let us try to understand what we see here, again in very simplified terms.

On the left, we have memory addresses. The second column shows increments in the memory space from the starting address. The third column shows the mnemonic. The fourth column includes actual registers and values.

There is a little arrow pointing at the memory address where our execution is right now. We are at offset 40054b, and we have moved the value that is stored 8 bytes below the base pointer into the RAX register. One line before that, we moved the value 0 into the RBP-8 address. So now, we have the value 0 in the RAX register.

```
   0x000000000040054b <+15>:      movq    $0x0,-0x8(%rbp)

=> 0x0000000000400553 <+23>:      mov     -0x8(%rbp),%rax
```

Our next instruction is the one that will cause the segmentation fault, as we have seen earlier while stepping through the code with the next command.

```
0x0000000000400557 <+27>:      mov     (%rax),%esi
```

So we need to understand what is wrong here. Let us examine the ESI register, which is supposed to get this new value. We can do this by using the examine or x command. You can use all kinds of output formats, but that is not important right now.

```
(gdb) x $rax

0x7ffff7ddaf40 <environ>:       0xffffe468

(gdb) x $esi

0xfffffffffffffe458:       Cannot access memory at address 0xfffffffffffffe458
```

And we get a message that we cannot access memory at the specified address. This is the clue right there, problem solved. We tried accessing an illegal memory address. As to why we breached our allocation and how we can know that, we will learn soon.

## NOT SO SIMPLE EXAMPLE

Now, we do something more complex. We will create a dynamic array called pointer. We will use the standard malloc (add reference) subroutine for this. We will then loop, incrementing *i* values by 1 every iteration, and then let pointer exceed its allowed memory space, also known as *heap overflow*. Understandable as a lab case, but let us see this happen in real life and how we can handle problems such as these. Most importantly, we will learn additional gdb commands. Here is the source:

```
#include <stdio.h>
#include <stdlib.h>

main()
```

```
{
    int *pointer;
    int i;
    pointer = malloc(sizeof(int));
    for (i = 0; 1; i++)
    {
        pointer[i]=i;
        printf("pointer[%d] = %d\n", i, pointer[i]);
    }
    return(0);
}
```

Let us compile:

```
gcc -g seg.c -o seg
```

When we run it, we see something like this:

```
./seg
...
pointer[33785] = 33785
pointer[33786] = 33786
pointer[33787] = 33787
Segmentation fault
```

Now, before we hit gdb and assembly, let us try some normal debugging. Let us say you want to try to solve the problem with one of the standard system admin and troubleshooting tools such as strace. After having heard of strace earlier, you know the tool's worth and you want to attempt the simple steps first. Indeed, strace works well in most cases. But here, it is of no use.

```
15715 write(1, "pointer[33784] = 33784\n", 23) = 23
15715 write(1, "pointer[33785] = 33785\n", 23) = 23
15715 write(1, "pointer[33786] = 33786\n", 23) = 23
15715 write(1, "pointer[33787] = 33787\n", 23) = 23
15715 --- SIGSEGV (Segmentation fault) @ 0 (0) ---
15715 +++ killed by SIGSEGV +++
```

Nothing is useful there, really. In fact, no classic tool will give you any indication what happens here. So we need a debugger, gdb in our case. Load the program.

```
gdb /tmp/seg
```

### Breakpoint

Like before, we set a breakpoint. However, using main() is not going to be good for us, because the program will enter main() once and then loop, never going back to the set breakpoint. So we need something else. We need to break in a specific line of code.

To determine the best place, we could run the code and try to figure out where the problem occurs. We can also take a look at our code and make an educated guess. This should be somewhere in the for loop of course. So perhaps, it is the start of it?

```
(gdb) break 10

Breakpoint 1 at 0x4005a9: file /tmp/seg.c, line 10.
```

### Condition

All right, but this is not good enough. We will have a break point at every entry to our loop, and from the execution run, we see there are going to be over 30K iterations. We cannot possibly manually type cont and hit Enter every time. So we need a condition, an if statement that will break only if a specific condition is met.

From our sample run, we see that the problem occurs when $i$ reaches the value of 33787, so we will place a conditional break some one or two loop iterations before that. Conditions are set per breakpoint. Notice the breakpoint number, after it is set, because we need that number to set a condition.

```
break 10
Breakpoint 1 at ...
```

And then:

```
(gdb) condition 1 i == 33786

(gdb) info breakpoint

Num     Type           Disp Enb Address            What
```

```
1          breakpoint     keep y   0x00000000004005a9 in main at /tmp/seg.c:10

           stop only if i == 33786
```

If you had multiple breakpoints and you wanted to set multiple conditions, then you would invoke the correct breakpoint number. Now, we are ready to roll; hit run and let the for loop churn for a while.

```
pointer[33782] = 33782

pointer[33783] = 33783

pointer[33784] = 33784

pointer[33785] = 33785



Breakpoint 1, main () at /tmp/seg.c:11

11              pointer[i]=i;

(gdb)
```

Now we walk through the code, step by step using the next command.

```
Breakpoint 1, main () at /tmp/seg.c:11

11              pointer[i]=i;

(gdb) next

12              printf("pointer[%d] = %d\n", i, pointer[i]);

(gdb)

pointer[33786] = 33786

9          for (i = 0; 1; i++)

(gdb)

13              }
```

```
(gdb)

11              pointer[i]=i;

(gdb)

12              printf("pointer[%d] = %d\n", i, pointer[i]);

(gdb)

pointer[33787] = 33787

9          for (i = 0; 1; i++)

(gdb)

13         }

(gdb)

11              pointer[i]=i;

(gdb)


Program received signal SIGSEGV, Segmentation fault.

0x00000000004005bc in main () at /tmp/seg.c:11

11              pointer[i]=i;

(gdb)
```

We know the problem occurs after pointer[i] = i is set, when the *i* value is 33787. Which means, we will rerun the program and then stop just short of executing the pointer[i] = i line of code after a successful print of pointer[33787] = 33787. Now, the next time we reach this point, we create the assembly dump.

```
(gdb) disassemble

Dump of assembler code for function main:

  0x000000000040058c <+0>:     push   %rbp

  0x000000000040058d <+1>:     mov    %rsp,%rbp

  0x0000000000400590 <+4>:     sub    $0x10,%rsp
```

```
   0x0000000000400594 <+8>:      mov     $0x4,%edi
   0x0000000000400599 <+13>:     callq   0x400478 <malloc@plt>
   0x000000000040059e <+18>:     mov     %rax,-0x10(%rbp)
   0x00000000004005a2 <+22>:     movl    $0x0,-0x4(%rbp)
=> 0x00000000004005a9 <+29>:     mov     -0x4(%rbp),%eax
   0x00000000004005ac <+32>:     cltq
   0x00000000004005ae <+34>:     shl     $0x2,%rax
   0x00000000004005b2 <+38>:     mov     %rax,%rdx
   0x00000000004005b5 <+41>:     add     -0x10(%rbp),%rdx
   0x00000000004005b9 <+45>:     mov     -0x4(%rbp),%eax
   0x00000000004005bc <+48>:     mov     %eax,(%rdx)
   0x00000000004005be <+50>:     mov     -0x4(%rbp),%eax
   0x00000000004005c1 <+53>:     cltq
   0x00000000004005c3 <+55>:     shl     $0x2,%rax
   0x00000000004005c7 <+59>:     add     -0x10(%rbp),%rax
   0x00000000004005cb <+63>:     mov     (%rax),%edx
   0x00000000004005cd <+65>:     mov     -0x4(%rbp),%esi
   0x00000000004005d0 <+68>:     mov     $0x4006e4,%edi
   0x00000000004005d5 <+73>:     mov     $0x0,%eax
   0x00000000004005da <+78>:     callq   0x400468 <printf@plt>
   0x00000000004005df <+83>:     addl    $0x1,-0x4(%rbp)
   0x00000000004005e3 <+87>:     jmp     0x4005a9 <main+29>
End of assembler dump.
(gdb)
```

We know the problem occurs at offset 4005bc, where we mov %eax value into %rdx. This is similar to what we saw earlier. But we need to understand what happens before that, one or two instructions back.

```
   0x00000000004005bc <+48>:      mov     %eax,(%rdx)
```

### *Stepping through assembly dump*

To this end, we will use the stepi command, which can walk the assembly dump, line by line. It is like next in a way, but you can control individual registers, so to speak. Take a look at the dump. The last line in the dump is the jump (jmp) instruction back to offset <main+29>, which brings us to mov 0x00000000004005a9 (%rbp), %eax. This is effectively our for loop. Now, when we hit stepi, we will execute line 4005ac. I omitted the line that reads cltq, because it merely extends the 2-byte EAX into a 4-byte value. That is because we are on a 64-bit system.

```
(gdb) stepi

0x00000000004005ac        11              pointer[i]=i;

(gdb) stepi

0x00000000004005ae        11              pointer[i]=i;
```

Now, we have several lines where the *i* value is incremented. But the crucial line is just one short of the segmentation fault. We need to understand what is inside those registers or whether we can access them at all.

```
(gdb) stepi

0x00000000004005b9        11              pointer[i]=i;

(gdb) stepi

0x00000000004005bc        11              pointer[i]=i;

(gdb) stepi



Program received signal SIGSEGV, Segmentation fault.

0x00000000004005bc in main () at /tmp/seg.c:11

11              pointer[i]=i;

(gdb)
```

And it turns out we cannot. It is like we had earlier. But why? How can we know that this address is off limits? How do we know that?

## Proc mappings

In Linux, you can view the memory maps of any process through /proc/ <pid>/ maps, as we have learned earlier. It is important to understand what a sample output provides before we can proceed. Let us recap briefly:

```
#cat /proc/self/maps | grep -iv lc

00400000-0040b000 r-xp 00000000 08:02 248                    /bin/cat

0060a000-0060b000 r--p 0000a000 08:02 248                    /bin/cat

0060b000-0060c000 rw-p 0000b000 08:02 248                    /bin/cat

0060c000-0062d000 rw-p 00000000 00:00 0                      [heap]

7ffff7a67000-7ffff7bd4000 r-xp 00000000 08:02 22             /lib64/libc-
2.11.3.so

7ffff7bd4000-7ffff7dd4000 ---p 0016d000 08:02 22             /lib64/libc-
2.11.3.so

7ffff7dd4000-7ffff7dd8000 r--p 0016d000 08:02 22             /lib64/libc-
2.11.3.so

7ffff7dd8000-7ffff7dd9000 rw-p 00171000 08:02 22             /lib64/libc-
2.11.3.so

7ffff7dd9000-7ffff7dde000 rw-p 00000000 00:00 0

7ffff7dde000-7ffff7dfd000 r-xp 00000000 08:02 788            /lib64/ld-
2.11.3.so

7ffff7fd7000-7ffff7fda000 rw-p 00000000 00:00 0

7ffff7ff3000-7ffff7ffa000 r--s 00000000 08:05 238067
/usr/lib64/gconv/gconv-modules.cache

7ffff7ffa000-7ffff7ffb000 rw-p 00000000 00:00 0

7ffff7ffb000-7ffff7ffc000 r-xp 00000000 00:00 0              [vdso]

7ffff7ffc000-7ffff7ffd000 r--p 0001e000 08:02 788            /lib64/ld-
2.11.3.so

7ffff7ffd000-7ffff7ffe000 rw-p 0001f000 08:02 788            /lib64/ld-
2.11.3.so

7ffff7ffe000-7ffff7fff000 rw-p 00000000 00:00 0

7fffffffde000-7fffffffff000 rw-p 00000000 00:00 0            [stack]

ffffffffff600000-ffffffffff601000 r-xp 00000000 00:00 0      [vsyscall]
```

The first line is the code (or text), the actual binary instructions. The second line shows data, which stores all initialized global variables. The third section is the heap, which is used for dynamic allocations, such as malloc. Sometimes, it also includes the .bss segment, which stores statically linked variables and uninitialized global variables. When the .bss segment is small, it can reside inside the data segment.

After that, you get shared libraries, and the first one is the dynamic linker itself. Finally, you get the stack. The two last lines are the Linux gating (add link) mechanisms for fast system calls, which replace the int 0x80 system call that was used in the past. As you may notice, there are still more memory addresses above the last line, reserved by the kernel.

So here, at a glance, you can examine how your process resides in the memory. When a program is executed through gdb, you can view its memory allocations using the info proc mappings command.

```
gdb) info proc mappings
process 44322
cmdline = '/tmp/seg'
cwd = '/tmp'
exe = '/tmp/seg'
Mapped address spaces:


       Start Addr          End Addr          Size     Offset objfile
        0x400000          0x401000        0x1000            0
/tmp/seg
        0x600000          0x601000        0x1000            0
/tmp/seg
        0x601000          0x602000        0x1000       0x1000
/tmp/seg
        0x602000          0x623000       0x21000            0
[heap]
    0x7ffff7a67000    0x7ffff7bd4000      0x16d000            0
/lib64/libc-2.11.3.so
    0x7ffff7bd4000    0x7ffff7dd4000      0x200000     0x16d000
/lib64/libc-2.11.3.so
    0x7ffff7dd4000    0x7ffff7dd8000        0x4000     0x16d000
/lib64/libc-2.11.3.so
    0x7ffff7dd8000    0x7f
/lib64/libc-2.11.3.so
    0x7ffff7dd9000    0x7ffff7dde000        0x5000            0
    0x7ffff7dde000    0x7ffff7dfd000       0x1f000            0
/lib64/ld-2.11.3.so
```

| | | | |
|---|---|---|---|
| 0x7ffff7fd7000 | 0x7ffff7fda000 | 0x3000 | 0 |
| 0x7ffff7ff9000 | 0x7ffff7ffb000 | 0x2000 | 0 |
| 0x7ffff7ffb000 [vdso] | 0x7ffff7ffc000 | 0x1000 | 0 |
| 0x7ffff7ffc000 /lib64/ld-2.11.3.so | 0x7ffff7ffd000 | 0x1000 | 0x1e000 |
| 0x7ffff7ffd000 /lib64/ld-2.11.3.so | 0x7ffff7ffe000 | 0x1000 | 0x1f000 |
| 0x7ffff7ffe000 | 0x7ffff7fff000 | 0x1000 | 0 |
| 0x7fffffffde000 [stack] | 0x7ffffffff000 | 0x21000 | 0 |
| 0xffffffffff600000 [vsyscall] | 0xffffffffff601000 | 0x1000 | 0 |

Three lines are of interest: code, data, and heap. And for heap, we can see that the end address is 0x623000. We cannot use that, so we get the segmentation fault. Back to C code; we will need to figure out what we did wrong.

| | Start Addr | End Addr | Size | Offset objfile |
|---|---|---|---|---|
| /tmp/seg | 0x400000 | 0x401000 | 0x1000 | 0 |
| /tmp/seg | 0x600000 | 0x601000 | 0x1000 | 0 |
| /tmp/seg | 0x601000 | 0x602000 | 0x1000 | 0x1000 |
| [heap] | 0x602000 | 0x623000 | 0x21000 | 0 |

We need to start counting bytes. In general, we use a single page for code because our executable is small. We use a single page for data. And then, there is some heap space, a total of 0x21000, which is 132 KB or more specifically 135,168 bytes.

On the other hand, we ran through 33,788 iterations of the for loop, each 4 bytes in size, as we are on a 64-bit system. Not 33,787 as you may assume from the print output in our program run, but one more, because we started counting $i$ at value 0.

So we get 135,152 bytes, which is 16 bytes less that our heap. So you may ask, where did the extra 16 bytes go? Well, we can use the examine command again and check more accurately what happens at the start address.

```
(gdb) x /8xw 0x602000

0x602000:      0x00000000    0x00000000    0x00000021    0x00000000

0x602010:      0x00000000    0x00000001    0x00000002    0x00000003

(gdb)
```

We print eight 4-byte hexadecimal values. The first 16 bytes are the heap header and the count starts at address 0x501010. The header size plus the total count of 4-byte increments sums to the total heap space. Any further allocation will exceed this space, resulting in a violation. So we are all good here, and we know why we got our nasty segmentation fault. We can examine our source code and try to figure out what we did wrong. Two examples, two problems solved.

## OTHER USEFUL COMMANDS

When working with application cores, there are several other useful commands you may want to use.

The show command lets you show contents, as simple as that. The set command lets you configure variables. For example, you may want to see the initial arguments your program started with and then change them. In our heap overflow example, we could try altering the value of *i* to see if that affects the program.

```
(gdb) show args

Argument list to give program being debugged when it is started is "".

(gdb)
```

And:

```
(gdb) set args Chapter 6

(gdb) show args

Argument list to give program being debugged when it is started is "Chapter 6".

(gdb)
```

The syntax for setting variables is quite simple. For instance, set i = 4. You can also set registers, but do not do this if you do not know what you are doing. The list command lets you dump your code. You can list individual lines, specific functions, or entire code. By default, you get ten lines printed, sort of like tail.

```
(gdb) list

77      #else

78

79      /* This is a "normal" system call stub: if there is an error,

80         it returns -1 and sets errno.  */

81

82      T_PSEUDO (SYSCALL_SYMBOL, SYSCALL_NAME, SYSCALL_NARGS)

83            ret

84      T_PSEUDO_END (SYSCALL_SYMBOL)

85

86      #endif
```

Another thing you may want to do is inspect stack frames in detail. We are already familiar with the info command, so what we need now is to invoke it against specific frames, as listed in the backtrace (bt) command. In our heap overflow example, there is only a single frame.

We break in main, run, display the backtrace, and then check info frame 0, as shown in the screenshot below. You get a wealth of information, including the instruction pointer (RIP), the saved instruction pointer from a previous frame, the address and the list of arguments, the address and the list of local variables, the previous stack pointer, and saved registers.

```
(gdb) break main

Breakpoint 1 at 0x400594: file /tmp/seg.c, line 8.

(gdb) run

Starting program: /tmp/seg
```

```
Breakpoint 1, main () at /tmp/seg.c:8

warning: Source file is more recent than executable.

8            pointer = malloc(sizeof(int));

(gdb) bt

#0   main () at /tmp/seg.c:8

 (gdb) info frame 0

Stack frame at 0x7fffffffe3a0:

 rip = 0x400594 in main (/tmp/seg.c:8); saved rip 0x7ffff7a85c16

 source language c.

 Arglist at 0x7fffffffe390, args:

 Locals at 0x7fffffffe390, Previous frame's sp is 0x7fffffffe3a0

 Saved registers:

 rbp at 0x7fffffffe390, rip at 0x7fffffffe398

(gdb)
```

We mentioned backtrace (bt) earlier, and indeed, it is a most valuable command and best used when you do not know what your program is doing. External commands can be executed using the shell command. For instance, showing the /proc/PID/maps can also be done by using the shell cat /proc/PID/maps instead of info proc mappings as we did before. If for some reason you cannot use either, then you might want to resort to readelf (add link) to try to decipher the binary. Just as we used next and stepi, you can use nexti and step. Let us not forget finish, jump, until, and call. The whatis command lets you examine variables.

## CONCLUSION

In this chapter, we focused on in-depth analysis and profiling of applications as well as the kernel itself, using different tools to create a more complete, multidimensional picture of our problem and present relevant solutions. A methodical approach helps ensure we do not diverge or lose track, and having several sources of data allow us to correlate our results with greater accuracy. Chapter 6 will take our investigation one step further, as we learn about kernel crash analysis and the use of the kernel debugger.

## REFERENCES

GDB: The GNU Project Debugger, n.d. Retrieved from: https://www.gnu.org/software/gdb/ (accessed May 2015).

Intel(R) VTune(TM) Amplifier XE 2013, n.d. Retrieved from: http://software.intel.com/en-us/intel-vtune-amplifier-xe (accessed May 2015).

Linux kernel profiling with perf, n.d. Retrieved from: https://perf.wiki.kernel.org/index.php/Tutorial (accessed May 2015).

Linux super-duper admin tools: OProfile, n.d. Retrieved from: http://www.dedoimedo.com/computers/oprofile.html (accessed May 2015).

lsof(8), n.d. Retrieved from: http://linux.die.net/man/8/lsof (accessed May 2015).

ltrace(1) – Linux man page, n.d. Retrieved from: http://linux.die.net/man/1/ltrace (accessed May 2015).

Oprofile, n.d. Retrieved from: http://oprofile.sourceforge.net/news/ (accessed May 2015).

Perfcounters added to the mainline, n.d. Retrieved from: http://lwn.net/Articles/339361/ (accessed May 2015).

ptrace(2) – Linux man page, n.d. Retrieved from: http://linux.die.net/man/2/ptrace (accessed May 2015).

Smashing performance with OProfile, n.d. Retrieved from: http://www.ibm.com/developerworks/library/l-oprof/ (accessed May 2015).

strace(1) – Linux man page, n.d. Retrieved from: http://linux.die.net/man/1/strace (accessed May 2015).

The GNU C Library, n.d. Retrieved from: http://www.gnu.org/software/libc/manual/html_node/System-Calls.html (accessed May 2015).

The Linux Cross Reference, n.d. Retrieved from: http://lxr.linux.no/linux/ (accessed May 2015).

Tuning Performance with OProfile, n.d. Retrieved from: http://people.redhat.com/~wcohen/Oprofile.pdf (accessed May 2015).

Valgrind, n.d. Retrieved from: http://www.valgrind.org/ (accessed May 2015).

CHAPTER

# Getting very geeky – application and kernel cores, kernel debugger

# 6

## COLLECTING APPLICATION CORES

If you have the privilege of debugging system issues in real time, you will most likely be able to rerun the suspected processes and perform all the necessary analyses. However, most of the time, problems will manifest themselves far away from the keyboard, and you will have to rely on automated, unattended mechanisms to collect all the necessary forensics information to troubleshoot the application hangs and crashes. To that end, you will want to be able to collect the memory cores of running processes for offline investigation.

In this section, we will talk about additional gdb features. Namely, we will learn the critical steps for collecting application cores and analyzing them. We will also learn how to attach the debugger to running processes, as well as other useful commands. Finally, we will explore yet another example, which illustrates a situation in which gdb is not really useful but the assembly dump will tell us all we need, even if we do not have source code available.

When a running application encounters an exception, it will stop running. Depending on the nature of the exception, the default action of certain signals is to cause a process to terminate and produce a *core dump* file (core(5) – Linux man page, n.d.), a disk file containing an image of the process's memory at the time of termination. This image can be used in a debugger to inspect the state of the program at the time that it terminated. A list of the signals that cause a process to dump core can be found in the signal(7) man page.

A process can set its soft RLIMIT_CORE resource limit to place an upper limit on the size of the core dump file that will be produced if it receives a "core dump" signal. However, it is important to note there are various circumstances in which a core dump file will not be produced:

- The process does not have permission to write the core file. By default the core file is called core, and is created in the current working directory. Writing the core file will fail if the directory in which it is to be created is nonwritable, or if a file with the same name exists and is not writable or is not a regular file (i.e., it is a directory or a symbolic link).
- A (writable, regular) file with the same name as would be used for the core dump already exists, but there is more than one hard link to that file.

137

- The file system in which the core dump file would be created is full, the file system has run out of inodes, the file system is mounted read-only, or the user has reached their quota for the file system.
- The directory in which the core dump file is to be created does not exist.
- The RLIMIT_CORE (core file size) or RLIMIT_FSIZE (file size) resource limits for the process are set to zero; we will discuss how to overcome this limitation using shell commands shortly.
- The binary being executed by the process does not have read permission enabled.
- The process is executing a set-user-ID (set-group-ID) program that is owned by a user (group) other than the real user (group) ID of the process.

Now, we will learn how to set up our Linux environment to enable the collection of memory cores of crashing applications.

## HOW TO DUMP APPLICATION CORES

You will have to make sure that you can create cores. This is governed via sysctl, but you can also make changes on the fly. Depending on your shell, you will use either the limit or ulimit built-ins (Shell Builtin Commands, n.d.). For instance, for BASH

```
ulimit -c unlimited
```

And for TCSH

```
limit coredumpsize unlimited
```

### Dump pattern

By default, the core will be dumped in the current directory in which the binary was executed. But, the core name might not be useful or meaningful. So you can change its format, which is governed by the core_pattern setting under /proc. For example

```
echo "/tmp/core-%p-%u" > /proc/sys/kernel/core_pattern
```

This will dump a core under /tmp, with the PID and UID suffixed. There are many other available options. You can also set this option permanently via sysctl.conf.

```
./seg
...
pointer[33785] = 33785
pointer[33786] = 33786
pointer[33787] = 33787
Segmentation fault (core dumped)
```

### Application core use

We can now invoke gdb for a core file. After the application crashes and creates a core, we will use gdb as follows:

```
gdb <binary> <core>
```

Using our example from Chapter 5

```
#gdb seg core-47335-0

GNU gdb (GDB) SUSE (7.3-0.6.1)

Copyright (C) 2011 Free Software Foundation, Inc.

License GPLv3+: GNU GPL version 3 or later <http://gnu.org/licenses/gpl.html>

This is free software: you are free to change and redistribute it.

There is NO WARRANTY, to the extent permitted by law.  Type "show copying"

and "show warranty" for details.

This GDB was configured as "x86_64-suse-linux".

For bug reporting instructions, please see:

<http://www.gnu.org/software/gdb/bugs/>...

Reading symbols from /tmp/seg...done.

[New LWP 47335]

Missing separate debuginfo for /lib64/ld-linux-x86-64.so.2

Try: zypper install -C "debuginfo(build-id)=31b3276dc0b305d25a213860d7d5a67601b1bb7a"

Missing separate debuginfo for
```

```
Try: zypper install -C "debuginfo(build-id)=31b3276dc0b305d25a213860d7d5a67601b1bb7a"

Core was generated by `./seg'.

Program terminated with signal 11, Segmentation fault.

#0  0x00000000004005bc in main () at /tmp/seg.c:11

11              pointer[i]=i;
```

The important thing is that gdb successfully read and loaded the symbols. We can now proceed with the analysis, like before. Some functions will not be available to us, as the core is not a running application, but we will still be able to figure out what went wrong. Do notice we are missing debug symbols for other system libraries.

### Attach to a running process

Similarly, you can attach gdb to a running process. You may want to do this if you assume the real-time debugging is of critical importance for your environment, and that if you do not do it right then, the problem will cause serious impact to your customer base. Moreover, you may not have the privilege of restarting the process or trying to reproduce the issue at a later stage. This may not be the most effective way of debugging problems, but it could give you additional information that may not be available otherwise.

The simplest way to demonstrate this is by altering our example with an extra sleep somewhere. Then, while the program is running, find its PID and attach to it.

```
gdb -p <process id>
```

We will start with a trivial example – a process that is currently sleeping, and we want to learn why.

```
#gdb -p 47684

GNU gdb (GDB) SUSE (7.3-0.6.1)

Copyright (C) 2011 Free Software Foundation, Inc.

License GPLv3+: GNU GPL version 3 or later <http://gnu.org/licenses/gpl.html>

This is free software: you are free to change and redistribute it.

There is NO WARRANTY, to the extent permitted by law.  Type "show copying"

and "show warranty" for details.
```

```
This GDB was configured as "x86_64-suse-linux".

For bug reporting instructions, please see:

<http://www.gnu.org/software/gdb/bugs/>.

Attaching to process 47684

Reading symbols from /tmp/segsleep...done.

Reading symbols from /lib64/libc.so.6...Reading symbols from
/usr/lib/debug/lib64/libc-2.11.3.so.debug...done.

done.

Loaded symbols for /lib64/libc.so.6

Reading symbols from /lib64/ld-linux-x86-64.so.2...Reading symbols from
/usr/lib/debug/lib64/ld-2.11.3.so.debug...done.

done.

Loaded symbols for /lib64/ld-linux-x86-64.so.2

0x00007ffff7b0ede0 in __nanosleep_nocancel () at ../sysdeps/unix/syscall-
template.S:82

82      T_PSEUDO (SYSCALL_SYMBOL, SYSCALL_NAME, SYSCALL_NARGS)
```

After the gdb loads, we will examine the backtrace for the traced process:

```
(gdb) bt

#0  0x00007ffff7b0ede0 in __nanosleep_nocancel () at ../sysdeps/unix/syscall-
template.S:82

#1  0x00007ffff7b0ec1c in __sleep (seconds=<optimized out>) at
../sysdeps/unix/sysv/linux/sleep.c:138

#2  0x0000000000400601 in main ()

(gdb)
```

This example also shows the fact the third-party libraries are stripped, so you get function names, but you do not know the exact lines of code or the variables. Moreover, using the backtrace (bt) command, we see the program is currently sleeping.

### Problem reproduction

The most important question here is when to use or not use gdb. The GNU Debugger is most useful when you have reproducible problems and your binaries have been compiled with symbols. You can also try using gdb on third-party functions, but this will not guarantee much success.

For instance, we know we are using printf() in our code. So maybe we need to break there? Well, gdb informs us that the function is not defined and will create a breakpoint pending future shared library load. Not a bad idea, but notice that we do not see any function names for libc.so.6, because we do not have symbols, and for that matter, we might not even have source code. Without either, it will not be easy figuring out what went wrong.

```
(gdb) break printf
Function "printf" not defined.
Make breakpoint pending on future shared library load? (y or [n]) y
Breakpoint 1 (printf) pending.
(gdb) run
Starting program: /tmp/segfaults/seg
Breakpoint 2 at 0x2aaaaac113f0
Pending breakpoint "printf" resolved
Breakpoint 2, 0x00002aaaaac113f0 in printf () from /lib64/libc.so.6
```

Finally, using gdb for sporadic, random problems that are not easily reproduced or those that might stem from hardware problems is a hard, grueling task that will yield few results. Even the trivial examples are not so trivial, so imagine what happens on a real production system, with binaries compiled from source files with thousands of lines of code. Still, you get a taste of the goodness, and you are hooked now.

Last, let us see an example in which gdb is both the worst and best tool for analysis. We will create an infinite loop program – while true. This kind of program will loop forever, churning CPU cycles. If you try strace, you will get no useful information.

```
#strace -p 29627

Process 29627 attached - interrupt to quit
```

We will now get attached to the process with gdb. Then, we will create a breakpoint in the main function, and resume the run of the application using the next command. You will notice that the debugger hangs at this point.

We will be forced to interrupt the execution, and then try a different set of gdb commands to try to understand what is happening. In our case, the use of the disassemble command will print the short stack of assembly instructions, showing a trivial jump (jmp) that is essentially the infinite loop program we ran.

```
#gdb -p 29894

GNU gdb 6.8

Copyright (C) 2008 Free Software Foundation, Inc.

License GPLv3+: GNU GPL version 3 or later <http://gnu.org/licenses/gpl.html>

This is free software: you are free to change and redistribute it.

There is NO WARRANTY, to the extent permitted by law.  Type "show copying"

and "show warranty" for details.

This GDB was configured as "x86_64-unknown-linux-gnu".

Attaching to process 29894

Reading symbols from /tmp/forever...done.

Reading symbols from /lib64/libc.so.6...done.

Loaded symbols for /lib64/libc.so.6

Reading symbols from /lib64/ld-linux-x86-64.so.2...done.

Loaded symbols for /lib64/ld-linux-x86-64.so.2

0x0000000000400500 in main () at /tmp/forever.c:2

2       void main () {

(gdb) bt

#0  0x0000000000400500 in main () at /tmp/forever.c:2

(gdb) disassemble

Dump of assembler code for function main:

0x00000000004004fc <main+0>:     push   %rbp

0x00000000004004fd <main+1>:     mov    %rsp,%rbp

0x0000000000400500 <main+4>:     jmp    0x400500 <main+4>
```

```
End of assembler dump.

(gdb) next
```

## COLLECTING KERNEL CORES (KDUMP)

The Linux kernel is a rather robust entity. It is stable and fault-tolerant and usually does not suffer irrecoverable errors that crash the entire system and require a reboot to restore to normal production. Nevertheless, these kinds of problems do occur from time to time. They are known as kernel crashes and are of utmost interest and importance to administrators in charge of these systems. Being able to detect the crashes, collect them and analyze them provides the system expert with a powerful tool for finding the root cause to crashes and possibly the solution to eliminate critical bugs.

There are several reasons that may cause the kernel to crash, all of them involving fatal, irrecoverable internal errors. Furthermore, the errors will usually manifest themselves in two specific conditions, known as *oops* and *panic*.

An oops (Oops tracing, n.d.) is a deviation from the correct behavior of the Linux kernel. When the kernel detects a problem, it prints an oops message and kills any offending process. The message is used by Linux kernel engineers to debug the condition that created the oops and fix the programming error that caused it. Once a system has experienced an oops, some internal resources may no longer be in service. Even if the system appears to work correctly, undesirable side effects may have resulted from the active task being killed. A kernel oops often leads on to a kernel panic once the system attempts to use resources that have been lost.

A kernel panic is an irrecoverable failure of the system, which can only be resolved by hard reboot. When the situation occurs, it is possible to dump an image of the crashed kernel memory to disk for later analysis. This has to be done from the context of a second kernel, which is invoked when an oops or a panic condition is encountered.

Oops and panic conditions may be caused by software bugs and faulty hardware. In this section, we will learn how to configure the system for kernel crash dump collection and analyze the saved memory cores. This will allow us to understand the root cause for the system failure and work toward resolving it, on both the hardware or software levels.

### KDUMP SERVICE OVERVIEW

The ability to save memory cores has existed for a number of years. Until several years back, the prevalent technology used for collecting crash dumps was Linux Kernel Crash Dump (LKCD) (LKCD, n.d.). However, LKCD, being an older project, exhibited several major limitations in its functionality: LKCD was unable to save memory dumps to local RAID (md) devices (Linux Raid, n.d.), and its network capability was restricted to sending memory cores to dedicated LKCD netdump servers only on the same subnet, provided the cores were under 4 GB in size. Memory cores exceeding the 32-bit size barrier were corrupt upon transfer and thus unavailable for analysis. The same-subnet requirement also proved impractical for large-scale operations with thousands of machines.

Kdump (Kdump, n.d.) is a much more flexible tool, with extended network-aware capabilities. It aims to replace LKCD, while providing better scalability. Indeed, Kdump supports network dumping to a range of devices, including local disks, but also NFS areas, CIFS shares, or FTP and SSH servers. This makes it far more attractive for deployment in large environments, without restricting operations to a single server per subnet.

In this section, we will learn how to set up and configure Kdump for memory core dumping to local disk and network shares. We begin with a short overview of basic Kdump functionality and terminology. Next, we review the kernel compilation parameters required to use Kdump. After that, we go through the configuration file and study each directive separately step by step. We also edit the GRUB menu as a part of the Kdump setup. Last, we demonstrate the Kdump functionality, including manually triggering kernel crashes and dumping memory cores to local and network devices.

### *Restrictions*

On one hand, this section examines the Kdump utility in great detail. On the other hand, a number of Kdump-related topics are only briefly discussed. It is important that you know what to expect from this tutorial.

### Kernel compilation

We will not explain the kernel compilation here, although we explain the parameters required for proper Kdump functionality. The kernel compilation is a delicate, complex process that merits separate attention, and it is beyond the scope of this book.

### Hardware-specific configurations

Kdump can also run on the Itanium (ia64) and Power PC (ppc64) architectures. However, due to relative scarcity of these platforms in both the home and business use, I will focus on the i386 (and x86-64) platforms. The platform-specific configurations for Itanium and PPC machines can be found in the official Kdump documentation.

### *Terminology*

To make things easier to understand, here is a brief lexicon of important terms we will use in this document:

- Standard (production) kernel – kernel we normally work with.
- Crash (capture) kernel – kernel specially used for collecting crash dumps.

We will sometimes use only partial names when referring to these two kernels. In general, if we do not specifically use the word crash or capture to describe the kernel, this means we are talking about the production kernel. Kdump has two main components: Kdump and Kexec.

## Kexec

Kexec is a fastboot mechanism that allows booting a Linux kernel from the context of an already-running kernel without going through BIOS. BIOS can be very time consuming, especially on big servers with numerous peripherals. This can save a lot of time for developers who end up booting a machine numerous times.

## Kdump

Kdump is a (relatively) new kernel crash dumping mechanism and is very reliable. The crash dump is captured from the context of a freshly booted kernel and not from the context of the crashed kernel. Kdump uses Kexec to boot into a second kernel whenever the system crashes. This second kernel, often called a crash or a capture kernel, boots with very little memory and captures the dump image.

The first kernel reserves a section of memory that the second kernel uses to boot. Kexec enables booting the capture kernel without going through BIOS; hence, the contents of the first kernel's memory are preserved, which is essentially the kernel crash dump.

## Kdump installation

There are quite a few requirements that must be met in order for Kdump to work. The production kernel must be compiled with a certain set of parameters required for kernel crash dumping.

The production kernel must have the kernel-kdump package installed. The kernel-kdump package contains the crash kernel that is started when the standard kernel crashes, providing an environment in which the standard kernel state during the crash can be captured. The version of the kernel-dump package has to be identical to the standard kernel.

If the operating system comes with a kernel already compiled to run and use Kdump, you will have saved quite a bit of time. If you do not have a kernel built to support the Kdump functionality, you will have to do quite a bit of work, including a lengthy compilation and configuration procedure of both the standard, production kernel, and the crash (capture) kernel.

In this section, we do not go into the details of kernel compilation. The compilation is a generic procedure that does not directly relate to Kdump and demands dedicated attention. Nevertheless, although we will not compile, we will have to go through the list of kernel parameters that have to be configured so that your system can support the Kexec/Kdump functionality and collect crash dumps. These parameters need to be configured before kernel compilation.

We will now go through the list of kernel parameters that need to be defined to enable Kdump/Kexec to function properly. For the sake of simplicity, this document focuses on the x86 (and x86_64) architecture.

## Standard (production) kernel

The standard kernel can be a vanilla kernel downloaded from kernel.org (The Linux Kernel Archives, n.d.) or one of your favorite distributions. Whichever you choose, you will have to configure the kernel with several parameters.

### Under processor type and features

**Enable Kexec system call.** This parameter tells the system to use Kexec to skip BIOS and boot (new) kernels. It is critical for the functionality of Kdump.

```
CONFIG_KEXEC=y
```

**Enable kernel crash dumps.** Crash dumps need to be enabled. Without this option, Kdump will be useless.

```
CONFIG_CRASH_DUMP=y
```

**Optional: enable high memory support (for 32-bit systems).** You need to configure this parameter in order to support memory allocations beyond the 32-bit (4 GB) barrier. This may not be applicable if your system has less than 4 GB RAM or if you are using a 64-bit system.

```
CONFIG_HIGHMEM4G=y
```

**Optional: disable symmetric multiprocessing (SMP) support.** On some older versions of Linux, Kdump can only work with a single processor. If you have only a single processor or run your machine with SMP support disabled, you can safely set this parameter to (*n*).

```
CONFIG_SMP=n
```

On the other hand, if your kernel must use SMP for whatever reason, you will want to set this directive to (*y*). However, you will have to remember this during the Kdump configuration. We will have to set Kdump to use only a single CPU. It is very important that you remember this!

To recap, you can either disable SMP during the compilation *or* enable SMP but instruct Kdump to use a single CPU. This instruction is done by changing the Kdump configuration file. It is not a part of the kernel compilation configuration.

The configuration file change requires that one of the options be configured in a particular manner. Specifically, the directive below needs to be set in the Kdump configuration file under /etc/sysconfig/kdump after the kernel has been compiled and installed.

```
KDUMP_COMMANDLINE_APPEND="maxcpus=1 "
```

## Under filesystems > pseudo filesystems

***Enable sysfs file system support.*** Modern kernels (2.6 and above) support this setting by default, but it does not hurt to check.

```
CONFIG_SYSFS=y
```

***Enable /proc/vmcore support.*** This configuration allows Kdump to save the memory dump to /proc/vmcore. We will talk more about this later. Although in your setup you may not use the /proc/vmcore as the dump device, for greatest compatibility, it is recommended you set this parameter to (y).

```
CONFIG_PROC_VMCORE=y
```

## Under kernel hacking

***Configure the kernel with debug info.*** This parameter means the kernel will be built with debug symbols. While this will increase the size of the kernel image, having the symbols available is very useful for in-depth analysis of kernel crashes, because it allows you to trace the problems not only to problematic function calls causing the crashes, but also the specific lines in relevant source codes. We will talk about this in great detail in the set of separate tutorials covering the crash, lcrash, and gdb debugging utilities.

```
CONFIG_DEBUG_INFO=y
```

## Other settings

***Configure the start section for reserved RAM for the crash kernel.*** This is a very important setting to pay attention to. To work properly, the crash kernel uses a piece of memory specially reserved for it. The start section for this memory allocation needs to be defined. For instance, if you intend to start the crash kernel RAM at 16 MB, then the value needs to be set to the following (in hexadecimal):

```
CONFIG_PHYSICAL_START=0x1000000
```

***Configure kdump kernel, so it can be identified.*** Setting this suffix allows kdump to select the right kernel for boot since there may be several kernels under /boot on your system. In general, the rule of thumb calls for the crash kernel to be named the same as your production kernel, save for the -kdump suffix. You can check this by running the uname -r command in terminal, to see the kernel version you run, and then check the files listed in the /boot directory.

```
CONFIG_LOCALVERSION="-kdump"
```

### Crash (capture) kernel

This kernel needs to be compiled with the same parameters as above, save one exception. Kdump does not support compressed kernel images as crash (capture) kernels. Therefore, you should not compress this image. This means that while your production kernels will most likely be named vmlinuz, the Kdump crash kernels need to be uncompressed, hence named vmlinux, or rather vmlinux-kdump.

### Kdump packages and files

This is the list of required packages that must be installed on the system for Kdump to work. Please note that your kernel must be compiled properly for these packages to work as expected. It is very likely that you will succeed in installing them anyhow, but this is no guarantee that they will work. The package names and their information are shown in Table 6.1.

The best way to obtain these packages is from your software repositories. This guarantees you will be using the most compatible version of Kdump and Kexec. Likewise, please note that the production kernel also must have the kernel-kdump package installed. This package contains the crash kernel that is started when the standard kernel crashes, providing an environment in which the standard kernel state during the crash can be captured. The version of this package has to be identical to the production kernel.

Table 6.2 lists the most important Kdump-related files[1].

**Table 6.1** List of Necessary Packages

| Package Name | Package Information |
| --- | --- |
| Kdump | Kdump package |
| Kexec-tools | Kexec package |
| Kernel-debuginfo* | Crash analysis package (optional) |

*The kernel–debuginfo package needs to match your kernel version – default, smp, and so on.

---

[1]The path as well as the names of files may change, depending on the Linux distribution and release.

**Table 6.2** Kdump Files

| Path | Information |
|------|-------------|
| /etc/init.d/kdump | Kdump service |
| /etc/sysconfig/kdump | Kdump configuration file |
| /usr/share/doc/packages/kdump | Kdump documentation |

The Kdump installation also includes the gdb Kdump wrapper script (gdb-kdump), which is used to simplify the use of gdb on Kdump images. The use of gdb, as well as other crash analysis utilities, requires the presence of the kernel-debuginfo package.

## KDUMP CONFIGURATION

In the last section, we went through the kernel configuration parameters that need to be set for Kexec/Kdump to work properly. Now, assuming you have a functioning kernel that boots to the login screen and has been compiled with the relevant parameters, whether by a vendor or yourself, we will see what extra steps we need to take to make Kdump actually work and collect crash dumps.

We will configure Kdump twice: once for local dump and once for network dump, similarly to what we did with LKCD. This is a very important step because LKCD is limited to network dumping only within the specific subnet of the crash machine. Kdump offers a much greater, more flexible network functionality, including FTP, SSH, NFS, and CIFS support.

### Configuration file

The configuration file for Kdump is /etc/sysconfig/kdump. We will start with the basic, local dump functionality. Later, we will also demonstrate a crash dump over network. You should save a backup before making any changes!

```
Configure KDUMP_KERNELVER
```

This setting refers to the CONFIG_LOCALVERSION kernel configuration parameter that we reviewed earlier. We specified the suffix -kdump, which tells our system to use kernels with -kdump suffix as crash kernels. As the short description paragraph specifies, if no value is used, the most recently installed Kdump kernel will be used. By default, crash kernels are identified by the -kdump suffix.

In general, this setting is meaningful only if nonstandard suffixes are used for Kdump kernels. Most users will not need to touch this setting and can leave it at the default value, unless they have very specific needs that require certain kernel versions.

```
KDUMP_KERNELVER=""
```

## Configure KDUMP_COMMANDLINE
This setting tells Kdump the set of parameters it needs to boot the crash kernel with. In most cases, you will use the same set as your production kernel, so you will not have to change it. To see the current set, you can issue the cat command against /proc/cmdline. When no string is specified, this is the set of parameters that will be used as the default. We will use this setting when we test Kdump (or rather, Kexec) and simulate a crash kernel boot.

```
KDUMP_COMMANDLINE=""
```

## Configure KDUMP_COMMANDLINE_APPEND
This is a very important directive. It is extremely crucial if you use or have to use an SMP kernel. We saw earlier during the configuration of kernel compilation parameters that Kdump cannot use more than a single core for the crash kernel. Therefore, this parameter is a *must* if you are using SMP. If the kernel has been configured with SMP disabled, you can ignore this setting.

```
KDUMP_COMMANDLINE_APPEND="MAXCPUS=1 "
```

## Configure KEXEC_OPTIONS
As we have mentioned earlier, Kexec is the mechanism that boots the crash kernel from the context of the production kernel. To work properly, Kexec requires a set of arguments. The basic set used is defined by the /proc/cmdline. Additional arguments can be specified using this directive. In most cases, the string can be left empty. However, if you receive strange errors when starting Kdump, it is likely that Kdump on your particular kernel version cannot parse the arguments properly. To make Kdump interpret the additional parameters literally, you may need to add the string –args-linux.

You should try both settings and see which one works for you. If you are interested, you can point your search engine to "--args-linux" and see a range of mailing list threads and bug entries revolving around this subject. Nothing decisive, so trial and error is your best choice here. We will discuss this some more later on.

```
KDUMP_OPTIONS="--args-linux "
```

## Configure KDUMP_RUNLEVEL

This is another important directive. It defines the runlevel into which the crash kernel should boot. If you want Kdump to save crash dumps only to a local device, you can set the runlevel to 1. If you want Kdump to save dumps to a network storage area, such as NFS, CIFS, or FTP, you need the network functionality, which means the runlevel should be set to 3. You can also use 2, 5, and s. If you opt for runlevel 5 (not recommended), make sure the crash kernel has enough memory to boot into the graphical environment. The default 64 MB is most likely insufficient.

```
KDUMP_RUNLEVEL="1"
```

## Configure KDUMP_IMMEDIATE_REBOOT

This directive tells Kdump whether to reboot out of the crash kernel once the dump is complete. This directive is ignored if the KDUMP_DUMPDEV parameter (see below) is not empty. In other words, if a dump device is used, the crash kernel will not be rebooted until the transfer and possibly additional postprocessing of the dump image to the destination directory are complete. You will most likely want to retain the default value.

```
KDUMP_IMMEDIATE_REBOOT="yes"
```

## Configure KDUMP_TRANSFER

This setting tells Kdump what to do with the dumped memory core. For instance, you may want to postprocess it instantly.

KDUMP_TRANSFER requires the use of a nonempty KDUMP_DUMPDEV directive. Available choices are /proc/vmcore and /dev/oldmem. This is similar to the LKCD utility. Normally, either /proc/vmcore or /dev/oldmem will point out to an unused swap partition.

For now onward, we will use only the default setting, which is just to copy the saved core image to KDUMP_SAVEDIR. We will talk about the KDUMP_DUMPDEV and KDUMP_SAVEDIR directives shortly. However, we will study the more advanced transfer options only when we discuss crash analysis utilities.

```
KDUMP_TRANSFER=""
```

## Configure KDUMP_SAVEDIR

This is a very important directive. It tells us where the memory core will be saved. Currently, we are talking about local dump, so for now, our destination will point to a directory on the local filesystem. Later on, we will see a network example. By default, the setting points to /var/log/dump.

```
KDUMP_SAVEDIR="file:///var/log/dump"
```

In our setup, we will change this to

```
KDUMP_SAVEDIR="file:///tmp/dump"
```

Please pay attention to the syntax. You can also use the absolute directory paths inside the quotation marks without a prefix, but this use is discouraged. You should specify what kind of protocol is used, with file:// for local directories, nfs:// for NFS storage, and so on. Furthermore, you should make sure the destination is writable and that it has sufficient space to accommodate the memory cores. The KDUMP_SAVE-DIR directive can be used in conjunction with KDUMP_DUMPDEV, which we will discuss a little later on.

## Configure KDUMP_KEEP_OLD_DUMPS

This setting defines how many dumps should be kept before rotating. If you are short on space or are collecting numerous dumps, you may want to retain only a small number of dumps. Alternatively, if you require a backtrace as long and thorough as possible, increase the number to accommodate your needs.

To keep an infinite number of old dumps, set the number to 0. To delete all existing dumps before writing a new one, set the number to −2. Please note the somewhat strange values as they are counterintuitive. Table 6.3 shows the special values; the default value is to retain five memory cores.

```
KDUMP_KEEP_OLD_DUMPS=5
```

**Table 6.3** Special Values for the Number of Old Dumps Retained on the Disk

| Value | Dumps Kept |
| --- | --- |
| 0 | All (infinite number) |
| −2 | none |

### Configure KDUMP_FREE_DISK_SIZE

This value defines the minimum free space that must remain on the target partition, where the memory core dump destination directory is located, after accounting for the memory core size. If this value cannot be met, the memory core will not be saved to prevent possible system failure. The default value is 64 MB. Please note it has nothing to do with the memory allocation in GRUB. This is an unrelated, purely disk space setting.

```
KDUMP_FREE_DISK_SIZE=64MB
```

### Configure KDUMP_DUMPDEV

This is a very important directive. We have mentioned it several times before. KDUMP_DUMPDEV does not have to be used, but you should carefully consider whether you might need it. Furthermore, please remember that this directive is closely associated with several other settings, so if you do use it, the functionality of Kdump will change.

First, let us see when it might be prudent to use KDUMP_DUMPDEV. Using this directive can be useful if you might be facing filesystem corruption problems. In this case, when a crash occurs, it might not be possible to mount the root filesystem and write to the destination directory (KDUMP_SAVEDIR), and consequently, the crash dump would fail. Using KDUMP_DUMPDEV allows you to write to a device or a partition in raw mode, without any consideration to underlying filesystem, circumventing any filesystem-related problems.

This also means that there will be no KDUMP_IMMEDIATE_REBOOT. The directive will also be ignored, allowing you to use the console to try to fix system problems manually, like checking the filesystem, because no partition will be mounted and used. Kdump will examine the KDUMP_DUMPDEV directive and if it is not empty, it will copy the contents from the dump device to the dump directory (KDUMP_SAVEDIR).

On the other hand, using KDUMP_DUMPDEV increases the risk of disk corruption in the recovery kernel environment. Furthermore, there will be no immediate reboot, which slows down the restoration to production. While such a solution is useful for small-scale operations, it is impractical for large environments. Moreover, take into account that the dump device will always be irrecoverably overwritten when the dump is collected, destroying data present on it. Second, you cannot use an active swap partition as the dump device.

```
KDUMP_DUMPDEV=" "
```

### Configure KDUMP_VERBOSE

This is a rather simple, administrative directive. It tells how much information is output to the user, using bitmask values in a fashion similar to the chmod command.

**Table 6.4** Kdump Verbosity Level

| Value | Action |
|---|---|
| 1 | Kdump command line written to syslog |
| 2 | Kdump progress written to STDOUT |
| 4 | Kdump command line written to STDOUT |
| 8 | Kdump transfer script debugged |

By default, the Kdump progress is written to the standard output (STDOUT) and the Kdump command line is written into the syslog. If we sum the values, we get command line (1) + STDOUT (2) = 3. See Table 6.4 for all available values.

### Configure KDUMP_DUMPLEVEL

This directive defines the level of data provided in the memory dump. Values range from 0 to 32. Level 0 means the entire contents of the memory will be dumped, with no detail omitted. Level 32 means the smallest image. The default value is 0.

You should refer to the configuration file for exact details about what each level offers and plan accordingly, based on your available storage and analysis requirements. You are welcome to try them all. We recommend using 0 as it provides the most information even though it requires a large amount of hard disk space.

### Configure KDUMP_DUMPFORMAT

This setting defines the dump format. The default selection is ELF, which allows you to open the dump with gdb and process it. You can also use compressed, but you can analyze the dump only with the crash utility. We will talk about these two tools in great detail in separate tutorials. The default and recommended choice is ELF, even though the dump file is larger.

This concludes the necessary changes in the configuration file for Kdump to work.

## GRUB menu changes

Because of the way it works, Kdump requires a change to the kernel entry in the GRUB (GNU GRUB, n.d.) menu. As you already know, Kdump works by booting from the context of the crashed kernel. In order for this feature to work, the crash kernel must have a section of memory available, even when the production kernel crashes. To this end, memory must be reserved.

In the kernel configurations earlier, we declared the offset point for our memory reservation. Now, we need to declare how much RAM we want to give our crash kernel. The exact figure will depend on several factors, including the size of your RAM and possibly other restrictions. If you read various sources online, you will notice that two figures are mostly used: 64 and 128 MB. The first is the default configuration and should work. However, if it proves unreliable for whatever reason, you may want to try the second value. Test-crashing the kernel a few times should give you a good indication whether your choice is sensible or not.

Now, let us edit the GRUB configuration file. We will demonstrate using the GRUB Legacy version. Changes for the GRUB2 bootloader are similar, and beyond the scope of this section. First, make sure you back up the file before any changes.

```
cp /boot/grub/menu.lst /boot/grub/menu.lst-backup
```

Open the file for editing. Locate the production kernel entry and append the following:

```
crashkernel=XM@YM
```

YM is the offset point we declared during the kernel compilation or that has been configured for us by the vendor. In our case, this is 16M. XM is the size of memory allocated to the crash kernel. As we have mentioned earlier, the most typical configuration will be either 64 or 128 MB. Therefore, the appended entry should look like

```
crashkernel=64M@16M
```

A complete stanza inside the menu.lst file:

```
title Some Linux
root (hd0,1)
kernel /boot/vmlinuz root=/dev/sda1 resume=/dev/sda5 ->
-> splash=silent crashkernel=64M@16M
```

### Set Kdump to start on boot

We now need to enable Kdump on startup. This can be done using chkconfig or sysv-rc-conf utilities on RedHat- or Debian-based distributions, respectively. For example, using the chkconfig utility

```
chkconfig kdump on
```

Changes to the configuration file require that the Kdump service be restarted. However, the Kdump service cannot run unless the GRUB menu change has been affected and the system rebooted. You can easily check this by trying to start the Kdump service:

```
/etc/init.d/kdump start
```

If you have not allocated the memory or if you have used the wrong offset, you will get an error, something like this:

```
/etc/init.d/kdump start
Loading kdump                                    failed
Memory for crashkernel is not reserved Please reserve memory by passing
"crashkernel=X@Y" parameter to the kernel Then try loading kdump kernel
```

If you receive this error, this means that the GRUB configuration file has not been edited properly. You will have to make the right changes, reboot the system, and try again. Once this is done properly, Kdump should start without any errors. We will mention this again when we test our setup.

## TEST CONFIGURATION

Before we start crashing our kernel for real, we need to check that our configuration really works. This means executing a dry run with Kexec. In other words, configure

Kexec to load with desired parameters and boot the crash (capture) kernel. If you successfully pass this stage, this means your system is properly configured and you can test the Kdump functionality with a real kernel crash.

Again, if your system comes with the kernel already compiled to use Kdump, you will have saved much time and effort. Basically, the Kdump installation and the configuration test are completely unnecessary. You can proceed straight away to using Kdump.

### Load Kexec with relevant parameters

Our first step is to load Kexec with desired parameters into the existing kernel. Usually, you will want Kdump to run with the same parameters your production kernel booted with. So, you will probably use the following configuration to test Kdump:

```
/usr/local/sbin/kexec -l /boot/vmlinuz-`uname -r` --initrd=/boot/initrd-`uname -r` --
command-line=`cat /proc/cmdline`
```

Then, execute Kexec (it will load the above parameters):

```
/usr/local/sbin/kexec -e
```

Your crash kernel should start booting. As mentioned earlier, it will skip BIOS, so you should see the boot sequence in your console immediately. If this step completes successfully without errors, you are on the right path. I would gladly share a screenshot here, but it would look just like any other boot, so it is useless.

The next step would be to load the new kernel for use on panic. Reboot and then test:

```
/usr/local/sbin/kexec -p
```

### Possible errors

At this stage, you may encounter a possible error, something like this:

```
kexec_load failed: Cannot assign requested address
entry = 0x96550 flags = 1
nr_segments = 4
segment[0].buf = 0x528aa0
```

```
segment[0].bufsz = 2044
segment[0].mem = 0x93000
segment[0].memsz = 3000
segment[1].buf = 0x521880
segment[1].bufsz = 7100
segment[1].mem = 0x96000
segment[1].memsz = 9000
segment[2].buf = 0x2aaaaf1f010
segment[2].bufsz = 169768
segment[2].mem = 0x100000
segment[2].memsz = 16a000
segment[3].buf = 0x2aaaab11e010
segment[3].bufsz = 2f5a36
segment[3].mem = 0xdf918000
segment[3].memsz = 2f6000
```

If this happens, this means you have one of the two following problems:

You have not configured the production kernel properly and Kdump will not work. You will have to go through the installation process again, which includes compiling the kernel with relevant parameters.

The Kexec version you are using does not match the kernel-kdump package. Make sure the right packages are selected. You should check the installed versions of the two packages: kernel-kdump and kexec-tools. Or you may be missing --args-linux in the configuration file, under KEXEC_OPTIONS.

Once you successfully solve this issue, you will be able to proceed with testing. If the crash kernel boots without any issues, this means you are good to go and can start using Kdump for real.

## KDUMP NETWORK DUMP FUNCTIONALITY

Being able to send kernel crash dumps to network storage makes Kdump attractive for deployment in large environments. It also allows system administrators to evade local disk space limitations. Compared to LKCD, Kdump is much more network-aware; it is not restricted to dumping on the same subnet, and there is no need for a dedicated server. You can use NFS areas or CIFS shares as the archiving destination. Best of all, the changes only affect the client side. There is no server-side configuration.

### Configuration file

To make Kdump send crash dumps to network storage, only two directives in the configuration file need to be changed for the entire procedure to work. The other settings remain identical to local disk functionality, including starting Kdump on boot, GRUB menu addition, and Kexec testing.

The configuration file is located under /etc/sysconfig/kdump. As always, before affecting a change, back up the configuration file.

### Configure KDUMP_RUNLEVEL

To use the network functionality, we need to configure Kdump to boot in runlevel 3. By default, runlevel 1 is used. Network functionality is achieved by changing the directive.

```
KDUMP_RUNLEVEL=3
```

### Configure KDUMP_SAVEDIR

The second step is to configure the network storage destination. We can no longer use the local file. We need to use either an NFS area, a CIFS share, an SSH server, or an FTP server. In this document, we will configure an NFS area because it seems the most sensible choice for sending crash dumps to. The configuration of the other two is very similar, and just as simple. The one thing you will have to pay attention to is the notation. You need to use the correct syntax

```
KDUMP_SAVEDIR="nfs:///<server>:/<dir>"
```

<server> refers to the NFS server, either by name or IP address. If you are using a name, you need to have some sort of a name resolution mechanism in your environment, like hosts file or DNS. <dir> is the exported NFS directory on the NFS server. The directory has to be writable by the root user. In our example, the directive takes the following form:

```
KDUMP_SAVEDIR="nfs:///nfsserver02:/dumps"
```

These are the two changes required to make Kdump send memory dumps to an NFS storage area in the case of a kernel crash. Now, we will test the functionality.

## KDUMP USE

We will now simulate a kernel crash to examine our configuration and make sure that everything works.

### Simulate kernel crash

To manually crash the kernel, you will have to enable the System Request (SysRq) functionality (also known as magic keys), if it has not already been enabled on your system(s), and then trigger a kernel panic. Therefore, first, enable the SysRq:

```
echo 1 > /proc/sys/kernel/sysrq
```

Then, crash the kernel

```
echo c > /proc/sysrq-trigger
```

Now watch the console. The crash kernel should boot up. After a while, you should see Kdump in action. Take a look at the console. After a while, a small counter should appear, showing you the progress of the dump procedure. This means you have most likely properly configured Kdump and it is working as expected. Wait until the dump completes. The system should reboot into the production kernel when the dump is complete. Indeed, checking the destination directory, you should see the vmcore file. The process of a memory core dump is shown in Figs. 6.1 and 6.2.

This concludes the long and thorough configuration and testing of Kdump. If you have successfully managed all the stages so far, this means your system is ready to be placed into production and collect memory cores when kernel panic situations occur.

```
Loading keymap i386/qwerty/us.map.gz                                done
Loading compose table winkeys shiftctrl latin1.add                  done
Start Unicode mode                                                  done
Loading console font lat9w-16.psfu  -m trivial G0:loadable          done
|------------------------------------------------|  0 MB of 8128 MB (0.0%)
```

**FIGURE 6.1  Kernel Memory Dump in Progress**

```
Start Unicode mode                                                  done
Loading console font lat9w-16.psfu  -m trivial G0:loadable          done
|################################################|  8128 MB of 8128 MB (100.0%)
                                                                    done

INIT: Switching to runlevel: 6
INIT: Sending processes the TERM signal
Master Resource Control: runlevel 3 has been                     reached
```

**FIGURE 6.2  Kernel Memory Dump Complete**

Analyzing the cores will provide you with valuable information that should hopefully help you find and resolve the root causes leading to system crashes.

## SUMMARY

Kdump is a powerful, flexible kernel crash dumping utility. The ability to execute a crash kernel in the context of the running production kernel is a very useful mechanism. Similarly, the ability to use the crash kernel in virtually all runlevels, including networking, and the ability to send cores to network storage using a variety of protocols, significantly extends our ability to control the environment.

Specifically, in comparison to the older LKCD utility, it offers improved functionality on all levels, including a more robust mechanism and better scalability. Kdump can use local RAID (md) devices, if needed. Furthermore, it has improved network awareness and can work with a number of protocols, including NFS, CIFS, FTP, and SSH. The memory cores are no longer limited by the 32-bit barrier.

## CRASH ANALYSIS (CRASH)

Kernel crash analysis is the next step in our investigation. After we have collected the memory cores, we now need to process them. The standard utility for this task is crash (Anderson, 2008) based on the SVR4 UNIX crash command and enhanced by merging it with the gdb tool. We will now expand on its use, and see how it can aid us in our troubleshooting.

## PREREQUISITES

You must have Kdump setup properly and working.

### Crash setup

Crash can be found in the repositories of all major distributions, including enterprise flavors.

### Memory cores

Memory cores are called vmcore and you will find them in dated directories inside the crash directory. On older versions of Kdump, the directories would only contain the vmcore file. Newer versions also copy the kernel and System map file into the directory, making the core processing easier.

### Invoke crash

The crash utility can be invoked in several ways. First, there is some difference between older and newer versions of Kdump in terms of what they can do and how they process the memory cores. Second, the crash utility can be run manually or unattended.

### Old (classic) invocation

The old invocation is done in the following manner:

```
crash <System map> <vmlinux> vmcore
```

<System map> is the absolute path to the System map file, which is normally located under /boot. This file must match the version of the kernel used at the time of the crash.

The System map file is a symbol table used by the kernel. A symbol table is a look-up between symbol names and their addresses in memory. A symbol name may be the name of a variable or the name of a function. The System.map is required when the address of a symbol name is needed. It is especially useful for debugging kernel panics and kernel oopses, which is what we need here.

- <vmlinux> is the uncompressed version of the kernel that was running when the memory core was collected on the host.
- vmcore is the memory core.

The System-map and vmlinux files remain in the /boot directory and are not copied into the crash directory. However, they can be manually copied to other machines, allowing portable use of crash against memory cores collected on other systems and/or kernels.

### New invocation

The newer versions of Kdump can work with compressed kernel images. Furthermore, they copy the System map file and the kernel image into the crash directory, making the use of crash utility somewhat simpler. Finally, there are two ways you can process the cores. Depending on your choice of distribution, the usage syntax might be somewhat different:

```
crash /usr/lib/debug/boot/<kernel>.debug vmcore

crash /usr/lib/debug/lib/modules/<kernel>/vmlinux vmcore
```

### Portable use

To process cores on other machines, you can either copy System map and the kernel or just the debug information file. Newer versions of Kdump and crash will work with compressed kernel images. The debug info must match the kernel version exactly, otherwise you will get a CRC match error, for instance

```
crash: /usr/lib/debug/boot/vmlinux-2.6.31-default.debug:

CRC value does not match
```

## RUNNING CRASH

All right, now that we know the little nuances, let us run crash. Kdump is working and doing its magic in the background. If you get to the crash prompt after invoking the crash command, either using the old or new syntax, then everything is ok.

```
crash 5.0.1

Copyright (C) 2002-2010  Red Hat, Inc.

Copyright (C) 2004, 2005, 2006  IBM Corporation

Copyright (C) 1999-2006  Hewlett-Packard Co

Copyright (C) 2005, 2006  Fujitsu Limited

Copyright (C) 2006, 2007  VA Linux Systems Japan K.K.

Copyright (C) 2005  NEC Corporation

Copyright (C) 1999, 2002, 2007  Silicon Graphics, Inc.

Copyright (C) 1999, 2000, 2001, 2002  Mission Critical Linux, Inc.

This program is free software, covered by the GNU General Public License,

and you are welcome to change it and/or distribute copies of it under

certain conditions.  Enter "help copying" to see the conditions.

This program has absolutely no warranty.  Enter "help warranty" for details.



NOTE: stdin: not a tty



GNU gdb (GDB) 7.0

Copyright (C) 2009 Free Software Foundation, Inc.

License GPLv3+: GNU GPL version 3 or later <http://gnu.org/licenses/gpl.html>

This is free software: you are free to change and redistribute it.
```

```
There is NO WARRANTY, to the extent permitted by law.  Type "show copying"

and "show warranty" for details.

This GDB was configured as "x86_64-unknown-linux-gnu"...

please wait... (gathering kmem slab cache data)

please wait... (gathering module symbol data)

please wait... (gathering task table data)

please wait... (determining panic task)

SYSTEM MAP: /boot/System.map-2.6.32.59-0.3.1-default

DEBUG KERNEL: /boot/vmlinux-2.6.32.59-0.3.1-default (2.6.32.59-0.3.1-default)

    DUMPFILE: /tmp/dump/2013-03-05-12:57/vmcore

       CPUS: 32

       DATE: Tue Mar  5 12:56:34 2013

     UPTIME: 57 days, 15:12:15

LOAD AVERAGE: 15.67, 15.93, 15.07

      TASKS: 882

   NODENAME: ics10745

    RELEASE: 2.6.32.59-0.3.1-default

    VERSION: #1 SMP 2012-04-27 11:14:44 +0200

    MACHINE: x86_64  (2600 Mhz)

     MEMORY: 128 GB

      PANIC: "[4968899.568159] Oops: 0000 [#1] SMP " (check log for details)

        PID: 27010

    COMMAND: "task.bin"

       TASK: ffff880a8e68a500  [THREAD_INFO: ffff880a77f98000]

        CPU: 19

      STATE: TASK_RUNNING (PANIC)
```

### *Crash commands*

Once crash is running and you are staring at the crash prompt, it is time to try some crash commands. In this tutorial, we will not focus too much on the commands or understanding their output. For now, it is a brief overview of what we need. Crash commands are listed in superb detail in the RedHat Crash White Paper (Anderson, n.d.). In fact, the document is pretty much everything you will need to work with crash. The following are a handful of important and useful commands you will need.

## Backtrace

The backtrace command displays a kernel stack backtrace. If no arguments are given, the stack trace of the current context is displayed.

```
PID: 27010   TASK: ffff880a8e68a500   CPU: 19   COMMAND: "task.bin"

 #0 [ffff880a77f99970] machine_kexec at ffffffff81020ac2

 #1 [ffff880a77f999c0] crash_kexec at ffffffff81088830

 #2 [ffff880a77f99a90] oops_end at ffffffff8139f790

 #3 [ffff880a77f99ab0] __bad_area_nosemaphore at ffffffff8102ed15

 #4 [ffff880a77f99ae0] put_rpccred at ffffffffa023f150

 #5 [ffff880a77f99af8] update_cpu_power at ffffffff8103ccf7

 #6 [ffff880a77f99b70] page_fault at ffffffff8139ea0f

 #7 [ffff880a77f99bf8] nfs_lookup_revalidate at ffffffffa02bafe9

 #8 [ffff880a77f99c20] nfs_lookup_revalidate at ffffffffa02baf75

 #9 [ffff880a77f99cb0] dput at ffffffff811127ea

#10 [ffff880a77f99cd0] nfs_lookup_revalidate at ffffffffa02bb01a

#11 [ffff880a77f99ce0] bit_waitqueue at ffffffff810657d0

#12 [ffff880a77f99d00] nfs_access_get_cached at ffffffffa02b8c87

#13 [ffff880a77f99d40] nfs_do_access at ffffffffa02b9059

#14 [ffff880a77f99dc0] __lookup_hash at ffffffff81108936

#15 [ffff880a77f99e00] lookup_one_len at ffffffff81109649
```

```
#16 [ffff880a77f99e30] nfs_sillyrename at ffffffffa02b8043

#17 [ffff880a77f99e60] nfs_unlink at ffffffffa02b9806

#18 [ffff880a77f99e90] vfs_unlink at ffffffff8110a0b1

#19 [ffff880a77f99eb0] do_unlinkat at ffffffff8110c911

#20 [ffff880a77f99f10] mntput_no_expire at ffffffff81119a43

#21 [ffff880a77f99f40] filp_close at ffffffff810fd096

#22 [ffff880a77f99f80] system_call_fastpath at ffffffff81002f7b

    RIP: 00002aaaacd99007  RSP: 00007fffffff6c68  RFLAGS: 00000202

    RAX: 0000000000000057  RBX: ffffffff81002f7b  RCX: 00002aaaad029e60

    RDX: 0000000000000041  RSI: 00002aaaacdf6650  RDI: 0000000001661238

    RBP: 00007fffffff6cc0   R8: 736a2e73746c7573   R9: 00000000016615d0

    R10: 00002aaaada82120  R11: 0000000000000202  R12: 00007fffffff6e00

    R13: 00007fffffff6d10  R14: 0000000001661238  R15: ffff88100e5d5a40

    ORIG_RAX: 0000000000000057  CS: 0033  SS: 002b
```

## Dump system message buffer
The log command dumps the kernel log_buf contents in a chronological order.

```
[    0.000000] Initializing cgroup subsys cpuset

[    0.000000] Initializing cgroup subsys cpu

[    0.000000] Linux version 2.6.32.59-0.3.1-default (geeko@buildhost) (gcc version
4.3.4 [gcc-4_3-branch revision 152973] (SUSE Linux) ) #1 SMP 2012-04-27 11:14:44
+0200

[    0.000000] Command line: root=/dev/disk/by-id/cciss-
3600508b1001c3794d87c4706c7c5dc6a-part2 resume=/dev/disk/by-id/cciss-
3600508b1001c7df40d7a8a6a2a2d146c-part1 splash=silent crashkernel=128M@32M

[    0.000000] KERNEL supported cpus:
```

```
[    0.000000]    Intel GenuineIntel

[    0.000000]    AMD AuthenticAMD

[    0.000000]    Centaur CentaurHauls

[    0.000000] BIOS-provided physical RAM map:

[    0.000000]  BIOS-e820: 0000000000000000 - 0000000000097400 (usable)

[    0.000000]  BIOS-e820: 0000000000097400 - 00000000000a0000 (reserved)

[    0.000000]  BIOS-e820: 00000000000f0000 - 0000000000100000 (reserved)

[    0.000000]  BIOS-e820: 0000000000100000 - 00000000bddcc000 (usable)

[    0.000000]  BIOS-e820: 00000000bddcc000 - 00000000bddde000 (ACPI data)

[    0.000000]  BIOS-e820: 00000000bddde000 - 00000000bdddf000 (usable)

[    0.000000]  BIOS-e820: 00000000bdddf000 - 00000000d0000000 (reserved)

[    0.000000]  BIOS-e820: 00000000fec00000 - 00000000fee10000 (reserved)

[    0.000000]  BIOS-e820: 00000000ff800000 - 0000000100000000 (reserved)

[    0.000000]  BIOS-e820: 0000000100000000 - 000000203ffff000 (usable)

[    0.000000] DMI 2.7 present.

[    0.000000] last_pfn = 0x203ffff max_arch_pfn = 0x400000000

[    0.000000] MTRR default type: write-back

[    0.000000] MTRR fixed ranges enabled:

[    0.000000]   00000-9FFFF write-back

[    0.000000]   A0000-BFFFF uncachable
```

## Display process status information

The ps command displays process status for selected, or all, processes in the system.
If no arguments are entered, the process data is displayed for all processes.

| PID | PPID | CPU | TASK | ST | %MEM | VSZ | RSS | COMM |
|---|---|---|---|---|---|---|---|---|
| 0 | 0 | 0 | ffffffff8180c020 | RU | 0.0 | 0 | 0 | [swapper] |
| 0 | 0 | 1 | ffff881030f70180 | RU | 0.0 | 0 | 0 | [swapper] |
| 0 | 0 | 2 | ffff882030f56080 | RU | 0.0 | 0 | 0 | [swapper] |

```
    0       0    3   ffff881030d6e2c0   RU   0.0      0      0   [swapper]
>   0       0    4   ffff882030f5a0c0   RU   0.0      0      0   [swapper]
>   0       0    5   ffff88103136c400   RU   0.0      0      0   [swapper]
>   0       0    6   ffff882030f5e100   RU   0.0      0      0   [swapper]
    0       0    7   ffff88103114c540   RU   0.0      0      0   [swapper]
>   0       0    8   ffff882030b48140   RU   0.0      0      0   [swapper]
    0       0    9   ffff881031164680   RU   0.0      0      0   [swapper]
>   0       0   10   ffff882031350180   RU   0.0      0      0   [swapper]
>   0       0   11   ffff88103117a140   RU   0.0      0      0   [swapper]
    0       0   12   ffff88203115a1c0   RU   0.0      0      0   [swapper]
>   0       0   13   ffff881031752280   RU   0.0      0      0   [swapper]
    0       0   14   ffff882031746200   RU   0.0      0      0   [swapper]
>   0       0   15   ffff8810315483c0   RU   0.0      0      0   [swapper]
    0       0   16   ffff88203176e240   RU   0.0      0      0   [swapper]
>   0       0   17   ffff881031562500   RU   0.0      0      0   [swapper]
>   0       0   18   ffff882031776280   RU   0.0      0      0   [swapper]
    0       0   19   ffff881031b62640   RU   0.0      0      0   [swapper]
>   0       0   20   ffff88203177c2c0   RU   0.0      0      0   [swapper]
    0       0   21   ffff881031942100   RU   0.0      0      0   [swapper]
    0       0   22   ffff882031540300   RU   0.0      0      0   [swapper]
    0       0   23   ffff88103197e240   RU   0.0      0      0   [swapper]
>   0       0   24   ffff882031544340   RU   0.0      0      0   [swapper]
```

## Other useful commands

You will also want to try help and h (command line history).

### *Create crash analysis file*

Processed command output can be sent to an external file. You merely need to use the redirection symbol (>) and specify a filename. This contrasts the usage of the lcrash utility (part of the LKCD framework), which specifically requires the -w flag to write to files.

### Crash running in unattended mode

Now that we know how to run crash commands and produce analysis files, why not do that entirely unattended? This can be done by specifying command line input from a file.

Commands can be sent to crash in two ways:

```
crash -i inputfile
```

Or using redirection

```
crash < inputfile
```

In both cases, the crash inputfile is a text file with crash commands one per line. For the crash utility to exit, you will also need to include the exit command at the end. Something like

```
bt
log
ps
exit
```

Thus, the complete, unattended analysis takes the form of

```
crash <debuginfo> vmcore < inputfile > outputfile
```

Or perhaps

```
crash <System map> <vmlinux> vmcore < inputfile > outputfile
```

And there are many other commands. The true study begins here. We will soon review the usage of these commands. We will also examine several simulated, study cases, as well as real crashes on production systems.

## Possible errors

When running the crash utility, you may encounter various errors. We will now elaborate on a number of typical problems that can occur when trying to open the crash cores.

### No debugging data available

After running crash, you may see this error:

```
crash: /boot/vmlinuz-2.6.18-164.10.1.el5: no debugging data available
```

This means you are probably missing the debuginfo packages. You should start your package manager and double-check. If you remember, I have repeatedly stated that having the debuginfo packages installed is a prerequisite for using Kdump and crash correctly.

### Vmlinux and Vmcore do not match (CRC does not match)

You may also get this error

```
crash: /usr/lib/debug/boot/vmlinux-2.6.31-default.debug:

CRC value does not match
```

If you see the following messages: "vmlinux and vmcore do not match!" or "CRC does not match," this means you have invoked crash for the wrong version of debuginfo, which does not match the vmcore file. Remember, you must use exactly the same version!

## No guarantee

There could be additional problems. Your dump may be invalid or incomplete. The header may be corrupt. The dump file may be in an unknown format. And even if the vmcore has been processed, the information therein may be partial or missing. For example, crash may not be able to find the task of the process causing the crash:

```
STATE: TASK_RUNNING

WARNING: panic task not found
```

There is no guarantee it will all work. System crashes are quite violent and things might not go as smoothly as you may desire, especially if the crashes are caused by hardware problems. For more details about possible errors, please consult the RedHat Crash White Paper mentioned earlier.

## ANALYSIS OF KERNEL CRASH CORES

Once you have successfully processed the core with the crash utility, the next step is to glean useful information stored inside the memory dump and try to understand what caused the kernel oops or panic in the first place. To that end, we will learn how to use several gdb-like crash commands. At a first glance, the collected output may seem like a new language, but we will soon learn how to interpret the alien syntax and understand the underlying issue that affected our system.

### First steps

Once you launch crash, you will get the initial report information printed to the console. This is where the analysis of the crash begins. This is a sample output of a typical crash run:

```
crash 4.0-8.9.1.el5.centos
Copyright (C) 2002, 2003, 2004, 2005, 2006, 2007, 2008, 2009  Red Hat, Inc.
Copyright (C) 2004, 2005, 2006   IBM Corporation
Copyright (C) 1999-2006   Hewlett-Packard Co
Copyright (C) 2005, 2006  Fujitsu Limited
Copyright (C) 2006, 2007  VA Linux Systems Japan K.K.
Copyright (C) 2005  NEC Corporation
Copyright (C) 1999, 2002, 2007  Silicon Graphics, Inc.
Copyright (C) 1999, 2000, 2001, 2002  Mission Critical Linux, Inc.
This program is free software, covered by the GNU General Public License, and you are
welcome to change it and/or distribute copies of it under certain conditions.  Enter
"help copying" to see the conditions. This program has absolutely no warranty.  Enter
"help warranty" for details.

NOTE: stdin: not a tty

GNU gdb 6.1
Copyright 2004 Free Software Foundation, Inc.
GDB is free software, covered by the GNU General Public License, and you are welcome
to change it and/or distribute copies of it under certain conditions.
Type "show copying" to see the conditions.
There is absolutely no warranty for GDB.  Type "show warranty" for details. This GDB
was configured as "x86_64-unknown-linux-gnu"...

bt: cannot transition from exception stack to current process stack:
    exception stack pointer: ffff810107132f20
      process stack pointer: ffff81010712bef0
        current_stack_base: ffff8101b509c000
```

```
       KERNEL: /usr/lib/debug/lib/modules/2.6.18-164.10.1.el5.centos.plus/vmlinux
     DUMPFILE: vmcore
         CPUS: 2
         DATE: Tue Jan 19 20:21:19 2010
       UPTIME: 00:00:00
 LOAD AVERAGE: 0.00, 0.04, 0.07
        TASKS: 134
     NODENAME: testhost2@localdomain
      RELEASE: 2.6.18-164.10.1.el5
      VERSION: #1 SMP Thu Jan 7 19:54:26 EST 2010
      MACHINE: x86_64  (3000 Mhz)
       MEMORY: 7.5 GB
        PANIC: "SysRq : Trigger a crashdump"
          PID: 0
      COMMAND: "swapper"
         TASK: ffffffff80300ae0  (1 of 2)  [THREAD_INFO: ffffffff803f2000]
          CPU: 0
        STATE: TASK_RUNNING (ACTIVE)
```

Let us walk through the report. The first thing you see is some kind of an error: you may or may not encounter it in your usage.

```
bt: cannot transition from exception stack to current process stack:
    exception stack pointer: ffff810107132f20
      process stack pointer: ffff81010712bef0
         current_stack_base: ffff8101b509c000
```

The technical explanation for this error is a little tricky. Quoted from the crash utility mailing list thread (Crash version 4.0.8-11 announcement, n.d.) about changes in the crash utility 4.0-8.11 release, we learn the following information:

```
If a kdump NMI issued to a non-crashing x86_64 cpu was received while
running in schedule(), after having set the next task as "current" in
the cpu's runqueue, but prior to changing the kernel stack to that of
the next task, then a backtrace would fail to make the transition
from the NMI exception stack back to the process stack, with the
error message "bt: cannot transition from exception stack to current
process stack". This patch will report inconsistencies found between
a task marked as the current task in a cpu's runqueue, and the task
found in the per-cpu x8664_pda "pcurrent" field (2.6.29 and earlier)
```

```
or the per-cpu "current_task" variable (2.6.30 and later). If it can
be safely determined that the runqueue setting (used by default) is
premature, then the crash utility's internal per-cpu active task will
be changed to be the task indicated by the appropriate architecture
specific value.
```

What does this mean? It is a warning that you should heed when analyzing the crash report. It will help us determine which task structure we need to look at to troubleshoot the crash reason. For now, ignore this error. It is not important to understanding what the crash report contains. You may or may not see it. Now, let us examine the code below this error.

- KERNEL: specifies the kernel running at the time of the crash.
- DUMPFILE: is the name of the dumped memory core.
- CPUS: is the number of CPUs on your machine.
- DATE: specifies the time of the crash.
- TASKS: indicates the number of tasks in the memory at the time of the crash. Task is a set of program instructions loaded into memory.
- NODENAME: is the name of the crashed host.
- RELEASE: and VERSION: specify the kernel release and version.
- MACHINE: specifies the architecture of the CPU.
- MEMORY: is the size of the physical memory on the crashed machine.
- PANIC: specifies what kind of crash occurred on the machine. There are several types that you can see.

SysRq (System Request) refers to magic keys, which allow you to send instructions directly to the kernel. They can be invoked by using a keyboard sequence or by echoing letter commands to /proc/sysrq-trigger, provided the functionality is enabled. We discussed this in the Kdump section.

Oops is a deviation from the expected, correct behavior of the kernel. Usually, the oops results in the offending process being killed. The system may or may not resume its normal behavior. Most likely, the system will enter an unpredictable, unstable state, which could lead to kernel panic if some of the buggy, killed resources are requested later on.

Panic is a state where the system has encountered a fatal error and cannot recover. Panic can be caused by trying to access prohibited addresses, forced loading or unloading of kernel modules, or hardware problems. In our first, most benign example, the PANIC: string refers to the use of magic keys. We deliberately triggered a crash.

- PANIC: "SysRq : Trigger a crashdump"
- PID: is the process ID of the task that caused the crash.
- COMMAND: is the name of the process, in this case swapper.
- COMMAND: "swapper"

Swapper, or PID 0, is the scheduler. It is the process that delegates the CPU time between runnable processes and, if there are no other processes in the runqueue, it takes control. You may want to refer to swapper as the idle task, so to speak.

There is one swapper per CPU, which you will soon see when we start exploring the crash in greater depth. But this is not really important. We will encounter many processes with different names.

- TASK: is the address in memory for the offending process. We will use this information later on. There is a difference in the memory addressing for 32-bit and 64-bit architectures.
- CPU: is the number of the CPU (relevant if more than one) where the offending process was running at the time of the crash. CPU refers to CPU cores and not just physical CPUs. If you are running your Linux with hyperthreading enabled, then you will also be counting separate threads as CPUs. This is important to remember because recurring crashes on just one specific CPU might indicate a CPU problem.

If you are running your processes with affinity set to certain CPUs (taskset), then you might have more difficulty in pinpointing CPU-related problems when analyzing the crash reports. You can examine the number of your CPUs by running cat /proc/cpuinfo.

- STATE: indicates the process state at the time of the crash. TASK_RUNNING refers to runnable processes, that is, processes that can continue their execution. Again, we will talk more about this later on.

### Additional crash core information

We have seen one benign example so far. It is just an introduction. We will take a look at several more examples, including real cases. For now onward, we know little about the crash, except for the process that caused it. We will now examine several more examples and try to understand what we see there.

Let us examine a different example. Take a look at the output below. While the information is arranged somewhat differently than what we have seen earlier, essentially, it is the same thing. We have an example from a Fedora 12 system crash.

```
Pid: 0, comm: swapper Not tainted 2.6.31.5-127.fc12.i686 #1

Call Trace:

 [<c0436d93>] warn_slowpath_common+0x70/0x87

 [<c0417426>] ? native_apic_write_dummy+0x32/0x3e
```

```
[<c0436dbc>] warn_slowpath_null+0x12/0x15

[<c0417426>] native_apic_write_dummy+0x32/0x3e

[<c040fd2c>] intel_init_thermal+0xc3/0x168

[<c040e8ce>] ? mce_init+0xa9/0xbd

[<c040f600>] mce_intel_feature_init+0x10/0x50

[<c040dcc9>] mce_cpu_features+0x1b/0x24

[<c0760681>] mcheck_init+0x249/0x28b

[<c075ea6e>] identify_cpu+0x37f/0x38e

[<c0990265>] identify_boot_cpu+0xd/0x23

[<c09903df>] check_bugs+0xb/0xdc

[<c0478a33>] ? delayacct_init+0x47/0x4c

[<c09898a3>] start_kernel+0x31c/0x330

[<c0989070>] i386_start_kernel+0x70/0x77
```

We have a different kind of information here:

```
Pid: 0, comm: swapper Not tainted.
```

Let us focus on the "Not tainted" string for a moment. What does it mean? This means that the kernel is not running any module that has been forcefully loaded. In other words, we are probably facing a code bug somewhere rather than a violation of the kernel. You can examine your running kernel by executing

```
cat /proc/sys/kernel/tainted
```

So far, we have learned another bit of information. We will talk about this later on. Now, let us explore another example, shown in the official Crash White Paper. Take a look at the following:

```
MEMORY: 128MB
 PANIC: "Oops: 0002" (check log for details)
   PID: 1696
COMMAND: "insmod"
```

What do we have here? We have a new piece of information. Oops: 0002. What does this mean?

### Kernel page error

The four digits are a decimal code of the Kernel Page Error. You can find this information under arch/arch/mm/fault.c in the kernel source tree:

```
/* Page fault error code bits */
#define PF_PROT  (1<<0) /* or no page found */
#define PF_WRITE (1<<1)
#define PF_USER  (1<<2)
#define PF_RSVD  (1<<3)
#define PF_INSTR (1<<4)
```

- If the first bit is clear (0), the exception was caused by an access to a page that is not present; if the bit is set (1), this means invalid access right.
- If the second bit is clear (0), the exception was caused by read or execute access; if set (1), the exception was caused by a write access.
- If the third bit is clear (0), the exception was caused while the processor was in Kernel mode; otherwise, it occurred in User mode.
- The fourth bit tells us whether the fault was an Instruction Fetch. This is only valid for 64-bit architecture. Since our machine is 64-bit, the bit has meaning here.

This is quite interesting. Seemingly incomprehensible information starts to feel very logical indeed. Oh, you may also see the Kernel Page Errors in the following format, as shown in Table 6.5.

Sometimes, invalid access is also referred to as Protection fault. Therefore, to understand what happened, we need to translate the decimal code into binary and

**Table 6.5** Kernel Page Errors, Reasons

|  | Value | |
|---|---|---|
| Bit | 0 | 1 |
| 0 | No page found | Invalid access |
| 1 | Read or Execute | Write |
| 2 | Kernel mode | User mode |
| 3 | Not instruction fetch | Instruction fetch |

**Table 6.6** Kernel Page Errors, Transposed

|  | Bit | 0 | 1 | 2 | 3 |
|---|---|---|---|---|---|
| Value | 0 | No page found | Read or Execute | Kernel mode | Not instruction fetch |
|  | 1 | Invalid access | Write | User mode | Instruction fetch |

then examine the four bits, from right to left. For clarify purposes, please consult this information in a transposed table (Table 6.6).

In our case, decimal 2 is binary 10. Looking from right to left, bit 1 is zero, bit 2 is lit, bit 3 and 4 are zero. Notice the binary count, starting from zero. In other words

```
0002 (dec) --> 0010 (binary) --> Not instruction fetch|Kernel mode|Write|Invalid
access
```

Therefore, we have a page not found during a write operation in Kernel mode; the fault was not an Instruction Fetch. Of course, it is a little more complicated than that, but still we are getting a very good idea of what is going on. Well, it is starting to get interesting, is it not?

Looking at the offending process, insmod, this tells us quite a bit. We tried to load a kernel module. It tried to write to a page it could not find, meaning protection fault, which caused our system to crash. This might be a badly written piece of code.

### Status check

OK, so far, we have seen quite a bit of useful information. We learned about the basic identifier fields in the crash report. We learned about the different types of panics. We learned about identifying the offending process, deciding whether the kernel is tainted and what kind of problem occurred at the time of the crash. But we have just started our analysis. Let us take this to a new level.

### Commands and detailed usage

Earlier, we learned about some basic commands. It is time to put them to good use. The first command we want is bt - backtrace. We want to see the execution history of the offending process, backtrace.

```
PID: 0        TASK: ffffffff80300ae0  CPU: 0    COMMAND: "swapper"
 #0 [ffffffff80440f20] crash_nmi_callback at ffffffff8007a68e
 #1 [ffffffff80440f40] do_nmi at ffffffff8006585a *
 #2 [ffffffff80440f50] nmi at ffffffff80064ebf *
    [exception RIP: default_idle+61]
    RIP: ffffffff8006b301  RSP: ffffffff803f3f90  RFLAGS: 00000246
    RAX: 0000000000000000  RBX: ffffffff8006b2d8  RCX: 0000000000000000
    RDX: 0000000000000000  RSI: 0000000000000001  RDI: ffffffff80302698
    RBP: 0000000000090000   R8: ffffffff803f2000   R9: 000000000000003e
    R10: ffff810107154038  R11: 0000000000000246  R12: 0000000000000000
    R13: 0000000000000000  R14: 0000000000000000  R15: 0000000000000000
    ORIG_RAX: ffffffffffffffff  CS: 0010  SS: 0018
--- <exception stack> ---
 #3 [ffffffff803f3f90] default_idle at ffffffff8006b301 *
 #4 [ffffffff803f3f90] cpu_idle at ffffffff8004943c
```

We have much data here, let us start digesting it slowly.

## Call trace

The sequence of numbered lines, starting with the hash sign (#), is the call trace. It is a list of kernel functions executed just before the crash. This gives us a good indication of what happened before the system went down.

```
#0 [ffffffff80440f20] crash_nmi_callback at ffffffff8007a68e
#1 [ffffffff80440f40] do_nmi at ffffffff8006585a *
#2 [ffffffff80440f50] nmi at ffffffff80064ebf *
   [exception RIP: default_idle+61]
   RIP: ffffffff8006b301  RSP: ffffffff803f3f90  RFLAGS: 00000246
   RAX: 0000000000000000  RBX: ffffffff8006b2d8  RCX: 0000000000000000
   RDX: 0000000000000000  RSI: 0000000000000001  RDI: ffffffff80302698
   RBP: 0000000000090000   R8: ffffffff803f2000   R9: 000000000000003e
   R10: ffff810107154038  R11: 0000000000000246  R12: 0000000000000000
   R13: 0000000000000000  R14: 0000000000000000  R15: 0000000000000000
   ORIG_RAX: ffffffffffffffff  CS: 0010  SS: 0018
```

```
--- <exception stack> ---
#3 [ffffffff803f3f90] default_idle at ffffffff8006b301 *
#4 [ffffffff803f3f90] cpu_idle at ffffffff8004943c
```

## Instruction pointer

The first really interesting line is this one:

```
[exception RIP: default_idle+61]
```

We have exception RIP: default_idle + 61. What does this mean? Let us discuss RIP. The three-letter acronym stands for Return Instruction Pointer; in other words, it points to a memory address, indicating the progress of program execution in memory. In our case, you can see the exact address in the line just below the bracketed exception line:

```
[exception RIP: default_idle+61]
RIP: ffffffff8006b301 RSP: ffffffff803f3f90 ...
```

For now, the address itself is not important. Note: on 32-bit architecture, the instruction pointer is called EIP.

The second part of information is far more useful to us. The name of the kernel function in which the RIP lies is default_idle: +61 is the offset, in decimal format, inside the said function where the exception occurred. This is the really important bit that we will use later in our analysis.

## Code segment (CS) register

The code between the bracketed string down to --- <exception stack> --- is the dumping of registers. Most are not useful to us, except the CS register.

```
CS: 0010
```

Again, we encounter a four-digit combination. In order to explain this concept, I need to digress a little and talk about privilege levels.

## Privilege levels

Privilege level is the concept of protecting resources on a CPU. Different execution threads can have different privilege levels, which grant access to system resources, like memory regions, I/O ports, and so on. There are four levels, ranging from 0 to 3.

Level 0 is the most privileged, known as Kernel mode. Level 3 is the least privileged, known as User mode.

Most modern operating systems, including Linux, ignore the intermediate two levels, using only 0 and 3. The levels are also known as rings.

## Current privilege level (CPL)

Code segment (CS) register is the one that points to a segment where program instructions are set. The two least significant bits of this register specify the Current Privilege Level (CPL) of the CPU: two bits, meaning numbers between 0 and 3.

## Descriptor privilege level (DPL) and requested privilege level (RPL)

Descriptor privilege level (DPL) is the highest level of privilege that can access the resource and is defined. This value is defined in the segment descriptor. Requested privilege level (RPL) is defined in the segment selector, the last two bits. Mathematically, CPL is not allowed to exceed MAX(RPL,DPL), and if it does, this will cause a general protection fault. Now, why is all this important, you ask?

Well, for instance, if you encounter a case where the system crashed while the CPL was 3, then this could indicate faulty hardware because the system should not crash because of a problem in the User mode. Alternatively, there might be a problem with a buggy system call. These are just some rough examples. Now, let us continue analyzing our crash log:

```
CS: 0010
```

As we know, the two least significant bits specify the CPL. Two bits means four levels; however, levels 1 and 2 are ignored. This leaves us with 0 and 3, the Kernel mode and User mode, respectively. Translated into binary format, we have 00 and 11.

The format used to present the descriptor data can be confusing, but it is very simple. If the rightmost figure is even, then we are in the kernel mode; if the last figure is odd, then we are in the user mode. Hence, we see that CPL is 0, since the offending task leading to the crash was running in the kernel mode. This is important to know. It may help us understand the nature of our problem. Just for reference, here is an example where the crash occurred in User mode:

```
#20 [ffff880a77f99f10] mntput_no_expire at ffffffff81119a43

#21 [ffff880a77f99f40] filp_close at ffffffff810fd096

#22 [ffff880a77f99f80] system_call_fastpath at ffffffff81002f7b

    RIP: 00002aaaacd99007  RSP: 00007fffffffff6c68  RFLAGS: 00000202

    RAX: 0000000000000057  RBX: ffffffff81002f7b  RCX: 00002aaaad029e60
```

```
RDX: 0000000000000041  RSI: 00002aaaacdf6650  RDI: 0000000001661238

RBP: 00007fffffff6cc0   R8: 736a2e73746c7573   R9: 0000000016615d0

R10: 00002aaaada82120  R11: 0000000000000202  R12: 00007fffffff6e00

R13: 00007fffffff6d10  R14: 0000000001661238  R15: ffff88100e5d5a40

ORIG_RAX: 0000000000000057  CS: 0033  SS: 002b
```

Back to our example, we have learned many useful, important details. We know the exact memory address in which the instruction pointer was at the time of the crash. We know the privilege level.

More importantly, we know the name of the kernel function and the offset where the RIP was pointing at the time of the crash. For all practical purposes, we just need to find the source file and examine the code. Of course, this may not be always possible, for various reasons, but we will do that, nevertheless, as an exercise.

So, we know that the crash_nmi_callback() function was called by do_nmi(), do_nmi() was called by nmi(), and nmi() was called by default_idle(), which caused the crash. We can examine these functions and try to understand more deeply what they do. We will do that soon. Now, let us revisit our Fedora example one more time.

```
Pid: 0, comm: swapper Not tainted 2.6.31.5-127.fc12.i686 #1

Call Trace:

 [<c0436d93>] warn_slowpath_common+0x70/0x87

 [<c0417426>] ? native_apic_write_dummy+0x32/0x3e

 [<c0436dbc>] warn_slowpath_null+0x12/0x15

 [<c0417426>] native_apic_write_dummy+0x32/0x3e

 [<c040fd2c>] intel_init_thermal+0xc3/0x168

 [<c040e8ce>] ? mce_init+0xa9/0xbd

 [<c040f600>] mce_intel_feature_init+0x10/0x50

 [<c040dcc9>] mce_cpu_features+0x1b/0x24

 [<c0760681>] mcheck_init+0x249/0x28b
```

```
[<c075ea6e>]  identify_cpu+0x37f/0x38e

[<c0990265>]  identify_boot_cpu+0xd/0x23

[<c09903df>]  check_bugs+0xb/0xdc

[<c0478a33>]  ? delayacct_init+0x47/0x4c

[<c09898a3>]  start_kernel+0x31c/0x330

[<c0989070>]  i386_start_kernel+0x70/0x77
```

Now that we understand what is wrong, we can take a look at the Fedora example again and try to understand the problem. We have a crash in an untainted kernel, caused by the swapper process. The crash report points to native_apic_write_dummy function.

Then, there is also a very long call trace, containing quite a bit of useful information that should help us solve the problem. We will see how we can use the crash reports to help developers fix bugs and produce better, more stable software. Now, let us focus some more on crash and the basic commands.

### Backtrace for all tasks
By default, crash will display backtrace for the active task. But you may also want to see the backtrace of all tasks. In this case, you will want to run foreach:

```
foreach bt
```

### Dump system message buffer
This command dumps the kernel log_buf content in a chronological order. The kernel log bugger (log_buf) might contain useful clues preceding the crash, which might help us pinpoint the problem more easily and understand why our system went down.

The log command may not be really useful if you have intermittent hardware problems or purely software bugs, but it is definitely worth the try. Here are the last few lines of our crash log:

```
ide: failed opcode was: 0xec
mtrr: type mismatch for f8000000,400000 old: uncachable new: write-combining
ISO 9660 Extensions: Microsoft Joliet Level 3
ISO 9660 Extensions: RRIP_1991A
SysRq : Trigger a crashdump
```

Or alternatively, a hardware-related issue

```
HARDWARE ERROR

CPU 6: Machine Check Exception:              5 Bank 3: b62000070002010a

RIP !INEXACT! 33:<00002aaac1de6224>

TSC 33241ebfff96 ADDR 7641b7080

This is not a software problem!

Run through mcelog --ascii to decode and contact your hardware vendor
```

## Display process status information

This command displays process status for selected, or all, processes in the system. If no arguments are entered, the process data is displayed for all processes.

The crash utility may load pointing to a task that did not cause the panic or may not be able to find the panic task. There are no guarantees. If you are using virtual machines, including VMware or Xen, then things might get even more complicated.

```
  STATE: TASK_RUNNING

WARNING: panic task not found
```

Using backtrace for all processes (with foreach) and running the ps command, you should be able to locate the offending process and examine its task.

## SUPER GEEKY STUFF: C CODE ANALYSIS

We will now attempt not just to understand the crash core reports, but also try to figure out how to resolve the problem on the code level. Let us say you may even want to analyze the C code for the offending function. Needless to say, you should have the C source files available and be able to read them. This is not something everyone should do, but it is an interesting mental exercise.

### Source code

All right, you want to examine the code. First, you will have to obtain the source files. You can also visit the Linux Kernel Archive and download the kernel matching your own, although some source files may be different from the ones used on your system, since some vendors make their own custom changes. Once you have the source files, it is time to examine them.

## Cscope

You could browse the sources using the standard tools like find and grep, but this can be rather tedious. A very neat utility for browsing C code is called cscope (CScope, n.d.). The tool runs from the command line and uses a vi-like interface. By default, it will search for source files in the current directory, but you can configure it any which way. Now, in the directory containing source files (by default, /usr/src/linux), run cscope:

```
cscope -R
```

This will recursively search all subdirectories, index the sources, and display the main interface. There are other uses as well; try the man page or --help flag. When launched the first time, cscope will take a few moments building its indexes. Then, on the main page, you can search for desired symbols, global definitions, functions, strings, patterns, and other information, as shown in Fig. 6.3.

We will begin with "Find this C symbol." Use the cursor keys to get down to this line, then type the desired function name and press Enter. The results will be displayed, as illustrated in Fig. 6.4.

Depending on what happened, you may get many results or none. It is quite possible that there is no source code containing the function seen in the crash report. If there are too many results, then you might want to search for the next function in the call trace by using the Find functions called by this function option. Use Tab to jump between the input and output section. If you have official vendor support, this is a good moment to turn the command over and let them drive.

If you stick with the investigation, looking for other functions listed in the call trace can help you narrow down the C file you require. But, there is no guarantee and this can

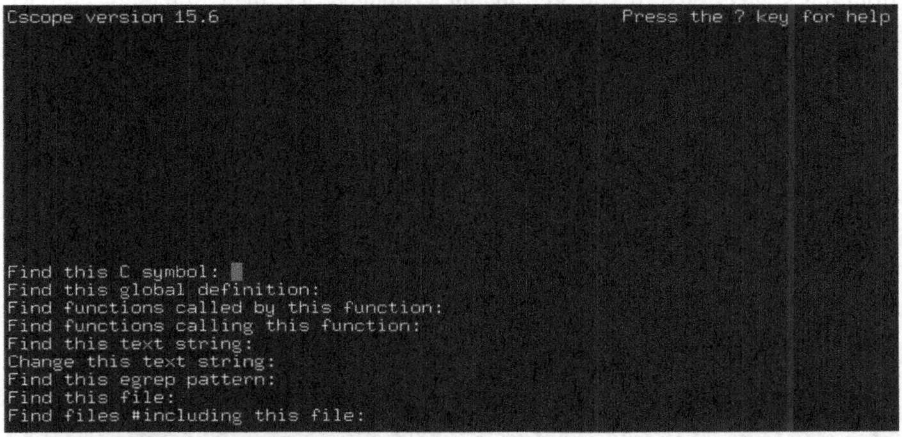

**FIGURE 6.3 Cscope Interface**

```
C symbol: default_idle

  File            Function            Line
0 process.c       <global>            170 void (*pm_idle)(void ) = default_idle;
1 system.h        <global>             87 void default_idle(void );
2 process.c       <global>             90 extern void default_idle(void );
3 process.c       <global>             71 void (*idle)(void ) = default_idle;
4 system.h        <global>            194 void default_idle(void );
5 process_mm.c    <global>             83 void (*idle)(void ) = default_idle;
6 process_no.c    <global>             63 void (*idle)(void ) = default_idle;
7 system.h        <global>             80 void default_idle(void );
8 system.h        <global>            142 void default_idle(void );

* 45 more lines - press the space bar to display more *
Find this C symbol:
Find this global definition:
Find functions called by this function:
Find functions calling this function:
Find this text string:
Change this text string:
Find this egrep pattern:
Find this file:
Find files #including this file:
```

**FIGURE 6.4 Cscope Search**

be a long, tedious process. Furthermore, any time you need help, just press ? and you will get a basic usage guide. Moreover, in the kernel source directory, you can also create the cscope indexes, for faster searches in the future, by running make cscope.

```
make cscope
```

### Disassemble the object

Assuming you have found the source, it is time to disassemble the object compiled from this source. First, if you are running a debug kernel, then all the objects have been compiled with the debug symbols. You are lucky. You just need to dump the object and burrow into the intermixed assembly-C code. If not, you will have to recompile the source with debug symbols and then reverse-engineer it.

This is not a simple or a trivial task. First, if you use a compiler other than the one used to compile the original, your object will be different from the one in the crash report, rendering your efforts difficult if not impossible.

## TRIVIAL EXAMPLE

We call this example trivial because it has nothing to do with the kernel. It merely demonstrates how to compile objects and then disassemble them.

Run make <object name>, for instance:

```
make object.o
```

Please note that make has no meaning without a Makefile, which specifies what needs to be done. But we have a Makefile. It was created after we ran ./configure. Otherwise, all this would not really work. Makefile is very important. We will see a less trivial example soon.

If you do not remove the existing object, then you probably will not be able to make it. Make compares timestamps on source files and the object, so unless you change the sources, the recompile of the object will fail.

Now, here is another simple example, and note the difference in the size of the created object, once with the debug symbols and once without:

```
#gcc memhog.c -o memhog.no.symbols

#ls -l memhog.no.symbols

-rwxr-x--- 1 iljubunc syseng 10417 2013-12-15 12:17 memhog.no.symbols


#gcc -g memhog.c -o memhog.symbols

#ls -l memhog.symbols

-rwxr-x--- 1 iljubunc syseng 12553 2013-12-15 12:18 memhog.symbols
```

If you do not have a Makefile, you can invoke gcc manually using all sorts of flags. You will need kernel headers that match the architecture and the kernel version that was used to create the kernel where the crash occurred; otherwise, your freshly compiled objects will be completely different from the ones you may wish to analyze, including functions and offsets.

## Objdump

A utility you want to use for disassembly is objdump (objdump(1) – Linux man page, n.d.). You will probably want to use the utility with the -S flag, which means display source code intermixed with assembly instructions. You may also want the -s flag, which will display contents of all sections, including empty ones. The -S implies -d, which displays the assembler mnemonics for the machine instructions from objfile; this option only disassembles those sections that are expected to contain instructions. Alternatively, use -D for all sections. Thus, the most inclusive objdump would be

```
objdump -D -S <compiled object with debug symbols> > <output file>
```

```
kernel/watchdog.o:        file format elf64-x86-64

Disassembly of section .text:

0000000000000000 <touch_softlockup_watchdog>:
        __this_cpu_write(watchdog_touch_ts, get_timestamp(this_cpu));
}

void touch_softlockup_watchdog(void)
{
        __this_cpu_write(watchdog_touch_ts, 0);
   0:   65 48 c7 04 25 00 00     movq    $0x0,%gs:0x0
   7:   00 00 00 00 00 00
}
   d:   c3                       retq
   e:   66 90                    xchg    %ax,%ax

0000000000000010 <touch_softlockup_watchdog_sync>:

#endif
watchdog lines 1-23/1681 0%
```

**FIGURE 6.5 Disassembled Object**

It will look something like this (Fig. 6.5).

### Moving on to kernel sources

Once you are confident practicing with trivial code, it is time to move to the kernel. Make sure you do not delete any important file. For the sake of the exercise, move or rename any existing kernel objects you may find lurking about.

Then, recompile them. You will require the .config file used to compile the kernel. It should be included with the sources. Alternatively, you can dump it from /proc/config.gz or under /boot. Make sure you use the one that matches the crashed kernel and copy it over into the source directory. If needed, edit some of the options, like CONFIG_DEBUG_INFO. More about that later.

Without the .config file, you will not be able to compile kernel sources. You may also encounter an error where the Makefile is supposedly missing, but it is there. In this case, you may be facing a relatively simply problem, with the wrong $ARCH environment variable set. For example, i585 versus i686 and x86-64 versus x86_64. Pay attention to the error and compare the architecture to the $ARCH variable. In the worst case, you may need to export it correctly. For example

```
export ARCH=x86_64
```

As a long-term solution, you could also create symbolic links under /usr/src/linux from the would-be bad architecture to the right one. This is not strictly related to the analysis of kernel crashes, but if and when you compile kernel sources, you may encounter this issue.

Regarding the CONFIG_DEBUG_INFO variable, if you recall the Kdump section earlier, this was a prerequisite we asked for, to be able to successfully troubleshoot kernel crashes. This tells the compiler to create objects with debug symbols. Alternatively, export the variable in the shell, as CONFIG_DEBUG_INFO = 1.

```
export CONFIG_DEBUG_INFO=1
```

Then, take a look at the Makefile. You should see that if this variable is set, the object will be compiled with debug symbols (-g). This is what we need. After that, once again, we will use objdump.

Now, Makefile might really be missing. In this case, you will get a whole bunch of errors related to the compilation process. But with the Makefile in place, it should all work smoothly.

```
#make kernel/watchdog.o

    CHK       include/linux/version.h

    CHK       include/generated/utsrelease.h

    CALL      scripts/checksyscalls.sh

    CC        kernel/watchdog.o
```

And then, there is the "object up to date" example again. If you do not remove an existing one, you will not be able to compile a new one, especially if you need debug symbols for later disassembly.

```
#make kernel/watchdog.o

    CHK       include/linux/version.h

    CHK       include/generated/utsrelease.h

    CALL      scripts/checksyscalls.sh

make[1]: `kernel/watchdog.o' is up to date.
```

```
kernel/watchdog.o:        file format elf64-x86-64

Disassembly of section .text:

0000000000000000 <touch_softlockup_watchdog>:
        __this_cpu_write(watchdog_touch_ts, get_timestamp(this_cpu));
}

void touch_softlockup_watchdog(void)
{
        __this_cpu_write(watchdog_touch_ts, 0);
   0:   65 48 c7 04 25 00 00      movq    $0x0,%gs:0x0
   7:   00 00 00 00 00 00
}

   d:   c3                        retq
   e:   66 90                     xchg    %ax,%ax

0000000000000010 <touch_softlockup_watchdog_sync>:

#endif
```
```
watchdog lines 1-23/1681 0%
```

**FIGURE 6.6 Disassembled Kernel Object File**

Finally, the disassembled object is as shown in Fig. 6.6.

### What do we do now?

Well, you look for the function listed in the exception RIP and mark the starting address. Then add the offset to this number, translated into a hexadecimal format. Then, go to the line specified. All that is left is to try to understand what really happened. You will have an assembly instruction listed and possibly some C code, telling us what might have gone wrong.

It is not easy. In fact, it is very difficult. But it is exciting and you may yet succeed, finding bugs in the operating system. What is more fun than that? Above, we learned about the compilation and disassembly procedures, without really doing anything specific. Now that we know how to go about compiling kernel objects and dissecting them into little bits, let us do some real work.

## INTERMEDIATE EXAMPLE

We will now try something more serious. Grab a proof-of-concept code that crashes the kernel, compile it, examine the crash report, then look for the right source files, do the whole process we mentioned above, and try to read the alien intermixed assembly and C code. Of course, we will be cheating because we will know what we are looking for, but still, it is a good exercise.

The most basic nontrivial example is to create a kernel module that causes panic. Before we panic our kernel, let us do a brief overview of the kernel module programming basics.

### Create problematic kernel module

This exercise forces us to deviate from the crash analysis flow and take a brief look at the C programming language from the kernel perspective. We want to crash our kernel, so we need kernel code. While we are going to use C, it is a little different from everyday stuff. The kernel has its own rules.

We will have a sampling of kernel module programing. We will write our own module and Makefile, compile the module, and then insert it into the kernel. Since our module is going to be written badly, it will crash the kernel. Then, we will analyze the crash report. Using the information obtained in the report, we will try to figure out what is wrong with our source codes.

### Step 1: kernel module

We first need to write some C code. Let us begin with a very simple and benign hello.c. Without getting too technical, here is the most basic of modules, with the init and cleanup functions. The module does nothing special except prints messages to the kernel logging facility.

```c
/*
 *  hello.c - The simplest kernel module.
 */

#include <linux/module.h>      /* Needed by all modules */
#include <linux/kernel.h>      /* Needed for KERN_INFO */

int init_module(void)
{
    printk(KERN_INFO "Hello world.\n");

    /*
     * A non 0 return means init_module failed; module can't be loaded.
     */
    return 0;
}

void cleanup_module(void)
{
    printk(KERN_INFO "Goodbye world.\n");
}
```

We need to compile this module, so we need a Makefile – again, the most basic example

```
obj-m += hello.o

all:
    make -C /lib/modules/$(shell uname -r)/build M=$(PWD) modules

clean:
    make -C /lib/modules/$(shell uname -r)/build M=$(PWD) clean
```

Now, just run the make command

```
#make

make -C /lib/modules/3.0.51-0.7.9-default/build M=/usr/src/linux/test modules

make[1]: Entering directory `/usr/src/linux-3.0.51-0.7.9-obj/x86_64/default'

make -C ../../../linux-3.0.51-0.7.9 O=/usr/src/linux-3.0.51-0.7.9-
obj/x86_64/default/. modules

  Building modules, stage 2.

  MODPOST 1 modules

make[1]: Leaving directory `/tmp/src/linux-3.0.51-0.7.9-obj/x86_64/default'
```

Our module has been compiled. Let us insert it into the kernel. This is done using the insmod command. However, a second before we do that, we can examine our module and see what it does. Maybe, the module advertises certain bits of information that we might find of value. Use the modinfo command for that.

```
#/sbin/modinfo hello.ko

filename:        hello.ko

srcversion:      67A7C9765BA14A0A1C8B6CF

depends:

vermagic:        3.0.51-0.7.9-default SMP mod_unload modversions
```

In this case, nothing special. Now, insert it:

```
/sbin/insmod hello.ko
```

If the module loads properly into the kernel, you will be able to see it with the lsmod command

```
#/sbin/lsmod | grep hello

hello                  12426   0
```

Notice that the use count for our module is 0. This means that we can unload it from the kernel without causing a problem. Normally, kernel modules are used for various purposes, such as communicating with system devices. Finally, to remove the module, use the rmmod command

```
/sbin/rmmod hello
```

If you take a look at /var/log/messages, you will notice the Hello and Goodbye messages, belonging to the init_module and cleanup_module functions:

```
Dec 22 14:47:47 test kernel: [  826.491060] hello: module license 'unspecified'
taints kernel.

Dec 22 14:47:47 test kernel: [  826.491065] Disabling lock debugging due to kernel
taint

Dec 22 14:47:47 test kernel: [  826.491592] Hello world.

Dec 22 14:48:20 test kernel: [  859.338064] Goodbye world.
```

That was just a quick demonstration of how to make kernel modules. No crash yet. But, we have a mechanism of inserting code into the kernel. If the code is bad, we will have an oops or a panic.

### Step 2: kernel panic

We will now create a new C program that uses the panic system call on initialization. Not very useful, but good enough for demonstrating the power of crash analysis. Here is the code, we call it kill-kernel.c:

```
/*
 * kill-kernel.c - The simplest kernel module to crash kernel.
 */

#include <linux/module.h>    /* Needed by all modules */
#include <linux/kernel.h>    /* Needed for KERN_INFO */

int init_module(void)
{
    printk(KERN_INFO "Hello world. Now we crash.\n");
    panic("Down we go, panic called!");

    return 0;
}

void cleanup_module(void)
{
    printk(KERN_INFO "Goodbye world.\n");
}
```

When inserted, this module will write a message to /var/log/messages and then panic. Indeed, this is what happens. Once you execute the insmod command, the machine will freeze, reboot, dump the kernel memory, and then reboot back into the production kernel.

### Step 3: Analysis

Let us take a look at the vmcore.

```
NODENAME: testhost1

 RELEASE: 3.0.51-0.7.9-default

 VERSION: #1 SMP Thu Nov 29 22:12:17 UTC 2012 (f3be9d0)

 MACHINE: x86_64   (2593 Mhz)

  MEMORY: 64 GB
```

```
      PANIC: "[  120.201319] Kernel panic - not syncing: Down we go, panic called!"

       PID: 8956

   COMMAND: "insmod"

      TASK: ffff88100d24a600  [THREAD_INFO: ffff88100d7e8000]

       CPU: 0

     STATE: TASK_RUNNING (PANIC)


PID: 8956   TASK: ffff88100d24a600  CPU: 0   COMMAND: "insmod"

 #0 [ffff88100d7e9d80] machine_kexec at ffffffff8102676e

 #1 [ffff88100d7e9dd0] crash_kexec at ffffffff810a3a3a

 #2 [ffff88100d7e9ea0] panic at ffffffff81441e53

 #3 [ffff88100d7e9f20] init_module at ffffffffa03da030 [kill_kernel]

 #4 [ffff88100d7e9f30] do_one_initcall at ffffffff810001cb

 #5 [ffff88100d7e9f60] sys_init_module at ffffffff8109930f

 #6 [ffff88100d7e9f80] system_call_fastpath at ffffffff8144ca12

   RIP: 00007ffff7b4135a  RSP: 00007fffffffe308  RFLAGS: 00010202

   RAX: 00000000000000af  RBX: ffffffff8144ca12  RCX: 00007ffff7b33130

   RDX: 0000000000603010  RSI: 0000000000014488  RDI: 0000000000603030

   RBP: 0000000000020000   R8: 00007fffffffe420   R9: 0000000000000001

   R10: 00007ffff7b33130  R11: 0000000000000202  R12: 0000000000020000

   R13: 0000000000014488  R14: ffffffff8109930f  R15: 0000000000603010

   ORIG_RAX: 00000000000000af  CS: 0033  SS: 002b
```

What do we have here? First, the interesting bit, the PANIC string:

```
"[  120.201319] Kernel panic - not syncing: Down we go, panic called!"
```

That bit looks familiar. Indeed, this is our own message we used on panic. Very informative, as we know what happened. We might use something like this if we encountered an error in the code to let the user know what the problem is.

Another interesting piece is the dumping of the CS register - CS: 0033. Seemingly, we crashed the kernel in user mode. As I have mentioned before, this can happen if you have hardware problems or if there is a problem with a system call. In our case, it is the latter.

## DIFFICULT EXAMPLE

Now let us examine another, more difficult example. We panicked our kernel with ... panic. Now, let us try some coding malpractice and create a NULL pointer testcase. We have seen earlier how to create a kernel module. Now, let us spice up our code. We will now create a classic NULL pointer example, the most typical problem with programs. NULL pointers can lead to all kinds of unexpected behavior, including kernel crashes. Our program, called null-pointer.c, now looks like this:

```
/*
 * null-pointer.c - A not so simple kernel module to crash kernel.
 */

#include <linux/module.h>      /* Needed by all modules */
#include <linux/kernel.h>      /* Needed for KERN_INFO */

char *p=NULL;

int init_module(void)
{
    printk(KERN_INFO "We is gonna KABOOM now!\n");

    *p = 1;
    return 0;
}

void cleanup_module(void)
{
    printk(KERN_INFO "Goodbye world.\n");
}
```

We declare a NULL pointer and then dereference it. Not a healthy practice. I guess programmers can explain this more eloquently than I, but you cannot have something pointing to nothing get a valid address of a sudden. In kernel, this leads to panic. Indeed, after making this module and trying to insert it, we get panic.

## Analysis

Looking at the crash report, we see a goldmine of information

```
   NODENAME: testhost1

    RELEASE: 3.0.51-0.7.9-default

    VERSION: #1 SMP Thu Nov 29 22:12:17 UTC 2012 (f3be9d0)

    MACHINE: x86_64   (2593 Mhz)

     MEMORY: 64 GB

      PANIC: "[  349.339852] Oops: 0002 [#1] SMP " (check log for details)

        PID: 9689

    COMMAND: "insmod"

       TASK: ffff88100e038140  [THREAD_INFO: ffff88100e438000]

        CPU: 0

      STATE: TASK_RUNNING (PANIC)


PID: 9689   TASK: ffff88100e038140  CPU: 0   COMMAND: "insmod"

 #0 [ffff88100e439b70] machine_kexec at ffffffff81026 76e

 #1 [ffff88100e439bc0] crash_kexec at ffffffff810a3a3a

 #2 [ffff88100e439c90] oops_end at ffffffff81446238

 #3 [ffff88100e439cb0] __bad_area_nosemaphore at ffffffff81032555

 #4 [ffff88100e439d70] do_page_fault at ffffffff8144887b

 #5 [ffff88100e439e70] page_fault at ffffffff814453e5

   [exception RIP: init_module+25]

 RIP: ffffffffa0402029  RSP: ffff88100e439f28  RFLAGS: 00010292

 RAX: 0000000000000000  RBX: ffffffffa0404000  RCX: 000000000000293b

 RDX: 000000000000293b  RSI: 0000000000000046  RDI: 0000000000000246
```

```
    RBP: 00000000000143ee    R8: 0000000000000000    R9: 0720072007200720

    R10: 0720072007200720    R11: 0720072007200720    R12: ffffffffa0402010

    R13: 0000000000000000    R14: 00007fffffffe78b    R15: 0000000000603030

    ORIG_RAX: ffffffffffffffff    CS: 0010    SS: 0018

 #6 [ffff88100e439f30] do_one_initcall at ffffffff810001cb

 #7 [ffff88100e439f60] sys_init_module at ffffffff8109930f

 #8 [ffff88100e439f80] system_call_fastpath at ffffffff8144ca12

    RIP: 00007ffff7b4135a    RSP: 00007fffffffe308    RFLAGS: 00010202

    RAX: 00000000000000af    RBX: ffffffff8144ca12    RCX: 00007ffff7b33130

    RDX: 0000000000603010    RSI: 00000000000143ee    RDI: 0000000000603030

    RBP: 0000000000020000    R8: 00007fffffffe420    R9: 0000000000000001

    R10: 00007ffff7b33130    R11: 0000000000000202    R12: 0000000000020000

    R13: 00000000000143ee    R14: ffffffff8109930f    R15: 0000000000603010

    ORIG_RAX: 00000000000000af    CS: 0033    SS: 002b
```

Let us digest the stuff displayed in the crash report.

```
PANIC: "[  349.339852] Oops: 0002 [#1] SMP " (check log for details)
```

We have an Oops on CPU 1. 0002 translates into 0010 in binary, meaning no page was found during a write operation in kernel mode. Exactly what we are trying to achieve. We are also referred to the log. Next, we have the exception pointer

```
[exception RIP: init_module+25]
```

The exception RIP says init_module + 25. This is useful information; however, if we consult the log, we get more details:

```
[  349.339505] null_pointer: module license 'unspecified' taints kernel.

[  349.339510] Disabling lock debugging due to kernel taint

[  349.339835] We will KABOOM now!

[  349.339841] BUG: unable to handle kernel NULL pointer dereference at
(null)

[  349.339844] IP: [<ffffffffa0402029>] init_module+0x19/0xff0 [null_pointer]

[  349.339849] PGD 80b9e5067 PUD 80bc6d067 PMD 0

[  349.339852] Oops: 0002 [#1] SMP

[  349.339861] CPU 0

[  349.339862] Modules linked in: null_pointer(PN+) autofs4 binfmt_misc edd
rpcsec_gss_krb5 nfs lockd fscache auth_rpcgss nfs_acl sunrpc cpufreq_conservative
cpufreq_userspace cpufreq_powersave pcc_cpufreq mperf microcode nls_iso8859_1
nls_cp437 vfat fat loop dm_mod joydev usbhid hid ipv6_lib hpilo hpwdt iTCO_wdt sg
pcspkr serio_raw tg3(X) iTCO_vendor_support container rtc_cmos acpi_power_meter
button ext3 jbd mbcache uhci_hcd ehci_hcd usbcore usb_common sd_mod crc_t10dif

thermal processor thermal_sys hwmon scsi_dh_hp_sw scsi_dh_alua scsi_dh_rdac

scsi_dh_emc scsi_dh ata_generic ata_piix libata hpsa scsi_mod

[  349.339908] Supported: Yes, External

[  349.339909]

[  349.339911] Pid: 9689, comm: insmod Tainted: P NX 3.0.51-0.7.9-default #1 HP
ProLiant DL360p Gen8

[  349.339914] RIP: 0010:[<ffffffffa0402029>]  [<ffffffffa0402029>]
init_module+0x19/0xff0 [null_pointer]

[  349.339918] RSP: 0018:ffff88100e439f28  EFLAGS: 00010292

[  349.339920] RAX: 0000000000000000 RBX: ffffffffa0404000 RCX: 000000000000293b

[  349.339922] RDX: 000000000000293b RSI: 0000000000000046 RDI: 0000000000000246

[  349.339924] RBP: 00000000000143ee R08: 0000000000000000 R09: 0720072007200720

[  349.339926] R10: 0720072007200720 R11: 0720072007200720 R12: ffffffffa0402010
```

```
[ 349.339928] R13: 0000000000000000 R14: 00007fffffffe78b R15: 0000000000603010

[ 349.339930] FS:  00007ffff7fd8700(0000) GS:ffff88083fa00000(0000)
knlGS:0000000000000000

[ 349.339932] CS:  0010 DS: 0000 ES: 0000 CR0: 0000000080050033

[ 349.339934] CR2: 0000000000000000 CR3: 000000080c4b4000 CR4: 00000000000406f0

[ 349.339936] DR0: 0000000000000000 DR1: 0000000000000000 DR2: 0000000000000000

[ 349.339938] DR3: 0000000000000000 DR6: 00000000ffff0ff0 DR7: 0000000000000400

[ 349.339940] Process insmod (pid: 9689, threadinfo ffff88100e438000, task
ffff88100e038140)

[ 349.339942] Stack:

[ 349.339943]  0000000000603010 ffffffff810001cb 0000000000603030 ffffffffa0404000

[ 349.339947]  00000000000143ee 0000000000603030 0000000000603010 ffffffff8109930f

[ 349.339951]  00000000000143ee 0000000000020000 0000000000020000 ffffffff8144ca12

[ 349.339955] Call Trace:

[ 349.339972]  [<ffffffff810001cb>] do_one_initcall+0x3b/0x180

[ 349.339979]  [<ffffffff8109930f>] sys_init_module+0xcf/0x240

[ 349.339985]  [<ffffffff8144ca12>] system_call_fastpath+0x16/0x1b

[ 349.339990]  [<00007ffff7b4135a>] 0x7ffff7b41359

[ 349.339991] Code: <c6> 00 01 31 c0 48 83 c4 08 c3 00 00 00 00 00 00 00 00 00 00
00

[ 349.340000] RIP  [<ffffffffa0402029>] init_module+0x19/0xff0 [null_pointer]

[ 349.340003]  RSP <ffff88100e439f28>

[ 349.340004] CR2: 0000000000000000
```

Among other things, we learn to have a classic case of a null pointer bug:

```
BUG: unable to handle kernel NULL pointer dereference at           (null)
```

Our module also tainted the kernel. Finally, the reference to the problematic off-set in the exception RIP is written in hexadecimal code, with the explicit information that we encountered a null pointer.

```
[  349.340000] RIP  [<ffffffffa0402029>] init_module+0x19/0xff0 [null_pointer]
```

We are making progress here. We know there was a problem with NULL pointer in the init_module function. Now, it is time to disassemble the object and see what went wrong.

```
objdump -d -S null-pointer.ko > /tmp/kernel.objdump
```

For the sake of brevity, we will not display all the fields shown in the dumped file. Instead, let us just focus on the init_module section

```
int init_module(void)
{
    10:    48 83 ec 08            sub     $0x8,%rsp
    14:    48 c7 c7 00 00 00 00   mov     $0x0,%rdi
    1b:    31 c0                  xor     %eax,%eax
    1d:    e8 00 00 00 00         callq   22 <init_module+0x12>


    22:    48 8b 05 00 00 00 00   mov     0x0(%rip),%rax        # 29 <init_module+0x19>
    29:    c6 00 01               movb    $0x1,(%rax)
    2c:    31 c0                  xor     %eax,%eax
    2e:    48 83 c4 08            add     $0x8,%rsp
    32:    c3                     retq
    ...
```

The problematic line is even marked for us with a comment: # 29 <init_module + 0x19>.

```
27:    c6 00 01              movb   $0x1,(%rax)
```

What do we have here? We are trying to load (assembly movb) value 1 ($0x1) into the RAX register (%rax). Now, why does it cause such a fuss? Let us go back to our log and see the memory address of the RAX register. RAX register is: 0000000000000000. In other words, zero. We are trying to write to memory address 0. This causes the page fault, resulting in kernel panic. Problem solved!

Of course, in real life, nothing is going to be *that* easy, but it is a start. In real life, you will face many difficulties, including missing source files, wrong versions of GCC, and all kinds of problems that will make crash analysis very, very difficult. Remember that!

For more information, please take a look at the case study shown in the RedHat Crash White Paper. Again, it is easier when you know what you are looking for. Any example you encounter online will be several orders of magnitude simpler than your real crashes, but it is really difficult demonstrating an all-inclusive, abstract case. Still, I hope my two examples are thorough enough to get you started.

## KERNEL CRASH BUG REPORTING

The big question is, what do crash reports tell us? Well, using the available information, we can try to understand what is happening on our troubled systems. First and foremost, we can compare different crashes and try to understand if there is any common element. Then, we can try to look for correlations between separate events, environment changes, and system changes, trying to isolate possible culprits to our crashes.

Combined with submitting crash reports to vendors and developers, the ample use of Google and additional resources, like mailing lists and forums, we might be able to narrow down our search and greatly simply the resolution of problems.

When your kernel crashes, you may want to take the initiative and submit the report to the vendor so that they may examine it and possibly fix a bug. This is a very important thing. You will not only be helping yourself but possibly everyone using Linux anywhere. What is more, kernel crashes are valuable. If there is a bug somewhere, the developers will find it and fix it.

### Kerneloops.org

Kerneloops.org (Linux kernel oopses, n.d.) is a website dedicated to collecting and listing kernel crashes across the various kernel releases and crash reasons, allowing kernel developers to work on identifying most critical bugs and solve them, as well as providing system administrators, engineers, and enthusiasts with a rich database of crucial information. The site's interface is shown in Fig. 6.7.

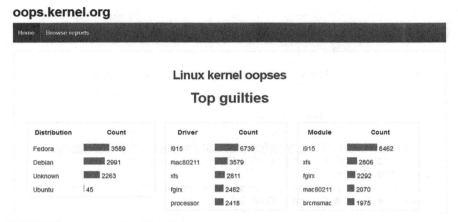

**FIGURE 6.7  oops.kernel.org Website**

### Search for information

Sounds trivial, but it is not. If you are having a kernel crash, there is a fair chance someone else saw it too. While environments differ from one another, there still might be some commonality for all of them. Then again, there might not. A site with 10 database machines and local logins will probably experience different kinds of problems than a 10,000-machine site with heavy use of autofs and NFS. Similarly, companies working with this or that hardware vendor are more likely to undergo platform-specific issues that cannot easily be found elsewhere.

The simplest way to search for data is to paste the exception RIP into the search box and look for mailing list threads and forum posts discussing same or similar items. Once again, using the Fedora case an example (Fig. 6.8).

### Reinstallation and software changes

Did the software setup change in any way that correlates with the kernel crashes? If so, do you know what the change is? Can you reproduce the change and the subsequent crashes on other hosts? Sometimes, it can be very simple; sometimes, you may not be able to easily separate software from the kernel or the underlying hardware.

If you can, try to isolate the changes and see how the system responds with or without them. If there is a software bug, then you might be just lucky enough and have to deal with a reproducible error. Kernel crashes due to a certain bug in software should look pretty much the same. But, there is no guarantee you will have it that easy.

Now, if your system is a generic machine that does not keep any critical data on local disks, you may want to consider wiping the slate clean – start over, with a fresh installation that you know is stable. It is worth a try.

native_apic_write_dummy kernel crash

Web     Images     Maps     Shopping     More ▾     Search tools

About 2,080,000 results (0.28 seconds)

### Kernel crashing, and problems reporting the crash - FedoraForum.org
forums.fedoraforum.org › Fedora 18/19/20 › Using Fedora ▾
Nov 25, 2009 - 2 posts
I keep getting notices that there is some sort of **kernel crash**. see cut and paste below.
... **native_apic_write_dummy**+0x32/0x3e() (Not tainted)

### Kernel crashing, and problems reporting the crash - FedoraForum.org
fourums.fedoraforum.org/showthread.php?t=234954 ▾
Nov 25, 2009 - **Kernel crashing**, and problems reporting the crash Using Fedora. ...
**native_apic_write_dummy**+0x32/0x3e() (Not tainted) Hardware name: ...

### Analyzing Linux **kernel crash** dumps with crash - The one tutorial ...
www.dedoimedo.com/computers/**crash**-analyze.html ▾
Jun 14, 2010 - This article is a part of my Linux **Kernel Crash** Book. It is available for
..... The crash report points to **native_apic_write_dummy** function. Fedora ...

### [PDF] Linux **Kernel Crash** Book Everything you need to know - Rogunix
rogunix.com/docs/Reversing.../Linux_**Kernel_Crash**_Book.pdf ▾
by IL aka Dedoimedo
11.2 Crash (capture) kernel . ... 16.1.3 **Kernel crash** dump NFS example . ...... The
crash report points to **native_apic_write_dummy** function. 108 ...

**FIGURE 6.8 Searching for Kernel Crash Exception Online**

### *Submit to developer/vendor*
Regardless of what you discovered or you think the problem is, you should send the kernel crash report to the relevant developer and/or vendor. Even if you are absolutely sure you know what the problem is and you have found the cure, you should still leave the official fix in the hands of people who do this kind of work for a living.

We have emphasized this several times throughout the chapter because we truly believe this is important, valuable, and effective. You can easily contribute to the quality of Linux kernel code by submitting a few short text reports. It is as simple and powerful as that.

## CRASH ANALYSIS RESULTS
After you have exhausted all the available channels, it is time to go through the information and data collected and try to reach a decision/resolution about the problem at hand.

We started with the situation in which our kernel is experiencing instability and is crashing. To solve the problem, we set up a robust infrastructure that includes a mechanism for kernel crash collection and tools for the analysis of dumped memory cores. We now understand what the seemingly cryptic reports mean.

The combination of all the lessons learned during our long journey allows us to reach a decision about what should be done next. How do we treat our crashing machines? Are they in for a hardware inspection, reinstallation, or something else? Maybe there is a bug in the kernel internals? Whatever the reason, we have the tools to handle the problems quickly and efficiently. Finally, there are some last-minute tips, very generic, very generalized, about what to do next.

### Single crash

A single crash may seem like too little information to work with. Do not be discouraged. If you can, analyze the core yourself or send the core to your vendor support. There is a fair chance you will find something wrong, either with software at hand, the kernel or the hardware underneath.

### Hardware inspection

Speaking of hardware, kernel crashes can be caused by faulty hardware. Such crashes usually seem sporadic and random. If you encounter a host that is experiencing many crashes, all of which have different panic tasks, you might want to consider scheduling some downtime and running a hardware check on the host, including memtest, CPU stress, disk checks, and more.

The exact definition of what is considered "many" crashes, how critical the machine is, how much downtime you can afford, and what you intend to do with the situation at hand is up to the individual and will vary from one admin to another.

But, it is important to distinguish between problems caused by software versus those caused by hardware problems. Since we assume that no user-space application may crash the kernel, whenever we encounter a trace that points to a user-space task, then it is quite likely the crash was caused by either a bad system call or a hardware error. This is an important piece of information if you are using third-party software that implements its own calls. Moreover, if you think there is no software problem, then it could be a hardware fault.

## KERNEL BUGS VS. HARDWARE ERRORS

Trying to discern between kernel bugs and hardware errors can be tricky, especially if the crash core reports do not specifically indicate either type. We have seen examples with memory issues and the use of the string BUG, which make our life easier.

```
[  349.339841] BUG: unable to handle kernel NULL pointer dereference at
(null)
```

```
HARDWARE ERROR

CPU 6: Machine Check Exception:          5 Bank 3: b62000070002010a

RIP !INEXACT! 33:<00002aaac1de6224>

TSC 33241ebfff96 ADDR 7641b7080

This is not a software problem!
```

However, what do you do when the exception is just a name of symbol and the offset in the function? Luckily, there is a relatively simply way of trying to discern between the two types.

Multiple crashes of a single host with different exception – this will most likely be a hardware-related problem caused by a buggy CPU or memory. The kernel will oops or panic in different places in the code, simply by hitting the underlying hardware issue.

Multiple crashes of several hosts with the same exception – if you encounter a number of kernel crashes with the same exception and offset string, you can assume this is a bug in the kernel or one of the loaded modules. In general, the exception RIP string is a unique identifier for kernel problems, and you can use it to understand and isolate your environment problems.

## SUMMARY

We worked carefully and slowly through the kernel crash analysis series. In this last part, we have finally taken a deep, personal look at the crash internals and now have the right tools and the knowledge to understand what is bothering our kernel. Using this new wealth of information, we can work on making our systems better, smarter, and more stable.

## KERNEL DEBUGGER

A full-blown kernel debugger (Wessel, 2010) is the last resort to trying to troubleshoot kernel-related issues. If you have encountered a rare problem that you suspect might not be easily replicated after a crash, and you need to perform initial investigation right then, in the live kernel, then your only option is to launch the kernel debugger.

This operation is rather destructive as the execution of the kernel will be halted while the debugger is running. From the perspective of any user running an active session or task on the host, it will appear as if the host has temporarily frozen, and most applications with network related activities will not handle the interruption in a graceful manner. Worse, they may recover with unexpected corruptions that may not be easily noticed, or with weird behavior that could affect the runtime outcome.

Debugging a live kernel also means that any mistake you make will change the kernel structures, and this could trigger a crash by itself. A very high level of knowledge is needed to perform a successful analysis, even more so than when using the crash utility in the offline mode. Last, you do need to connect to the host using a serial console because any network-based connection, such as a remote shell or VNC, will hang.

## KERNEL COMPILATION

Kernel debugging can be performed using either kdb or kgdb. For the sake of simplicity, in this chapter, we will only focus on kdb. The program comes with a shell-like interface, and you can use it to inspect memory, registers, process lists, kernel log, and set breakpoints. To be able to use kdb, the kernel must be compiled with certain options. You can inspect your kernel configuration to determine whether you can use kdb in the first place. Most enterprise distributions do offer the necessary support out of the box.

```
CONFIG_FRAME_POINTER=y

CONFIG_KGDB=y

CONFIG_KGDB_SERIAL_CONSOLE=y

CONFIG_KGDB_KDB=y

CONFIG_KDB_KEYBOARD=y
```

## ENTER THE DEBUGGER

You can configure your systems to enter the debugger on an irrecoverable error, but then, the host will hang and wait until you perform your analysis. This is practical for very small deployments and test machines, in which you can afford lengthy and possibly arbitrary downtimes. For large environments, using the kdump + crash combination is a much more favorable alternative. Manually, kdb can be entered by echoing the right value into the /proc/sysrq-trigger tunable, as illustrated below:

```
echo g > /proc/sysrq-trigger

[    132.2101919] SysRq : DEBUG

Entering kdb (current=0xffff88005a15e5c0, pid 1579) on processor 1 due to Keyboard
Entry

[1]kdb>_
```

## BASIC COMMANDS

Once inside the debugger shell, you can start analyzing your system. If you are not familiar with the available commands, you can always use the help option to get the list (Fig. 6.9).

```
[1]kdb> help
Command         Usage                Description
----------------------------------------------------------
md              <vaddr>              Display Memory Contents, also mdWcN, e.g. md
8c1
mdr             <vaddr> <bytes>      Display Raw Memory
mdp             <paddr> <bytes>      Display Physical Memory
mds             <vaddr>              Display Memory Symbolically
mm              <vaddr> <contents>   Modify Memory Contents
go              [<vaddr>]            Continue Execution
rd                                   Display Registers
rm              <reg> <contents>     Modify Registers
ef              <vaddr>              Display exception frame
bt              [<vaddr>]            Stack traceback
btp             <pid>                Display stack for process <pid>
bta             [D|R|S|T|C|Z|E|U|I|M|A]
                                     Backtrace all processes matching state flag
btc                                  Backtrace current process on each cpu
btt             <vaddr>              Backtrace process given its struct task addr
ess
env                                  Show environment variables
set                                  Set environment variables
help                                 Display Help Message
more> _
```

**FIGURE 6.9 Kdb Help**



In essence, the commands are very similar to what we have used with crash. We can display the stack traceback, display stack for specific or all processes, including matching state flag, filter by processor, show and set environment variables, display and modify registers, and more. All of these operations require a very good understanding of what is being done, and there is no easy, simple way to generalize, as each use case will be different. Several simple examples are presented in the images just below (Figs. 6.10–6.12).

```
[1]kdb> ps
1 idle process (state I) and
66 sleeping system daemon (state M) processes suppressed,
use 'ps A' to see all.
Task Addr           Pid   Parent [*] cpu State Thread             Command
0xffff88005a15e5c0  1579     692  1    1   R   0xffff88005a15eab8 *bash

0xffff88005cd86040     1       0  0    0   S   0xffff88005cd86538  systemd
0xffff8800366f2400   235       1  0    1   S   0xffff8800366f28f8  systemd-jo
urnal
0xffff880059d9a740   265       1  0    0   S   0xffff880059d9ac38  systemd-ud
evd
0xffff88005acac340   495       1  0    0   S   0xffff88005acac838  avahi-daem
on
0xffff880036594640   498       1  0    1   S   0xffff880036594b38  nscd
0xffff88005a354640   511       1  0    1   S   0xffff88005a354b38  nscd
0xffff88005a358680   512       1  0    1   S   0xffff88005a358b78  nscd
0xffff88005a35c6c0   513       1  0    0   S   0xffff88005a35cbb8  nscd
0xffff88005a360700   514       1  0    1   S   0xffff88005a360bf8  nscd
0xffff88005a364740   515       1  0    1   S   0xffff88005a364c38  nscd
0xffff88005a368780   516       1  0    1   S   0xffff88005a368c78  nscd
0xffff88005a36c7c0   517       1  0    0   S   0xffff88005a36ccb8  nscd
0xffff88005a370800   518       1  0    0   S   0xffff88005a370cf8  nscd
more>_
```

**FIGURE 6.10 Kdb ps Command**

```
[1]kdb> bt
Stack traceback for pid 1579
0xffff88005a15e5c0     1579     692  1   1  R  0xffff88005a15eab8 *bash
 ffff88005aff3eb8 0000000000000018 0000000000000000 0000000000000000
 0000000000000000 0000000000000000 0000000000000000 0000000000000000
 0000000000000000 0000000000000000 0000000000000000 0000000000000000
Call Trace:
 [<ffffffff81004a18>] dump_trace+0x88/0x310
 [<ffffffff81004d70>] show_stack_log_lvl+0xd0/0x1d0
 [<ffffffff810061bc>] show_stack+0x1c/0x50
 [<ffffffff810e01ab>] kdb_show_stack+0x6b/0x80
 [<ffffffff810e0256>] kdb_bt1.isra.0+0x96/0x100
 [<ffffffff810e062e>] kdb_bt+0x36e/0x460
 [<ffffffff810dda6f>] kdb_parse+0x24f/0x670
 [<ffffffff810de5d4>] kdb_main_loop+0x514/0x750
 [<ffffffff810e114a>] kdb_stub+0x1ba/0x3e0
 [<ffffffff810d7644>] kgdb_cpu_enter+0x314/0x570
 [<ffffffff810d7ae2>] kgdb_handle_exception+0x142/0x1c0
 [<ffffffff810382ac>] __kgdb_notify+0x6c/0xd0
 [<ffffffff81038375>] kgdb_ll_trap+0x35/0x40
 [<ffffffff815b15ad>] do_int3+0x2d/0xf0
 [<ffffffff815b0e1b>] int3+0x2b/0x40
 [<ffffffff810d6dfb>] kgdb_breakpoint+0xb/0x20
 [<ffffffff81389ac0>] __handle_sysrq+0x90/0x160
more>
```

**FIGURE 6.11  Kdb bt Command**

```
[1]kdb> btp 598
Stack traceback for pid 598
0xffff8800367fa140     598      1  0   0  S  0xffff8800367fa638  kdm
 ffff88005a783948 0000000000000086 0000000000013900 ffff88005a783fd8
 ffff88005a783fd8 0000000000013900 ffff8800367fa140 0000000000000000
 00000000ffffffdc 0000000000002000 000000000000000d 000000000000000d
Call Trace:
 [<ffffffff815ad7bd>] schedule_hrtimeout_range_clock+0x13d/0x160
 [<ffffffff811983c4>] poll_schedule_timeout+0x54/0xb0
 [<ffffffff81198d31>] do_select+0x6e1/0x7c0
 [<ffffffff81198f9f>] core_sys_select+0x18f/0x2b0
 [<ffffffff81199165>] SyS_select+0xa5/0xf0
 [<ffffffff815b782d>] system_call_fastpath+0x1a/0x1f
 [<00007ffd5b6b48f3>] 0x7ffd5b6b48f2
[1]kdb>
```

**FIGURE 6.12  Kdb btp Command**

## SUMMARY

The essential difference between offline analysis with crash and online analysis using kdb is that you may not have the luxury of time and error when using the latter, because any potential mistake could complicate the problem further, as well as remove all traces of the original issue and its symptoms. However, in some cases, it may be the only way to try to find the reason for an elusive, complex kernel-related issue.

## CONCLUSION

This chapter wraps the most complex piece of the investigation process, starting with the setup of the Kdump utility, followed by in-depth kernel crash analysis, and finally a brief overview of the kdb facility. Kernel crashes are one of the last pieces of troubleshooting that you can perform on an individual host. After that, we step back and look horizontally, trying to figure out how our problems manifest themselves on the data center scale. In the next several chapters, we will focus on expanding our skillset and understanding into a complete, holistic situational awareness approach.

## REFERENCES

Anderson, D., 2008. Crash. Available at: http://people.redhat.com/anderson/ (accessed May 2015).

Anderson, D., n.d. White Paper: the RedHat crash utility. Available at: http://people.redhat.com/anderson/crash_whitepaper/ (accessed May 2015)

core(5) – Linux man page, n.d. Available at: http://linux.die.net/man/5/core (accessed May 2015)

Crash version 4.0.8-11 announcement, n.d. Available at: http://www.mail-archive.com/crash-utility@redhat.com/msg01699.html (accessed May 2015)

CScope, n.d. Available at: http://cscope.sourceforge.net/ (accessed May 2015)

GNU GRUB, n.d. Available at: http://www.gnu.org/software/grub/ (accessed May 2015)

Kdump, n.d. Available at: http://lse.sourceforge.net/kdump/ (accessed May 2015)

Linux kernel oopses, n.d. Available at: http://www.kerneloops.org/ (accessed May 2015)

Linux raid, n.d. Available at: https://raid.wiki.kernel.org/index.php/Linux_Raid (accessed May 2015)

LKCD, n.d. Available at: http://lkcd.sourceforge.net/ (accessed May 2015)

objdump(1) – Linux man page, n.d. Available at: http://linux.die.net/man/1/objdump (accessed May 2015)

Oops tracing, n.d. Available at: https://www.kernel.org/doc/Documentation/oops-tracing.txt (accessed May 2015)

Shell builtin commands, n.d. Available at: http://www.gnu.org/software/bash/manual/html_node/Shell-Builtin-Commands.html (accessed May 2015)

The Linux kernel archives, n.d. Available at: https://www.kernel.org/ (accessed May 2015)

Wessel, J., 2010. Using kgdb, kdb and the kernel debugger internals. Available at: https://www.kernel.org/pub/linux/kernel/people/jwessel/kdb/ (accessed May 2015)

# Problem solution

## 7

So far, in the previous chapters, we have learned about a range of technologies and techniques that can be helpful in problem solving in mission-critical, high-performance compute environments. We started with basic, top-level investigation and climbed down the stack all the way to the kernel. Now, we will zoom up and wrap up our investigation in a meaningful way.

Without a highly methodical and efficient post-mortem strategy, including proper collection and analysis of data while keeping the business prime objectives and environment criticality in mind, it is very difficult to derive a successful way of running the data center. We will now follow up with a layer approach to isolating problems, implementing fixes, and most importantly, closing up with a tangible, measurable resolution.

## WHAT TO DO WITH COLLECTED DATA

System troubleshooting entails much data collection. Logs, reports, bug errors, crash dumps – all of these will find a way onto your hard disk. The question is, what do you do with the lessons learned from your problem solving and the amassed evidence?

### DOCUMENTATION

For engineers and senior system administrators, the concept of having to document their hard work, intuition, years of experience, the hunches, as well as the way they think, is often a difficult task. It is perceived as unnecessary, beneath their skill level and detrimental to their work, especially *after* the problem has been resolved.

In a sense, they are right. Most natural problem solvers are not good project managers, and they detest the nontechnical parts of their job. Once the suspense and thrill of fixing a problem dissipate, the mopping-up process is an arduous, painful objective. This is one of the chief reasons why most problem stories remain undocumented and why they resurface so often. In large companies, the problem is even more acute due to increased complexity and overlap of departments, roles, and functions.

However, good documentation is an excellent source of solutions, when used properly. If you think about it, the Internet is a great example. Most people treat their search engine of choice as the one portal for information. No matter what bothers you, there is a good chance you will come up with a handful of tips and tricks that can help you with whatever you are facing, no matter how obscure and complex. Unfortunately, intranet sites and local databases are notoriously unhelpful. A combination of outdated information, a multitude of formats, a variety of backend technologies, an inconsistent presentation layer, and no easy way to really search the content makes the company's internal resources a virtual waste bin without a real purpose.

## Rebound effect

People in all big companies are well aware of the problem. To solve it, grand initiatives are periodically launched in an attempt to harmonize the knowledge across the departments and business groups and gain control of the information. Once again, unfortunately, the problem is addressed with the same inefficient brute-force approach that led to documentation being neglected or not used well.

Large portals are created, and users are encouraged to start logging their work into the system, by following any one of the popular, contemporary IT practices. This leads to yet more conflict, including confusion, more resistance from skilled employees who refused to be "dumbed down" into a formula, and the practical impossibility of creating a step-by-step template to problem solving that replaces investigative thinking. On the technical side, the gap persists, and the data center issues and their fixes are reinvented all the time.

## Effective documentation

If you step aside from the fundamental loopback nature of this situation, you can try to approach the documentation as another data center issue. How can you guarantee that it will be resolved in a flexible way with a long-lasting effect?

To date, no one has really cracked the secret to making information realize its potential like it does in the outside world (Internet). However, we believe that you can attempt to approach the ideal state asymptotically, just by following a small number of unusual practices.

The first one would be to hire a technical writer, a person skilled and possibly passionate about writing detailed documents containing information about processes. That person could then work with engineers and problem solvers and offload their knowledge onto paper.

The second one is to decide where the information ought to go. Since we know that the Intranet sites are not easily searchable or indexable, we must exclude them from the equation. Any attempt to create a beautiful new site that will become "the mother of all sites" is likely bound to fail, just like the previous 1000 iterations of the same, noble idea. You might be enamored by the powerful content management systems such as Drupal, WordPress, and others, and while they do wonders in the outside world, they cannot survive on an Intranet or local database, for the same reason all other databases could not.

The answer might sound counterintuitive, but the idea is to put the knowledge in the public domain. Most companies will shy away from this practice, fearing disclosure of technology and business secrets, but with some discretion and care, this can be a very powerful way of managing information. It will be stored in the same dimension like all the rest of the data on the Internet, making it easily accessible. Utilizing proven public services and bug systems makes a lot of sense.

Mind you, there is no need for an exclusive black and white approach. Intranet resources can continue to exist and even flourish and grow. Alongside these, you can keep a public record of problem-solving practices that can be used by everyone. The concepts of application tracing, kernel debugging, or component search are universal methodologies that can always be applied and tried, regardless of the intellectual property specific to this or that company.

Some of the large IT businesses have a healthy practice of sharing their methods with the world. This also helps position them as leaders in the industry, without any compromise to the integrity of their business.

## DATA CLUTTER

Quite often, investigation and problem analysis can lead to an accumulation of large quantities of raw data. Usually, once data is collected, it never goes away. It becomes a sort of a shrine, revered, and feared, but rarely put to any great practical use.

You can treat data collection as a sort of obsessive-compulsive disorder on a company scale. Metrics are created and then logged for the sole purpose of being there. For instance, information security teams are notoriously well known for this practice, and they lead the field with data collection. Unfortunately, the backlog rarely leads to meaningful results in the process of problem solving.

### *Intelligent guessing*

One of the ways to cope with large amounts of data is not to create them in the first place. Sometimes, it may appear necessary to collect everything, but it is possible to narrow down the information through past experience and some skill. Your history of problem solving will often include several typical, representative scenarios that will revolve around one or two critical parameters, whereas your systems will mostly be agnostic to all others.

Let us consider the following example. In a data center with a thousand servers, CPU metrics are reported to a central database every minute. When certain thresholds are exceeded, alerts are raised. At this point, system administrators are expected to take corrective actions to restore the CPU activity below the thresholds. This is the way CPU data has been sampled for many years, and the practice remains.

However, you observe little to no correlation in CPU load to actual problems being experienced by your customers. You find the total memory usage to be far more accurate in foretelling the situations in which the servers may deviate from their expected behavior. Most of the time, no action will be taken. In the best case, the monitoring team may raise thresholds to a higher bar, this way reducing the noise, and hoping that increased loads will eventually correlate to problems. Or they may ignore the CPU alerts altogether.

However, the smart thing to do is to remove the CPU metric because it yields no useful results. Naturally, the concept of letting go sounds frightening, and most people will hesitate to implement, just in case some terrible corner case occurs, and they are held accountable for the resulting damage.

The correct way to perform analysis and manage data is to narrow down the number of parameters being sampled and trim away those with flat or random response. Sometimes, it will be necessary to collect everything, but without deep knowledge in statistics, few people will know how to interpret the results. There are several useful industry methods that can help system administrators manage their data more effectively though. We will discuss them in a few moments.

### Housekeeping

Over time, data collection tends to grow, both in size and scope. Whenever a new problem with a seemingly large impact is found and resolved, metrics and alerting rules are added to avoid the future manifestation of the problem. Most of the time, new rules are added without an expiration date, running forever. After a while, months or years, both the original problem and the technology where it happened become irrelevant, the technical team handling the issue has since moved to new job roles, but the data rules remain, shrouded in ambiguity and the fear of breaking tradition, practices, and the overall flow of things.

You should consider reviewing the production environment on a periodic basis and pruning old and unnecessary data collectors and monitoring directives that are no longer relevant in the current reality. You should also seek correlations to problems, and if none are found, aggressively remove the mechanisms introduced to find these correlations in the first place. Once again, you should refer to statistical methods and tools to help you make the right decision.

If we go back to our earlier CPU example, removing the CPU monitor as well as the logged data is the correct, logical way of managing the environment. It will also reduce the overall quantity of data, allowing for a much better, more effective situational awareness of the production setups.

### Meaningful retention

You may assume that data retention and housekeeping are one and the same. It is not quite true. Meaningful retention is what will help reduce clutter and the need for housekeeping, after you have decided a certain metric is worth logging and keeping. Moreover, you will retain only the data you really need, instead of collecting vast amounts of information that you can barely store, let alone process with any kind of timely and intelligent response.

When you start investigating a problem, it does make sense to begin collecting large amounts of data, especially if you are not really certain where the issue origins, or if you do not even fully know what the issue might be. However, later on, after you have gained statistical confidence, you should narrow down the collection to only the relevant data.

A good example of data retention is always related to information security. One of the common practices with security teams is to report local system logs on every single server in the data center to a remote, centralized database, wherein a supposedly smart business intelligence engine will parse the log entries and detect anomalies.

However, this data collection is often done without a precise objective in mind, making everything and anything potentially suspicious. This leads to a lot of storage and CPU cycles being used, and detection normally being based on loosely generated patterns, often without any real statistical significance.

The end result is a huge database with logs kept for weeks and months, without any action being taken. Sometimes, the engines processing the data simply cannot keep up, or the actual technology is missing, and the logs are waiting for future data to be parsed and analyzed. This acute demand has led to a flourishing industry of security companies developing tools specifically designed to filter huge amounts of data in near real-time periods.

Retention of data may be enforced by legal demands, in which case there is little you can do. However, if there are no restrictions on how the data should be kept, you should consider a more pragmatic approach. You can assess how often you used old, saved data to relate to new problems, or how often you accessed the ancient logs after the fact. That will give you a good estimate of how useful the retained information really is, and whether you should bother keeping it in the *first* place.

Furthermore, you should also consider the natural cycle of information on your systems. For example, system logs may be rotated once a week, with five copies kept, after which they are purged completely. This means that your data – and consequently – problem analysis lifetime based on these specific system logs is about 5 weeks. If you have not resolved the issue in that time frame, or taken any actions toward the resolution, there is probably little to no chance the problem will be found and fixed using only this pool of data.

This does not mean you should completely neglect useful information found in your logs, reports, and alerts. But that is exactly what knowledge sharing and documentation are made for. You can reduce the data to small amounts of critical information, tips, and tricks that can help tie down the problems together, without the original raw data. Using statistics and proper industry methods will help you guess the right data and reduce the overhead.

### If no one reads it, it is worthless

The second aspect of great accumulations of data is its readability. Even if you do maintain a lean database on only the important information, it can still be a great waste of time and space if the data is not used in any meaningful way.

Let us examine the system process accounting. On Linux, it is logged under /var/account/pacct and rotated periodically. Sometimes, system administrators will parse the pacct logs to try to understand what may have happened with a particular host at a particular time. However, most of the time, the logs will be completely and utterly neglected. So why not just throw them away?

A classic counter-argument you may hear is: "But it does not hurt" or "It only takes a miniscule amount of CPU to run this service" or "We have always done this, and we need the data, just in case something happens."

Despite the cautious attitude of "just in case," you might need to be bolder in your approach here. The negative impact may indeed be low, but the positive impact may be even lower. And while it does not hurt, it sure does not help.

This is a good example in which you log massive amounts of data, with millions of entries per day, and multiple zipped logs kept, awaiting that critical moment when someone might deign to look at the information. Ask yourself how often you accessed this data, and when it was useful for you in identifying critical problems? If the answer is once a year, then you probably do not need it all. Even if the data is not retained for a long time, and you are not hogging databases and file servers with huge backlogs, you are still processing unneeded information.

To use a crude analogy, data collection is no different than the arsenal of shirts you keep in your closet. If you never bother wearing some of them, you might as well throw them away. Likewise here, if you or some business intelligence engine is not making any good use of the collected bytes, you can safely stop collecting them and save your organization some resource wastage.

## BEST PRACTICES

If you need to troubleshoot a problem, and you have the privilege of defining the test conditions, then you might want to consider several handy ways of collecting and analyzing data. We will begin with a difficult example that illustrates the problem and then present a practical approach to resolving it.

Your monitoring team is actively scanning your servers for so-called "runaway" processes to ensure there is no wastage of resources of processes that have been alive for longer than necessary. Indeed, a runaway, or a suspected runaway, is a process that has had a wall time beyond an expected quota. The emphasis is on the word expected because the entire process is empirical.

The team reports seeing a very large number of runaways in the environment, mostly for customer processes. There are no defined actions for these processes beyond the default threshold. They would like to get rid of these processes, or at least, be able to configure intelligent thresholds, but they do not know how to do that, because no one, including the customers themselves, can tell them the exact runtime for these processes. How would you go about solving this issue? Please take a moment for the information to sink in.

There is no single method of fixing this, but the most common is to arbitrarily raise thresholds. A brute force approach would be to sample customers one by one, trying to glean some kind of meaningful data from them. The midway solution is what we propose below.

The idea is to configure threshold to zero and then increment it by powers of two, each time measuring the total number of runaway processes in the environment until there are no more left. We then repeat this process for each of the affected processes, using its name and arguments as an identifier. In large environments, it is possible to complete the data collection within several hours or days using this approach. Sample data is shown in Table 7.1.

What do we have here? The data we collected provides us with several vectors of information. First, we learn about the distribution of task runtimes. Ideally, you will want to have a normal distribution with a narrow distribution, because that will indicate your tasks all run in a predictable manner and there is little noise and variation between different hosts. On the other hand, if you encounter a situation in which the

**Table 7.1** Sample Data Set Emphasizing the Importance of Data Analysis Best Practices

| Runtime Threshold [min] | Number of Runaways |
| --- | --- |
| 0 | 1000 |
| 1 | 998 |
| 2 | 996 |
| 4 | 994 |
| 8 | 991 |
| 16 | 987 |
| 32 | 892 |
| 64 | 793 |
| 128 | 688 |
| 256 | 576 |
| 512 | 481 |
| 1024 | 79 |
| 2048 | 2 |

standard deviation is greater than average runtime, you may discover you have several separate groups of tasks that should be relabeled as individual tasks rather than a single category, or that the environmental noise is so large that it completely skews the results. In that case, you will have to consider not using the runtime as a reliable metric and consider a different one. We can see the distribution of this experiment in Fig. 7.1. For brevity, the axes are scaled logarithmically.

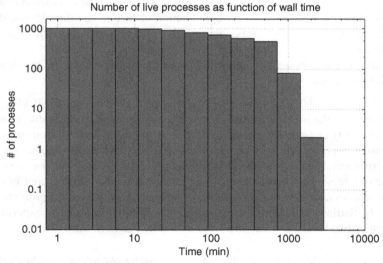

**FIGURE 7.1  Process Runaways Graph**

Furthermore, the binary threshold increase approach also allows you to determine the point where 50% of your processes completed their run. You can consider this point the half-life time for the particular task. If your processes have a normal[1] distribution, then you will be interested in the cutoff point for approximately 68% of the total population.

Then, you can configure your monitor to alert for thresholds that are twice the half-life for linear distributions or two standard deviations above the mean value. This can be considered an acceptable, sensible way of creating smart and highly accurate thresholds that will describe runaways in a meaningful manner. You will be certain that any leftover process has experienced a real problem and it should be investigated separately.

### Design of experiment

*Design of experiment*, sometimes also called *design of experiments* (DoE), is a branch of applied statistics that deals with planning, conducting, analyzing, and interpreting controlled tests to evaluate the factors that control the value of a parameter or group of parameters.

It differs from the classical X→Y approach in that it allows efficient analysis of an experimental set when changing several factor levels simultaneously. In a standard experiment, the level of one factor is changed whereas others are held constant, and the response is measured (Design of Experiments (DOE), n.d.). This approach, also known as one-factor-at-a-time (OFAT), can be very time consuming, as it may involve a huge number of parameter changes, and it does not offer valuable information when there is interaction between factors.

Without going too deeply into statistics, which is beyond the scope of this book, the simplest, most comprehensive way of conducting DoE is the full factorial design, which studies the response of every combination of factors and their levels. Blocking and randomization may also be introduced to narrow down the scope of complex experiments.

If you wish to conduct a full factorial experiment, you need to be familiar with the following terms:

- *Factors (inputs):* They can be classified as controllable or uncontrollable variables. In the high-performance compute environment, controllable variables are normally quantifiable elements, such as network bandwidth, number of running processes, memory usage, and others. Factors that also depend on environmental settings, such as latency, overall router utilization, the response time of a remote file server, and similar factors, are not within the control of a system administrator trying to run the experiment and analyze the problem.
- *Levels:* Settings of each factor in the study. Normally, the simplest experiment includes two levels, low and high. For example, you may want to test the

---

[1] The measurement of the number of running processes as shown above will not yield the distribution function in an accurate manner. Instead, you should create fixed-sized bins and measure the total number of processes that completed their runtime within the specified window.

behavior of a system with low disk utilization (e.g., nothing or slow read/write) and heavy disk utilization. In this kind of scenario, you assume a linear response between the two levels. If you believe there might be a nonlinear behavior involved, you might want to test additional midrange points.

- *Response:* There can be one or more outputs to the experiment, and they will differ based on the specific case. In some situations, you may want to measure the total runtime of a process, or you might be interested in the number of bytes written to storage. You might also want to know other finer details. Most of the time, problem solving in data centers will revolve around pass/fail criteria and runtime figures.

The analysis can be performed manually, with some understanding of statistics. However, a much easier way is to use statistics data analysis packs available in a variety of spreadsheet software.

Once again, without delving too deeply into statistics, we will just briefly touch on the basics of analysis once the design of experiments is completed. You will be interested in the analysis of variance (ANOVA) analysis, or more specifically the *F*-ratio, which is available as a function in most statistical software.

The *F*-ratio (*F*-Ratio The Statistics Glossary, n.d.) is the ratio of the variance between groups to the variance within groups, that is, the ratio of the explained variance to the unexplained variance. The *F*-ratio is used to test whether or not two variances are equal. The *F*-ratio is calculated as follows:

$$F = \frac{\text{explained variance}}{\text{unexplained variance}}$$

On its own, the number does not tell us much. However, we need to account the number of degrees of freedom for each sample and their respective variance. Then, either calculate manually or consult an F-Distribution Table (F-Distribution Tables, n.d.). If the value is greater than the expected critical number shown in the table, the results can be considered significant. However, you also need the confidence level to determine whether your test hypothesis is true or not.

Indeed, we are also interested in the P-Value, which is the probability of obtaining a test statistic at least as extreme as the one that was actually observed. Since no test condition is perfect, there is always a certain significance level used, and normally, under most circumstances, it is set to 0.05. In other words, there is a 5% probability that a model *F*-ratio could occur due to noise (random chance).

When running a DoE, you can analyze individual factors, as well as their interactions, and then filter out those with $P > 0.05$, narrowing down the experiment to important parameters.

You might be interested in the following study (Ljubuncic, n.d.), which illustrates the impact of memory size (RAM), the use of software firewall and antivirus on the boot time, and scan time performance of a third-party anti-malware program. The study demonstrates the full-factorial experiment in the information technology world, with three inputs, two levels, and two responses. The general idea is highly applicable to the world of data centers and high-performance compute environments.

### Statistical engineering

Statistical engineering is another set of methods and tools that can help you try to find and understand quantifiable underlying orders in a seemingly random system, which can then be controlled and changed. Like the design of experiments, it relies on statistical thinking and tools to achieve its goals. This branch of applied science could also be said to cover the design of experiment, but since the latter can be used with good results on its own, we have separated the two for clarity.

In general, statistical engineering is well suited to IT environments, often because compute setups do not allow for lengthy, detailed experiments that cover all angles and possibilities. Especially in the production environment, you will be forced to make quick, seemingly intuitive decisions based on a small subset of parameters. Statistical engineering can help you narrow down your investigation of problems and point out the most significant vectors affecting your systems.

In reality, in most companies, statistics narrow down to the following two phenomena: people look at the graph of their data points and then draw a trend line using Microsoft Office Excel. If the deflection angle points above the artificial horizon, it is called a positive trend, and if the angle is negative, then it is a negative trend.

This method is very simple to implement and understand. Unfortunately, it masks the complex reality that exists in data centers, with hundreds and thousands of systems and system components interacting among them. In turn, there is little real understanding of the cause and effect for most problems, leading to massive collection of every possible vector of data, in a hope that some will exhibit linear, easily predictable behavior.

A radically opposite approach is to use genuine statistics to try to analyze problems and find the root cause. Normally, engineers and system administrators simply try to resolve problems by studying symptoms and guessing the cause. Then, they follow up by suggesting a change they believe might fix the problem. Sometimes, they may suggest several changes as there could be several potential causes involved. Regardless, the fundamental approach is that the problem stems from a flaw in how the system is designed or used. This is the classic approach to problem solving, and it can be referred to simply as the X→Y approach.

Statistical engineering recognizes the fact there could be multiple inputs affecting any one output. Instead of checking all possible permutations of a system, which might not be technically or practically feasible, the general idea is to search for statistically significant relationships. One way of doing this is through the design of experiment, which we have just studied above. In general, statistical engineering is a Y→X approach.

This kind of problem solving is counterintuitive, because you never speculate about the possible sources for the variation in outputs, until you have found a clear cause–effect relationship. Finding the relationship begins with a so-called Red X paradigm (Shainin, 2012). In a nutshell, there is always one relationship whose contribution to the variation is stronger than others.

When solving problems in a data center, understanding which factors contribute the most to the output will significantly reduce your effort on trying to tweak systems without any considerable improvement or running extremely long tests trying to affirm known relationships.

Let us consider the following example. In a special pool of high-memory machines (1 TB and above) inside your data center, the customers execute special computation jobs, which they consider critical to their project. The technical definition is "critical-path jobs," and you want them to run as fast as possible. You are assigned as a member of an expert's team, whose job is to optimize the system so that you achieve the shortest turnaround time. To make things a little more complicated, the servers used for these tasks are not identical, and they feature different storage solutions, CPU models, and other parameters.

Your first step is to profile the critical-path jobs to get the basic understanding of how they behave. After the initial few runs, you may decide they are CPU-bound, or memory-bound, or there could be some other factor limiting the performance. Most of the time, your results will be based on the wall time of executed tasks. For the sake of this exercise, let us assume that the jobs are mostly CPU intensive.

At this point, you may decide to start tweaking the systems to get the best results, since you already have a basic hunch what could be improved. Enter kernel and system tunables.

One of the options is to change the CPU scheduler (SUSE Linux Enterprise Server 11 SP3 System Analysis and Tuning Guide, n.d.), for instance from noop to cfq. Another worthwhile tunable is sched_compat_yield, available on the specific kernel for your operating system. It enables the aggressive yield behavior of the old 0(1) scheduler. Reading from the man page, you learn that you should expect applications that depend on the sched_yield() syscall behavior to perform better with the value set to 1 rather than the default value of 0.

Then, since you know that the customer tasks involve running multiple threads and a lot of migration between cores, you also consider changing the sched_migration_cost. This tunable is the amount of time after the last execution that a task is considered to be "cache hot" in migration decisions. A "hot" task is less likely to be migrated, so increasing this variable reduces task migrations. The default value is 500,000 ns.

If the CPU idle time is higher than expected when there are runnable processes, reducing this value might help. If tasks bounce between CPUs or nodes too often, increasing it might help land on the sweet spot.

Also worthy of consideration is sched_latency_ns. This tunable determines targeted preemption latency for CPU-bound tasks. Increasing this variable increases a CPU-bound task's timeslice. A task's *timeslice* is its weighted fair share of the scheduling period. The task's weight depends on the task's nice level and the scheduling policy. Timeslices become smaller as the load increases. Furthermore, this value also specifies the maximum amount of time during which a sleeping task is considered to be running for entitlement calculations. Increasing this variable increases the amount of time a waking task may consume before being preempted, thus increasing scheduler latency for CPU-bound tasks. The default value is 20,000,000 ns.

Finally, we have sched_wakeup_granularity_ns, controlling the wakeup preemption granularity. Increasing this variable reduces wakeup preemption, reducing disturbance of compute-bound tasks. Lowering it improves wakeup latency and throughput for latency critical tasks, particularly when a short duty cycle load component must compete with CPU-bound components. The default value is 5,000,000 ns.

With this in mind, you can begin your profiling. Which of these parameters do you think will yield the best results? Indeed, this is the kind of problem that a highly experienced system administrator or engineer will face, and the results will most likely be quite puzzling to understand and interpret. It is doable, as we will see an example of this same use case later on.

But perhaps the problem should be analyzed from a different perspective. First, try to determine which of the components actually causes the most variation in task runtime, *regardless* of the fact that they seem to be CPU bound.

Without decent statistical knowledge, you will probably struggle to correlate between three versions of CPU, two types of disk storage (SAS versus SSD), 1-Gbps versus 10-Gbps network, local and NFS work areas, four different memory bus sizes and total RAM sizes, and finally, different versions of the customer application.

A full test set would include at least 96 permutations in order to cover all test conditions, and this cannot be done with any practical expectations in a production environment. Moreover, you cannot repeat the test set at least 20 times to get the desired 95% confidence level.

The simple answer is to use the statistical engineering to your aid. Run a small number of tests, keeping all the parameters fixed and changing just one at a time. The most obvious choice is the customer application because it merely requires running a different binary. However, this is contrary to intuition, as well as your problem-solving approach as the IT systems expert.

This example illustrates a real-life scenario that we had to cope with, and we learned a number of valuable lessons, just by using statistical engineering. The impact of all hardware components was much less than the choice of the application version, even though it may not seem apparent by looking at the wall time as a function of CPU model or frequency, the choice of memory, storage, and network. But the variations showed a distinct Red X pointing at the application version, making CPU tuning a noble but misplaced effort. Indeed, we later proved that the CPU tweaks did yield minor improvements, but they were negligible compared to the randomness imposed by the internal application logic.

Without the statistical engineering, our task of finding the most significant X would have been much more difficult. Furthermore, we were able to demonstrate value in our testing, without full coverage and without multiple repetitions of the test scenario to gain the needed confidence.

As highlighted in Shainin's paper, if finding and controlling the Red X is the key to system or process improvement, then a mathematical model in the form of $Y = f(x)$ is not necessary. In fact, it is unproductive. Too much time is spent reconfirming relationships that are already known and controlled.

## Component search

When troubleshooting system problems, you may sometimes encounter a situation in which you have to investigate the manifestation of an issue in two disparate setups. For example, server A might be running a 2-year old processor with eight cores, 64 GB RAM and an older version of an operating system, whereas server B could be a latest model with 12 CPU cores, 128 GB RAM, and a newer operating system. And yet, you may find that you get better results on the seemingly inferior hardware/software combination.

When the overall pool of test options is relatively limited, you might not have the privilege of running a full-factorial design of experiment or use statistical engineering to your aid. In this kind of scenario, you might want to consider the *component search*, a subset of the statistical engineering approach.

The general idea is to swap parts between the supposedly good and bad systems. Normally, this method applies to mechanical systems, with thousands of components, but it can also be used in the software and hardware world. In the example illustrated above, the simple swapping of parts would be to install the newer version of the operating system on server A and vice versa, and then retest the application behavior. If the performance improves, you will know for certain that the issue is in the software rather than the underlying metal. Should it prove that the operating system is not at fault, you can then focus on trying to understand which of the hardware components might cause the degradation in the application behavior.

### Pairwise comparison

Another interesting method of trying to choose a preferable solution among two available options is the *pairwise comparison*. This kind of analysis can help you find the importance of a number of options, relative to one another. A typical scenario from the data center world might be choosing the best caching solution, based on the performance of your customer tools. Instinctively, you may want to run $N \times M$ permutations of tests, and then compare the results. The question is, how do you interpret the results and choose the preferable solution?

Pairwise comparison can help in this situation. The basic idea is to examine any two parameters at the same time – let us call them A and B – and check the number of times A was preferable over B, the number of times B was preferable over A, and when they were tied.

The total number of binary comparisons is $N(N - 1)/2$, and you merely need to sum the times either A or B offered superior results. In the end, the solution with the highest score can be considered the best.

### Summary

Documentation is an important part of data center health and problem solving. It can save you the time needed to analyze or explain the same problems and solutions over and over again, as well as raise the technical bar across the organization. While there is no silver bullet to how knowledge sharing should be affected, using public services can help with the redundancy of content management systems and the lack of overall visibility of data, procedures, and skills.

Furthermore, clutter-free, effective data management comes down to three basic things:

- Decide which parameters bear checking and monitoring in the first place; use proven statistical methods to narrow down the scope. In the short term, you can use the methods for pinpoint problem solving. In the long term, use the methods to determine the strategy for managing data in your compute environment.

- Periodically clean up data collection based on existing monitoring statistics. Do not be afraid to get rid of a legacy mechanism or those that show no added value to the stability and efficiency of your environment.
- Retain data in a meaningful manner that reflects your problem solving. If you keep so much data that it becomes unreadable, or no one bothers to analyze it, you can submit your data strategy to a lean diet that reflects the reality.

## SEARCH ENGINES, MAILING LISTS, AND VENDOR SUPPORT

Let us assume that you have good documentation in place, that you practice industry methods for making your problem solving more effective, and that you do not clutter your databases with unnecessary data. So far so good, but most of the issues you encounter and try to fix will not be isolated, internal incidents. Most often, underlying problems will reside with the hardware and software you use in your environment.

### Do not fire and forget

The follow-up step after the problem has been found is just as important as the investigation itself. If you have identified a new bug in the operating system, knowing it is there will not make your systems any more stable or introduce control into your environment. You will have to actively engage outside your organizations to bring proper closure to the issues you are facing.

### Vendor engagement and industry impact

One of the most important things you can do is engage your vendor. Normally, in most companies, there will be an external entity responsible and accountable for the products and solutions deployed in your data center, no matter how big it is. This is true for home users and SOHO businesses as well as large companies, with the scale and importance matching accordingly. When problems occur, and you believe you know how they manifest, you should engage the parent entity for complete resolution.

Some people steer away from this communication because it can be frustrating and time-consuming. You might be redirected to a first-level support technician who will start asking silly questions, or you may be asked to collect vast amounts of debug data before sending it to the vendor. Better yet, you might even be asked to open a BugZilla account.

Even after you have established your first contact (no *Star Trek* reference here), you still might find yourself bogged in more emails, slow response, evasive answers, yet more silly questions, and the resolution process could take weeks or even months. Regardless, you should not give up, and follow up until the necessary change has been acknowledged by the vendor, and publicly released as a bug fix, improvement, or patch of some kind.

We would like to give you a personal example here – from the world of kernel crashes. Several years ago, when we started deploying a fully automated kernel crash solution in our global environment spanning tens of data centers, we had a relatively high kernel crash monthly incidence rate of about 6%. Stepping out, in large setups, this can easily translate into hundreds of kernel crashes every month, leading to a big loss of productivity. Even more importantly, in homogenous environments, the presence of even one kernel crash bug poses a huge risk because it can theoretically affect the entire install base. This kind of situation cannot be controlled and requires constant vendor engagement.

Going back to our story, we would report every single crash instance to our vendor, indeed, almost religiously, in addition to our internal investigation and mitigation. We would make sure that the vendor followed up with the right kernel patches.

Approximately 18 months into the project, we reduced the incidence rate from several hundred hosts crashing every month to just a handful, if not outright zero. In that time period, we reported more than 70 unique kernel crash exceptions to the vendor, most of which had been pushed upstream.

Not only did we positively affect our own environment, bringing it out of the uncontrollable phase into one that we fully control, we also demonstrated significant impact on the industry and market. And while we may not get public credit for the work done in this sphere, it clearly illustrates the critical importance of following up with your problems, especially in large companies. Remember, you might be in a position in which your unique, high-demand setup offers an unprecedented test ground for bugs and problems that others cannot detect and find, and you have an industry leadership responsibility to see them through.

### Someone saw it already

The other side of the coin is that there are many large companies doing much hard work, and reporting problems all the time. This means that there is a good chance that someone may have already seen the problem you are facing. In some situations, you will be at the forefront of technologies, writing those articles and how-to's for other people. In other situations, you will be learning from others. If you happen to use legacy technologies and operating systems, the industry may already have had much experience with the problems related to them, and the Internet will know something about it.

When trying to resolve a problem, if you do have some kind of an error trace, consider searching online – minus the confidential company information, of course. There is a good chance you will come up with hints or leads or even complete solutions for your problem. In turn, this may help you narrow down the scope of your problem and even accelerate the provisioning of a fix by the vendor.

### Confidentiality

With information leaving the virtual premises of your organization, there is always a chance that you may accidentally expose confidential data. Part of the external interface with vendors, public forums, and mailing lists, as well as vendors, should include a fair dose of discretion on your end.

With vendors and written support contracts, there will normally be some kind of a nondisclosure agreement (NDA) in place. In fact, any good support contract should include it. Elsewhere, you will have to exercise a different level of self-censorship, knowing there are no legal barriers preventing leaks of data.

There is no reason to bunker down, but if you do decide to ask for help outside your company, you should remove any absolute values and benchmarks from your reports and stick to percentages and comparisons instead. You should also mask hostnames and IP addresses, as well as any other sensitive pieces of information. You will still be able to get the needed help without any risk to your business and intellectual property.

## ROOT CAUSE FOUND

If your problem solving is progressing well, then there is a relatively good chance that you will find a clear root cause to the issue at hand. While we did discuss the need for proactive engagement and follow-up, there are additional aspects that you need to consider.

### A solution exists, but is the problem solved?

If your engineering and system work converges toward a certain solution, it does not mean your work, or your responsibility, ends there. One of the most critical parts is doing the boring part of making sure everything clicks into place. Many engineers find the switch from the excitement of being Sherlock Holmes in their data center to a bureaucracy champion hard and uninspiring, but the necessity remains nonetheless.

Perhaps it sounds trivial, but often as not, this part is left untouched. The notion that someone will handle it is wrong. As a problem investigator, you have the best visibility and understanding of the problem, and you cannot expect the operations teams to see your solution through to the end. You need to make sure that the technical and business solution that fixes your problem is fully implemented. Only then will you regain full control of your environment and be able to move to other, more exciting topics.

### Test and verify

After you receive a solution to your problem, you must test it to make sure that it resolves the original problem. Even more importantly, you must verify that it does *not* introduce any new regressions. The testing must be more extensive than saying, "it seems okay" and leaving it at that. You must run a series of tests that will prove that the specific original issue that kick-started the investigation in the first place has been fixed. Once again, you may use statistics to your aid to avoid bias and opinion taking over.

The testing should be done in a phased manner. You should first make basic go/no-go checks to verify the integrity of the patch. Then, you should test on a small subset of isolated hosts to make sure the raw functionality has changed accordingly, and that your problem does not come to bear. After that, the solution needs to be introduced into some kind of integration environment or a special production pool where real tests will be executed. Indeed, for complex problems that only manifest in special conditions, the test may require several weeks and hundreds of hosts before you may decide you have sufficient confidence to approve the solution for standard, production use. Last but not the least, your monitoring system should be capable of checking the environment sanity and report on the expected behavior and any deviations from it. Just the fact something seems to run fine does not mean there are no problems, new or old.

### Be ready to roll back if needed

A very hard part of problem solving is letting go of your hypotheses and going back to square one. Sometimes, seemingly good solutions may not yield adequate results, or they may introduce new bugs of their own. In those situations, you must be willing to stop the testing, roll back to where you started, and retry with a different approach.

The ability to detect and undo changes will necessitate a solid monitoring framework and a robust configuration management system. Without those in place, new hardware and software will merely become potential vectors for downtime and uncontrolled behavior in your data center.

### Summary

Testing the solution for a problem is just as important as finding the cause to the problem in the first place. You must be thorough and methodical in your work, and flexible enough to change directions when new issues occur. You need to use monitoring and configuration management tools to assist in problem solving and controlled introduction of changes into your environment.

## ELIMINATING THE PROBLEM

Let us explore the resolution step in greater detail. In general, we discussed the follow-up step, and how you need to make sure solutions indeed satisfy your demands and resolve the original problem. However, most often the full resolution will require patching or fixing a large percentage of your install base, especially in homogenous data centers. This means that the fixes will not be a plug-and-play affair, but a detailed, complex operation instead.

### Devise a resolution plan

Let us consider the following scenario. You have identified a new kernel bug that caused 12% of your install base to undergo unexpected crashes and reboot in the past quarter. After a close engagement with the vendor, you have a new kernel release that resolves the problem. Indeed, you have thoroughly tested and verified the patch. Now, the tricky part is making sure some 3800 hosts in your data center get the patch in time. To make things worse, they are all running important computational jobs 24/7, the capacity needs are dire, and there are a large number of infrastructure servers also affected by this particular bug.

Handling this issue is surely not a trivial matter of connecting to each one of these hosts and firing up a quick installation of a few packages, followed by a reboot.

You must take into account the overall business need, you must make sure that you carefully stage the fix, and you must take into account the compute backbone, which needs to be handled separately.

Some companies will opt for full shutdowns, where the entire capacity is taken offline, and necessary patching is done. Others may choose rolling upgrades, working on smaller subsets of hosts at any given time. Either way, you must plan carefully; otherwise, your solution could become just as severe as the problem it comes to eliminate.

### Operational constraints

The gray area reality of data centers will dictate how much freedom you have in implementing your solutions. Even though everyone fully acknowledges the problem, they may not be able to do much about it. Sometimes, it could take months before the entire affected install base is patched, and you will have a lot of fragmentation along the way, with several kernel or application versions being used.

However, rather than treating these scenarios as a system administration hell, you should treat them as an opportunity. If you know similar problems will crop up again in several months, and you will have to redo it all over again, only with a different patch for some other issue, you might want to consider a more strategic path. Consider testing and implementing technologies that will allow you more seamless changes in the environment.

For kernel upgrades, it might be that you want to use some kind of rebootless patching solution. Or you might use high-availability utilities for critical services. Virtualization can also help, as well as having abstracted layers between users and hardware. In all cases, the operational constraints will shape the way you think and work, and help you make the right technological decisions.

### Sometimes you will not like it but do it anyway

In the worst case, no matter what you decide, you will have to choose between lesser evils. The final outcome will be less than ideal. You will not be able to deploy your solution in time, on all hosts, or both. There will be gaps left, and you will have a significant portion of your environment out of control. A tendency could be just to drop the whole thing, but it is important to realize the necessity and minimize the impact. The work of the system administrator is, after all, mostly about damage control, and that should be your main driver for improving the environment.

### Defining real success criteria does not equal "no one sees the problem anymore"

This is the golden trap of all data centers and compute environments worldwide. If you have watched an episode or three of the legendary British series *Yes, Prime Minister,* you are well aware of the dread the administrative team exercises over the notion of success criteria. But, it is the most important piece of the whole puzzle.

If projects and problems do not have a clear definition of how they should be managed and resolved, anything and everything could constitute as a success. You are having many alerts on some metric? No problem, raise the threshold, and it is fixed! Or perhaps your customers have stopped complaining? Great, the problem is not there anymore – it went away on its own!

Wrong. The laws of physics mandate that an interference needs to be introduced into a system before it can change. Data centers are no exception, and even though philosophers may disagree, having issues happen when no one sees them does not negate their existence.

This is why having clear and, more importantly, *quantifiable* success criteria *before* performing any kind of change is critical. Consequently, you will be able to monitor key factors that govern your setup and measure the outcome in an objective manner. Otherwise, you will be able to construe anything and everything as a success and use it to justify your work. Last but not the least, having robust methods and well-defined goals could expose gaps in your understanding of the environment and your inability to predict and respond to problems and changes, which can be just as severe as the actual operational issues that crop up from time to time. Luckily, understanding that you may lack understanding will allow you to step back and address the fundamental shortcomings in your problem-solving procedures before proceeding with additional, potentially futile tests and tweaks.

### Summary

Eliminating a problem in a large environment is often proportional to the complexity of the environment. It starts with having a proper plan in place, with clear objectives. You will have to take into account your operational constraints and exercise some flexibility where your proposed ideas and the reality do not match.

Hopefully, you will use industry best practices to create controlled setups in which you can measure your success. Here, we see again the importance of the monitoring component, which will be your tool for developing and maintaining situational awareness, as well as being able to respond to problems in a timely and intelligent manner. We will discuss this key component very soon.

## IMPLEMENT AND TRACK

If you are certain you control your environment well, you have a good way of measuring how and where changes come to bear, and you think you want to proceed with a solution to a problem, you need to implement it in your setup. This could be a small hive of several hosts, or a huge data center with thousands of servers. At this point, the complexity of your environment will expose additional challenges, in addition to the actual technical issues that you are trying to fix.

### If you stub a toe, when does the head register this?

You know your solution works. You verified it, tested it, and used real statistics to back your data up. You have also done extensive testing and gradually phased in the solution into your environment. However, problems do not always cooperate with your best intentions, and there can be a nonlinear effect on any mass rollout of solutions into complex environments. A new, negative side-effect may result from your one solution to one specific problem. In that scenario, when will you know that you are facing a fresh, uncontrolled vector in your space?

The ability to see, grasp, and respond to problems is one of the great challenges of any compute environment, and the bigger it gets, the more complicated it becomes. Sometimes, weird, odd, obscure, and rare phenomena will only come to haunt you when you deploy your solutions on tens of thousands of hosts, and you will swear you have never seen them before during the test phase. This could happen months after the fact. Moreover, it could take much time correlating the new issue with a fix for an old one.

The ability to gauge all of the above is probably the best indicator of how robust and smart your environment really is. If you cannot connect the dots quickly and easily enough, then you will never really be fully in control of your setup, and any change and adverse effect thereafter will be treated with suspicion. You may assume a defensive mode, slowing down rollouts or freezing them altogether, perpetuating problems and increasing fragmentation. You need to work hard to avoid these situations.

### Difficulties in 24/7 environments

Size and scope will only be a fraction of your operational challenges. You will most likely be constrained by your customer needs, the reason why your environment exists and runs in the first place. The people paying the bills for the hardware and software may require certain portions of your data center to run at all times, and they might never afford downtime for patching and fixes. Others will gladly accept them in their own due time, which could be a year from now, once their critical project is complete. Others will reject them because it is the easy way.

On top of that, if you frequently experience whiplash effects from your solutions, or if you do not respond quickly enough to problems, you will also be riddled with over-defensiveness, which will further stifle your flexibility and innovation. With this difficult mission statement, you will have to devise the right ways of making everything move forward.

There is no silver bullet solution here, either. However, rigorous methodology and thorough testing will go a long way toward making your case heard. Letting the numbers talk is the best way to assuage fears, reduce friction and opposition, and allow your solutions to move forward. Industry standards are a part of the picture. Phased testing and deployment are another.

### Monitoring is a must

The third component is the monitoring part, and it goes beyond checking whether your one specific change has any effect on the environment. Monitoring, as a whole, and this includes a complex collection of tools, agents, collectors, analyzers, and people, is the only sensible way of managing data centers without resorting to hunches and guesses. You need to know what happens in a way that cannot be given to misinterpretation. And you must be able to do that when the problem is relevant, not days or months later. Once again, like everything else we have outlined so far, this component, too, must be based on smart methods, mathematics, and facts.

## CONCLUSION

Problem solving shapes up to be a complete doctrine with multiple layers of tools and practices. It begins with organizing your data in a practical, useful manner, followed by internal and external engagement with vendors and the industry. It follows with the resolution of the problem, a complex cycle of tests, verification, and phased implementation. There are several key components that will help you make the right decisions along the way.

- Industry methods – you need them because your intuition might be wrong, and you do not have the luxury of manually testing every single component when needed.
- Configuration management – this layer will allow you to stage changes in a controlled manner and be aware of all that happens in your setup. You will be able to follow and time the introduction of technologies, bug fixes, and patches, and you will have a clear path from the problem to the solution.
- Integration environment – in order to minimize potential negative impact on your install base and customers, you will want to test the proposed solution in a very thorough way. You will start with go/no-go decisions, followed by more rigorous regression tests, full executions, and other checks inside a large, sandboxed environment that simulates your real setup as closely as possible. Only after you are satisfied with the tests that verify all the different elements in your data center will you allow a change to propagate into the customer space.
- Monitoring – all of the above need a very good monitoring component. Situational awareness is the key ingredient that will determine the long-term success of your environment. Either you will develop and maintain it, or you will always struggle at the brink of control, assuming a defensive mode that kills any healthy risk taking and innovation.

With this in mind, we move on to Chapter 8, which elaborates in great detail on the considerations, methods, and tools for setting up a robust and efficient monitoring environment.

## REFERENCES

Design of Experiments (DOE), n.d. Retrieved from: <http://asq.org/learn-about-quality/data-collection-analysis-tools/overview/design-of-experiments.html> (accessed April 2015)
F-Ratio The Statistics Glossary, n.d. Retrieved from: <http://www.stats.gla.ac.uk/glossary/?q=node/168> (accessed April 2015)
F-Distribution Tables, n.d. Retrieved from: <http://www.socr.ucla.edu/applets.dir/f_table.html> (accessed April 2015)

Ljubuncic, I., n.d. Design of Experiment. Retrieved from: <http://www.dedoimedo.com/computers/Design-of-Experiment-www.dedoimedo.com-latex.pdf> (accessed April 2015)

Shainin, R.D., 2012. Statistical engineering – six decades of improved process and systems performance. Retrieved from: <https://shainin.com/library/statistical_engineering> (accessed April 2015)

SUSE Linux Enterprise Server 11 SP3 System Analysis and Tuning Guide, n.d. Retrieved from: <https://www.suse.com/documentation/sles11/singlehtml/book_sle_tuning/book_sle_tuning.html#cha.tuning.taskscheduler> (accessed April 2015)

# Monitoring and prevention

Our work so far has been focused on investigating problems and following industry best practices of problem solving. In a large compute environment, it is very important to use data in the correct manner, avoid hasty assumptions, and analyze issues and their symptoms in a structured way. The next step in problem solving is making sure we can spot patterns in our data, correlating them with the sources generating the data, and trying to prevent the problems from occurring in the first place. The common word for this practice is monitoring, but it can be much more than that.

## WHICH DATA TO MONITOR

One of the big questions any system administrator will ask themselves is what subset of data, for any given problem or case, really matters? Sometimes, it is quite easy, and you can make rather trivial guesses and correlations based on typical events and data thresholds. In many cases, you can also use well-established monitoring rules to try to prevent service outages or disruptions to your customers, even without fully understanding all the fine mechanics taking place in the background. But most often, as we have seen in Chapter 7, monitoring will be more about trial and error, and less about precise mathematics. However, if we can somehow fully understand the cause and effect for occurrences and patterns in our environment, we can then actively control it, and monitoring becomes more of a way of alerting us of changes than a system that tells us something is wrong.

## TOO MUCH DATA IS WORSE THAN NO DATA

We have seen that the inability to process data in a reasonable time and volume often leads system administrators and engineers to compensate with guesses, incomplete solutions, rule-of-thumb estimates, and other compromises that make monitoring tools into a part of the problem rather than a neutral observer.

This often happens as businesses grow and accumulate more information from their internal systems. With the natural, and sometimes legally required, tendency to hoard data, data center environments quickly become overwhelmed with so much useful stuff that no one can make any sense out of it. The end result is that data becomes neglected, thresholds are raised, and events are ignored. In the end, the monitoring becomes rather useless.

It is a controversial argument, but it makes more sense not to collect data at all, if you do not understand what it is used for, than to store it somewhere and then search for ways to analyze it. It is always possible to find correlations between vectors of data and environment events, but correlation does not imply causality. Unfortunately, people with analytical minds often rush to seek patterns and make these kinds of links in the data they use, and over time, a significant bias in the quality of reported metrics develops. Most notably, the link between the symptoms of a problem once reported and the actual root cause disappears. Too much data simply breeds apathy.

With no data in place, there is no bias, and people working at problem solving will be challenged in thinking what might have caused the issue they are seeing. Arguably, this always happens at some point somewhere, and from there on, semi-automated and automated monitoring solutions are developed and tweaked. However, it is possible to create robust and relatively simple solutions that bridge the two ends of the spectrum.

## Y TO X WILL DEFINE WHAT YOU NEED TO MONITOR

Statistical engineering is the key to creating correct monitoring solutions. The actual software tools are less important. We are looking at the mathematical link between cause and effect, and to that end, we want to use the $Y \rightarrow X$ approach.

Practically, this means letting engineers, developers, system administrators, and solutions architects suggest all possible variables that could lead to negative results, and suggest thresholds that they believe could be indicative of a problem. With thousands and possibly millions of permutations of hardware and software combinations in the environment, to run classic experiments in which a single parameter is changed in linear or exponential increments and then measure the outcome is impossible. This is the main reason why monitoring solutions, which are supposed to be *proactive*, are designed in a *reactive* manner, simply because the classic approach does not provide the necessary visibility into critical parameters and their values.

Instead, with the statistical engineering approach, only a small number of runs are required, basically one for each selected parameter, and then the highest variation in measured outcome is observed. In this way, the problem complexity is one of $o(n)$ rather than $o(n!)$. This is a first step toward creating a robust monitoring formula.

## DO NOT BE AFRAID TO CHANGE

After a monitoring solution has been in production for a while, it will become as critical and fragile as the environment it looks after, and a large percentage of the system support personnel may find it difficult to introduce changes, especially if original architects and developers are no longer involved with the project. What if the monitoring rules break? What if the thresholds are wrong?

Data centers may appear to be large buildings with tons of plastic and metal, but they are living things, with thousands of changes happening all the time. New hardware platforms are introduced, new software installed or updated, and most importantly, customer tools and applications often change, and the support teams are not always aware of these changes. The assumption that the environment remains the same must often be examined and challenged, and old monitors must be removed when they are no longer useful.

In general, there are several very simple criteria that can help determine whether the monitoring tool and its rules are still valid and useful for the business. Namely:

- Has the monitor alerted in the past week? Or month? Or year? If not, perhaps there is no reason for it to be present as an active, 24/7 ingredient in the environment. Moreover, if it has been introduced because of a one-time issue a long time ago, this also has to be examined and, if necessary, updated. Last, if the monitor is in place for a potentially large problem that could happen once a year or at even lesser frequency, then monitoring is not the correct way of identifying the issue. Active monitoring should focus on everyday data samples, and problem symptoms need to be correctly translated into available data views.
- Has the monitor been altered too frequently? Is the environment, or a portion thereof, still running despite the alerts? Indeed, if you ever need to adjust the monitor because it is too noisy, and your overall setup is working fine, then the tool is not doing its job. The same applies to ignoring and suppression of alerts, frequent changes or thresholds, and activities focused on the monitoring itself rather than the actual source causing the monitor to fire off.
- Have you had disasters related to a certain domain that relevant monitors have not been able to capture? If so, the monitors need to be decommissioned or updated to reflect the reality.
- Do you understand what the monitor is doing? And why? If you struggle to answer both questions, you may have legacy systems that no longer reflect the reality, and they should be challenged and tested for validity. Large, classic enterprise environments are notorious for their long tail of backward-compatible solutions, including monitoring tools and solutions, that are never properly managed and refreshed, resulting in a huge tool and data overhead.

## HOW TO MONITOR AND ANALYZE TRENDS

Another important aspect of monitoring is being able to spot tendencies in the system behavior, which we might as well call trends. When it comes to monitoring, trends usually indicate a deviation from an accepted pattern, for an unknown reason, and managers often use them to support their business decisions, even if the cause is not always understood.

Technically, even the nominal behavior of the environment, as defined and hopefully checked through monitoring systems, can also be referred to as a trend, but most often, the word will be used only for data, usually graphs, that stand out from the norm. Unfortunately, in most cases, a graph showing a set of data points with an approximate linear function ($y = ax + b$) having a negative $a$ coefficient will be simplistically categorized as a negative trend, and the one with a positive coefficient will be named accordingly.

Bad data analysis will ultimately lead to bad business decisions. In the long run, the data center setup will be run on hunches and kneejerk responses, leading to over and under capacity planning, sudden needs for burst capacity that cannot be provisioned, serious shortages in resources, inability to respond quickly enough, and many other problems. Monitoring, in this sense, is also a tool for helping shape the business correctly. Once again, a classic and over-simplified approach to data analysis does not cut it.

## SET UP MONITORS FOR WHAT YOU CARE ABOUT

Reducing the environment noise also means analyzing trends in a conservative manner. This means reducing the monitored data to a minimal functional set that provides real value. In other words, monitor a small number of "golden" parameters that have real and highly measurable impact on the environment when they deviate from the established (and well-tested) thresholds.

We have seen how difficult it is to let go, but sometimes, it is the only way to bridge the gap between clutter and a lack of mathematical capabilities (often called big data). Start with small data, and then expand as you build knowledge and expertise. Focus on the specific events and metrics that are known to have caused significant outage to your services or your customers, while being actively engaged to fix them.

In general, monitors are there to help you step in when there is a problem, preferably some time *before* it happens. But they are also a barometer for how you manage your data center. If the monitors keep alerting on the same issues over and over, and they never get resolved at their source, then you might have a much bigger problem. In theory, you should ever have only one alert, and upon receiving the alert, the problem should be systematically solved. That would allow you to keep the monitoring set to a minimum and focus on the most critical data.

## MONITORING != REPORTING

Which brings us back to trends. Because they are so significant to the culture of IT, trends have become synonymous with information, rather than being one aspect thereof. Moreover, trends should be normally built from informational resources rather than actionable metrics. Unfortunately, monitoring tools are often used to report noncritical postproblem metrics, which are then aggregated and dissected to create trends, which are then used for management and growth of the data center resources. Many organizations do not distinguish between monitoring and reporting, and they often confuse different data types.

The phenomenon only becomes more severe as the complexity of the environment grows, and there is added pressure on management to try to master the chaos, which has grown beyond the means of most engineers to evaluate using everyday tools. However, system and solutions architects should remain vigilant and remember a few core points:

- Problem solving is about finding root causes to manifestations of problems through the analysis of symptoms. Sometimes, there might be a mathematical model. If the problem cannot be predicted or modeled, a monitoring system might be used to alert when the problem occurs, to mitigate and shorten its impact. If the issue can be fully resolved, monitoring is not really needed. Instead, a reporting facility should be set up to measure and pace the ability of the organization to implement the solution.
- Monitoring systems are designed to alert us of anomalies in expected behavior of systems, be they individual parameters on a single host, the overall health of a machine, or entire pools and groups of hardware or software or even logical resources. Reporting systems should be used to track compliance and offer some mathematical estimation of how the data center changes, across various business dimensions. In most companies, it will often be impossible to separate the two mechanisms, but it is important to understand them and classify different metrics accordingly.

## DO NOT MONITOR RANDOM METRICS

Inability to properly conduct problem solving from one end to the other can create desperate scenarios in which data is monitored for the sake of monitoring. If we may borrow a quote from the famous British 1980s political satire *Yes, Prime Minister*, much like the Ministry of Administrative Affairs, the purpose of monitors may be to generate activity (The BBC, 1986–1988). Not necessarily useful activity, but definitely a great volume of it.

The phrase random metrics does not necessarily mean people going through a long list of potential hardware and software phrases and ticking them off on a whim. Instead, it means that sometimes people will wildly seek for solutions, hoping to find something that could explain why systems fail without an early warning, and why no one seems to be able to catch the issue.

From a purely mathematical perspective, if there is an equation or a model that can be applied to a problem, then it can be measured and predicted. Some system behaviors may appear to have no discernible pattern, but that does not mean they are random, it may merely mean that they do not play any part in observed problems, or that the interaction is much more complex than expected. For example, bugs in code definitely defy mathematical prediction models implemented on the hardware or software levels. But bugs can be fixed, and therefore, they should not be considered when monitoring rules are created.

This emphasizes the importance of statistical engineering and carefully executed designs of experiments, because not only do they help solve problems in a consistent and accurate manner, they shed light on the important metrics that should be taken into consideration. As a rule, anything that does not have a clear link between a suspected problem source and its manifestation should not be included in monitoring.

## DEFINE MATHEMATICAL TRENDS

This is probably the trickiest part, because few engineers working in the IT field have an intimate knowledge of how to really define data. But, it is cardinal in understanding the environment and how to respond to issues.

We must assume that monitoring systems in most organizations will have been in place and that changing them is a very arduous and prolonged task, sometimes quite impossible. We must also assume that off-the-shelf products are being used, sometimes with only minimal tweaks to their configurations. Most of the people working in the monitoring teams are not statisticians or mathematicians, and neither are their peers in the development and engineering teams. All combined, these factors leave a prospecting, problem-solving-hungry system administrator or solutions architect with the challenge of having to manage polluted, biased, possibly useless data, often already highly processed into what the business calls trends. It sounds like a lost battle, but there is some hope.

Even if data points on a graph are already averaged averages of raw data sampled and passed through several collection tools and spreadsheets, it is still possible to derive interesting and useful facts about the system generating the data. The over-simplistic *positive* and *negative* trend terms are rather meaningless, and we should strike them from our lexicon.

Now, we have data, which possibly represents a time report of the environment status at some point, for a specific subset of its resources, or it might be a historical view of what the monitoring system captured. Either one will help us trace a path back to the problem and understand whether we are focusing our energy on the wrong kinds of efforts.

Before we can claim there is a deviation from our established norms, we need to figure out if our norms are what we expected them to be in the first place. Let us consider the following example. You have a customer running computationally intense regressions in a pool of 1000 identical servers. The customer is interested in the runtimes for each task, and they want to know if certain changes in the server configuration or scheduling policy might affect the overall execution times.

Setting up a monitor, even for a temporary purpose of profiling the customer jobs, seems like a prudent thing. Over time, the execution of these tasks becomes a routine, and the monitor is in place, sometimes triggering alerts on defined anomalies, for which both system engineers and the customers take a variety of actions. The thresholds have mostly been defined using Excel, with some use of PivotTables and average values. This is often how things are done.

However, there is a big problem with this kind of approach. Most people assume that their data has a normal distribution. This may be true for most things in nature, but it is not necessarily correct for data centers.

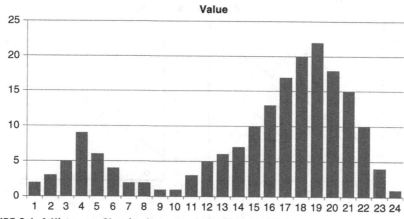

**Value**

**FIGURE 8.1  A Histogram Showing Nonnormal Distribution of Values**

The problem is compounded when system administrators and engineers try to apply some basic statistics to their data sets. They try to help, but the numbers are all wrong. For instance, you may want to alert if and when test results vary from the average value by one standard deviation. This sounds like a cool idea, but consider the following example, illustrated in Fig. 8.1.

We have a graph with 24 buckets of data, and a corresponding number of test samples that fit into each bucket. Let us assume that these are numbers of customer's regression flows, and that the x-axis is the runtime in minutes. We can see that there are two distinct groups of data points in our set.

However, if we'd not looked at the graph, we just might assume that we have a single set, and then, the average runtime for our set is 15.4 minutes, and the standard deviation roughly 6.5 minutes. This means that all the results 1–8 minutes, as well as those with a runtime of greater than 22 minutes, would be flagged as wrong, and we might have to take some action.

But what happens if we looked at our data as two separate groups, 1–10 minutes, and then 11–24 minutes? In that case, the average runtimes become 4.6 and 17.9 minutes, respectively, and standard deviations become 2.5 and 6.8 minutes. When we consider the second scenario, the criteria for analyzing the results change, and we would be flagging different data points for further inspection.

Sampling also plays a critical part. What if we bucketed our results every 2 minutes? Or every 5 seconds? Would we be undersampling or oversampling? Furthermore, do all these results belong to the same group, and have they been collected under the same test conditions?

Going back to trends, it is critical to understand what kind of data we are dealing with. Different distributions of data points may render similar linear approximations and trends, even if their fit might be completely wrong. For instance, Anscombe's Quarter clearly demonstrates the importance of data inspection and understanding

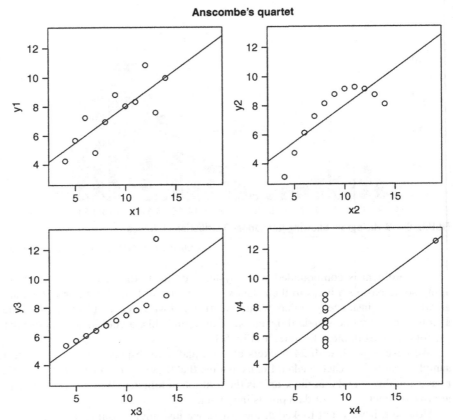

**Anscombe's quartet**

**FIGURE 8.2** Anscombe's Quarter Demonstrates the Importance of Understanding of Data Before Statistical Models Can Be Applied

before any models – and in the case of IT monitoring, alerts – can be configured and used. We can see that in Fig. 8.2.

Another classic mistake is creating line graphs and connecting dots when there is no historical correlation between data points. They help visualize the passage of time and allow human observers to see the behavior of the system, but if there is no history between any two points, such representation may be misleading. That also raises a question, how can we decide which data points we ought to filter from our sets?

Things become even more complicated when we account for outliers and how to separate them from meaningful data. Many methods are available, such as Grubb's Test, Pierce's Test, Dixon's Q Test (Dixon's Q Test, n.d.), and others, complicating our work further.

All of this emphasizes the importance of making deliberate decisions based on mathematics when creating monitoring solutions. Otherwise, most of the tools in place and their corresponding alerts will revolve around poorly understood links and errors.

## HOW TO RESPOND TO TRENDS

Let us call this proactive failure trending. If you have monitoring set up in the environment, and you are looking at trend graphs for anomalies, then you are trying to predict the future based on past information. In large, mission-critical setups, this becomes even more important. For example, a mere increase of just 1% in power utilization may seem negligible, but the actual amount and cost could be huge. Being able to discern a small change and respond before it becomes a well-established phenomenon is crucial.

The same applies to all changes in which the response cycle might be long. Introducing new hardware could take a long time, especially if it requires provisioning additional racks in the data center, physical installation of new hosts, network infrastructure setup, and similar. On the software level, problems with the operating system could cause significant downtime to customers, or slow down projects.

Ideally, we want to have a simple, robust way of identifying trends, so that we can plan and prepare accordingly. We want a mechanism that has a forecast window that is longer than the time it takes for the monitored parameter to be changed, if necessary.

## WHEN IT BECOMES TOO LATE

Monitoring is easy to set up. However, good monitoring is extremely tricky, and it often eludes most companies. There are many reasons for this, with the lack of proper mathematics and problem-solving culture as one of the primary issues. Then, some of it is institutional. Typical IT organizations have their monitoring tools set up in the following manner:

- Different departments take care of data center facilities (power, cooling), backbone (network), and operations (hardware, software).
- In the software stack, operating system and services are usually considered backend tools, and they are monitored separately from customer-facing systems, which include applications and sometimes business intelligence tools.
- Monitoring rules are historical (based on past experience).
- Monitoring is skewed toward closing events as quickly as possible.
- Monitoring is skewed toward operational efficiency.
- Most monitors are there to alert IT about problems that are not well understood and have not been systematically eradicated from the environment.
- Quantity of data exceeds the ability of existing facilities to process the data in a meaningful and timely manner.

- Fragmentation creeps in over time, with the legacy tail of the monitoring infrastructure outgrowing the critical piece.
- Companies often seek software solutions to compensate for the lack of real knowledge of what is happening in their environments; that is, they will buy business analytics programs and services and install additional data collection agents on their hosts, hoping to build new hierarchies and links, which might shed light on the correlations between different components of the whole system.

In the end, monitoring tools are often useful for alerting when something is horribly wrong, like a critical service outage, a host crash, or the like. They are also good for alerting when thresholds are exceeded, with memory, disk, and processor usage being the most popular – and often overrated – metrics. But they are not good in helping prevent issues.

There is nothing inherent in the concept of monitoring that should dictate what pieces of the system should be kept under scrutiny. But given a chance to choose between using a monitor that could tell you the host is going to suffer a kernel panic in 30 seconds versus the one that only reports on the problem afterward, would you not prefer to have the first one implemented in your environment?

In the software world, such monitors are incredibly tricky, but that does not mean they are impossible. Unfortunately, the knowledge vacuum is best filled with additional monitors, which leads most companies to have dedicated operations centers fully staffed 24/7, just to minimize damage for when the problems happen. It is sort of a lost cause. Organizations assume they cannot fix the root cause, so they just look after the symptoms of the disaster, or at least a near approximation (based on previous failures), and try to react as soon as the issue surfaces.

This is normally a phenomenon of a classic IT setup that chases its tail and has little to no prediction ability. It is also a good indication that the monitoring piece has been built after that fact and not as an integral part of the original solution. At some point in the past, the quantity of data outgrew the ability of the support team to manage, and scripts and services were put in place to help with that.

## HOUSEKEEPING

We come back to the issue of too much information. Finding patterns in numbers and graphs is a natural human response. Unfortunately, we all have limited time, and we cannot focus on all the parameters and trends that crop up in the environment. The phrase "big data" emphasizes the challenge organizations face in trying to decipher what goes on in their data centers.

The combination of historical behavior, deep lack of understanding of cause–effect pairs, insufficient technical expertise, little knowledge in the methods of problem solving and testing, as well as the torrents of seemingly random data creates an insurmountable obstacle for most IT departments, whether they handle pure system administration or HPC engineering. For most companies, at any given time, this will be a reality. There will always be significant legacy that has led to the existing situation. Most businesses choose to continue the traditional way, investing more money in tools, hiring more first- and second-level support personnel, and firefighting the problems, juggling between cost and customer satisfaction scores.

Our approach is different, and monitoring/trending is another layer in the top-down, systematic approach to problem solving. The correct way of handling issues across the board includes data-driven decisions, design of experiment, statistical engineering, and careful examination of the outcome. With the monitoring, the same principles apply. Data vectors that provide no useful information need to be taken out of the equation. In this case, it means ceasing monitoring operations on random or badly correlated segments of the environment.

Trends are sometimes a reflection of inertia in the organization. But often as not, they do not given any real useful, proactive guidelines, which could help drive the business or prevent errors. Frequently, the trends are used too late, with gut feeling being the chief deciding factor. Indeed, this cycle of information overload and information has kept IT departments busy for the better part of the last four decades.

## PREVENTION IS THE KEY TO GOOD PROBLEM SOLVING

A much cheaper and more efficient way is to find the root cause for every "bug" in the environment. It is easy to say, but it emphasizes the need for strict problem solving. If you use a methodical approach when troubleshooting system issues, you will be able to significantly improve your understanding about where the issue exists and to fix it. It comes down to two major areas:

- Bugs in code.
- Performance related problems.

Few if any software bugs can be foreseen – but failures can be analyzed in depth, and code fixes provided. This is true for applications as well as the operating system. We have learned how to trace software execution, collect memory cores, and analyze them.

Performance issues may not have a direct root cause, so to speak; they might result from inadequate resource planning, overbooking of existing hardware, improper use, and other issues. Again, if you address these with the same systematic, top-down approach we have seen in the previous chapters, then you can find the reasons for performance issues and resolve them. This could be optimization of kernel tunables, configuration of software, when and how your customers' tools ought to be run, and more.

In the end, you will be able to find equilibrium in the environment and master its behavior. Bugs will never be fully eradicated, and they will remain a challenge, in which case automated solutions for collection and analysis of forensics data will be the most useful way of handling them.

However, when it comes to performance issues, once you learn how your system behaves, you will be able to model a formula, and once you have a formula, you have prediction. Once you can predict possible issues (basically trends), then you can prevent them. As we have mentioned before, necessarily, this means focusing *only* on the core parameters that actually influence the outcome of whatever you are measuring.

# CONFIGURATION AUDITING

Monitoring does not necessarily have to revolve around live pulse checks or system parameters. It should also involve the environment topology. In other words, if and when a change occurs in your data center, you want to be able to register it, and then understand or project how it may affect your systems. For instance, are your customers going to be affected when a new kernel is introduced on their host? Will their applications or tools require any modification?

## WHY AUDITING CAN BE USEFUL

Being able to know how your system configurations change is critical in building the necessary situational awareness. It is another step to making your control of the environment complete. Initially, we focused on thorough examination and resolution of issues, starting with simple tools, going deeper with application tracing, and then handling kernel crashes, profiling, and tuning. Next, we define monitoring as a mathematical extension of problem solving; if we cannot define a relation between parameters we want to keep under watch and their expected outcome, then we do not require them.

The next piece in the puzzle is auditing what we have in place. Data centers sometimes host hundreds of different platforms, with possibly thousands of software permutations. We cannot always account for all of them, and we may not have the luxury of running any kind of tests to determine their exact behavior, or the impact on every single application flow they may run. Problem solving will allow us to understand many of these, but not all. Quite often, the conditions under which we tested the problems will also change, and in theory, we might have to redo all out hard work from scratch.

Auditing can help us mitigate this to a degree. We can decide that specific configurations are our golden standards, or at least, predictable setups that we can control and for which we can understand the outcome of software behavior and performance. As long as we can maintain those configurations, we should be fine. And if we deviate, then our assumptions may no longer be valid – and this means, our monitors might throw false positives.

Before we can maintain configurations, we need to be able to know that they may change. This is why we want to use auditing mechanisms, to watch for changes in system configurations and files, kernel boot parameters, BIOS configurations, partition scheme and filesystem formats, mount options, and other core settings that we know can affect our customers.

Creating the minimal auditing setup is actually a very important step in problem solving. This means you have reduced the scope of your problems to quantifiable, measurable values. You can now also set up your monitors accordingly.

## CONTROL THE CHANGES IN YOUR ENVIRONMENT

Ask yourself, your colleagues, and your boss what they think about the title of this subsection. What is the answer going to be? Write it down. Now, let us consider what it is not. Being in control of the environment does not mean having the knowledge of all the little pieces and what they do at any given time. It also is not about fundamental ITIL (ITIL, n.d.) service management underpinnings. Last, controlling the changes in the environment is not about reflecting these changes in reports, spreadsheets, or even monitors.

Being in control means one very simple thing. This means you do not react to changes, they do not surprise you, and if they happen outside your awareness cycle, which could be auditing or monitoring systems, the adverse effect the changes have is minimal and short-lived before a return to normalcy. Control of changes in the environment is all about knowing what is going to happen if one of the critical pieces in the whole data center stack is affected. Irrelevant parameters are not even taken into consideration.

A full mathematical understanding of data center environments will be very difficult to gain in most situations. However, as a compromise, you can have certain models and tools in place that will help you govern the core components of your environment. You will have the means of knowing when things have changed and then putting them back into the right order and shape. This can be a fully automated process, and in fact, it should be. As a concept, the control of changes is a fundamental piece in the post-problem-solving phase. Now that you know what is wrong, you make sure it never happens again. And if it does, you quickly undo the changes. We shall learn more about how we can control the environment in the next chapter.

## SECURITY ASPECTS

Being able to know if and when your system changes also has security implications. If you are handling or hosting customer data, the integrity of your environment plays just as an important role as any performance issue or a software bug. There are many ways to approach security, but we can treat it as another facet of our mission. It needs to be understood, we need to isolate core parameters, and then, we need to set an audit in place to know when we might deviate from the known, secure setup.

In classic IT setup, third-party security tools are used to perform wide sweeps of the environment, audit and log everything, seek irregularities and patterns in data streams, and isolate suspicious behavior. But often as not, much like the monitoring, tools are put in place, just to be there, without a real visibility of all the components through the stack. Sometimes, the use of security software may be mandated by laws, regulations, or compliance, but it does not mean it cannot be done with analytic understanding.

## SYSTEM DATA COLLECTION UTILITIES

Some of the tools we have used for troubleshooting can also be used for monitoring, as well as auditing. For instance, SAR is a versatile utility that can perform both these functions, as well as be used for live troubleshooting. The built-in Linux audit mechanism (System Auditing, n.d.) provides a way to track changes in filesystem objects, and it can be used as a security mechanism.

Logging facilities available in most distributions can also be used to some degree as data collection tools, although they are most useful when coupled to business intelligence systems, as the analysis of raw logs can be a slow, tedious, and often misleading process. In fact, due to the very modular nature of how Linux is designed, there are dozens of tools that can be used in the monitoring function, including specific utilities for network utilization and performance, I/O activities, hardware configuration, and more. Most business places emphasize on infrastructure monitoring tools that provide more comprehensive metrics, or at least, they combine data from multiple sources into combined views. The most popular mainstream open-source software includes the following:

- Nagios (Nagios, n.d.), a comprehensive monitoring suite capable of aggregating networking data, system resource metrics, and information collected by environmental probes. It offers remote scripting and monitoring, service checks, event handling, log rotation, as well as visualization. The functionality can be extended using plugins, and the tool relies on text files for data store rather than a database.
- Zabbix (Zabbix: The enterprise class monitoring solution for everyone, n.d.) is a monitoring application that can be used in an agent-based or agentless mode, capable of tracking the status of network services, servers, and network hardware. It uses a database backend for data storage, and comes with a Web-based interface and a reporting facility.

### CUSTOM TOOLS

However, many large organizations will have their own custom monitoring tools. There are a variety of reasons for this, including a significant legacy tail, which probably spans a much wider (and older) range of products, operating system and application versions, as well as types of possibly obscure products that typical off-the-shelf monitoring solutions normally support. Furthermore, the desire to control the business top to bottom, the usual not-invented-here philosophy, and specialized needs in high-performance environments all add their layers of complexity.

In most cases, engineers, system administrators, and support specialists will have inherited a setup with its own monitoring rules, and they will need to adapt to working in this scenario, often at a disadvantage. The big question is, how does one manage the monitoring piece in less than ideal conditions, with limited visibility and inadequate tools?

Due to budget, time, and risk constraints, it will be impossible to start from scratch. The alternative is to take the existing toolbox as the starting point and then build from there using the methodologies we have discussed here, one system layer at a time. Every new problem will be an opportunity to try to understand how your business runs, inside out, and then develop correct, meaningful metrics. Over time, you will optimize the environment. Custom tools are not necessarily good or bad, but they do reflect the complexity of the setup – and the understanding thereof. The more complex the monitoring solutions are, the less likely it is that the organization lacks in-depth, strategic knowledge of their own turf. In that case, the only escape from a never-ending struggle against a flood of meaningless alerts, elusive numbers, and firefighting is to adhere to a very strict regime of careful, step-by-step troubleshooting and rigorous statistically driven testing.

## COMMERCIAL SUPPORT

The other side of the coin is commercial support for stock products, sometimes with small modifications tailored toward large businesses. In general, commercial support is a double-edged sword. It provides structure, it has a name, and it comes with accountability. The price is that the core understanding of cause and effect and its exposure through the organization and its support structure is being delegated to a third party that does not have sufficient knowledge of the environment. Invariably, placing third-party vendor products into your data centers and hoping they work as advertised will ultimately almost always fail. If some of these tools were that good at perfectly fitting every single scenario, after a while, there would be little to no need for problem solving.

So what can be done? The answer is, commercially supported software can and should be used where it matches the requirements, but it must be accompanied with internal expertise, especially in large, complex, high-performance compute environments. If an organization does not fully and completely master the products it is using, they will become another puzzle, another problem, another unknown factor in the larger equation.

Buying software is an easy answer to a bigger problem. It creates the illusion of activity, of decision making, but it can be just as problematic as the original issue it aims to solve. Moreover, quite often, software purchases, especially monitoring and business intelligence systems, are done based on cost rather than scientific data. Furthermore, these systems are bought to try to help the business resolve the mystery surrounding its own data, which just makes the problem that much bigger.

Large companies do expect commercial support, and that is perfectly acceptable. But at the same time, when it comes to problem solving, monitoring tools cannot replace core knowledge; rather, they complement it. The process of how an IT organization manages its software is a good indication of how well it understands itself. On a larger scale, this is another problem that can be resolved through a methodical, step-by-step approach.

## CONCLUSION

Monitoring the environment is not about software, which is why we have not discussed any in this chapter. Software can and will reflect your business decisions, but it is not a replacement for hard work, thorough problem solving, and systematic profiling of your environment toward a deterministic, surprise-free model that you can manage and control.

The most immediate way to reduce the information overload is to reduce the amount of data, which we almost instinctively hoard and retain, to avoid classic pitfalls of "office mathematics" and to focus on a statistical approach driven by cause and effect. Then, auditing and change control can help contain and stabilize the environment, allowing you to focus on proactive management of your data center. Last, but not the least, you may go with commercial software, but it is important to remember that on its own, it does not and cannot ever truly replace human expertise and understanding inside your own business.

## REFERENCES

Dixon's Q test, n.d. Available at: <http://en.wikipedia.org/wiki/Q_test> (accessed April 2015)
ITIL, n.d. Available at: <http://en.wikipedia.org/wiki/ITIL> (accessed April 2015)
Nagios, n.d. Available at: <http://www.nagios.org/> (accessed April 2015)
System auditing, n.d. Available at: <https://access.redhat.com/documentation/en-US/Red_Hat_Enterprise_Linux/6/html/Security_Guide/chap-system_auditing.html> (accessed April 2015)
Zabbix: the enterprise class monitoring solution for everyone, n.d. Available at: <http://www.zabbix.com/> (accessed April 2015)
The BBC, 1986–1988. Yes, Prime Minister. Available at: <http://www.bbc.co.uk/comedy/yesprimeminister/>

# Make your environment safer, more robust

# 9

In the ITIL world, unexpected issues that crop up in the environment normally fall into two categories: problems and incidents. The former can be regarded as scenarios that require a deeper investigation and analysis, usually culminating in a large change, whereas the latter are often unexpected deviations from the normal state. Sometimes, incidents evolve into problems.

Classification notwithstanding, both types of issues require proper handling and closure. A critical piece of problem solving is in providing a quantifiable, repeatable set of tools, metrics, and methods that can be used by the technical personnel in the environment to be able to mitigate and control the issues. So far, we have learned how to identify issues, how to fix them, and how to monitor them. But what about control?

## VERSION CONTROL

In small setups and startup companies, problem solving often starts and ends with the technical personnel and sometimes with ad hoc solutions. But as we scale and grow into massive, mission-critical scenarios that span data centers, thousands of hosts and millions of dollars' worth of business logic, a different approach becomes necessary.

On a larger scale, problem solving is a question of process rather than skill or software. The issue and its resolution transform into an abstract definition, encapsulated by the IT Service Management (ITSM) way of work. Monitoring plays an important role, but so does change control. Indeed, the Change Management (CM) service of the ITSM framework dictates that, in order to be successful, IT departments need to ensure that standardized methods and procedures are used for efficient and prompt handling of all changes to control IT infrastructure to minimize the number and impact of any related incidents upon service. On the software side, this manifests itself in version control tools.

## WHY YOU NEED VERSION CONTROL

If you are a software developer, you will probably have naturally developed your own version control methodology. You often save your changes, and you keep them in different files: code1.c, code2.c, code3.c, and so on. For system administrators and engineers, the need for rigorous housekeeping is often trumped by workload, haste, and priorities, which revolve around more pressing matters. Indeed, in the so-called firefighting mode, which becomes the de-facto modus operandi as IT organizations rapidly scale from SOHO to big data centers, there is little to no time for any strategic thinking and planning. The reactive, defensive way is the reality on the ground.

But, the developer's way applies equally well to data centers as it does to one's coding studio. Data centers are large ecosystems, and changes need to be captured so that people in charge can see the temporal history of how their environment is changing, spot "bad" changes, and contain them. This is done by using version control software – also sometimes known as revision or source control.

## SUBVERSION, GIT, AND FRIENDS

There are many version control platforms available. The most popular ones include Subversion (Apache Subversion, n.d.) and Git (Git, n.d.). The basic principle is simple: users check in and check out their software changes against central repositories so that branches and flows in code, configuration files, and other core pieces of the environment can be fully tracked, and if necessary, reverted.

Revision control also comes with additional advantages, like the ability to test changes before rolling them out into the production, the ability to compare work, and the ability to track down people responsible for specific changes in software.

## ROLL BACK WITH EASE

Let us briefly consider a scenario. One of your engineers is responsible for optimizing the company's Apache Web servers. Diligently, he keeps all changes to the main configuration file httpd.conf stored using version control. The engineer leaves on holiday, and a couple of days later, your customers complain that one of their servers is not performing well.

At this point, in a classic scenario, troubleshooting the issue would require comparing the configuration setup with other servers that are not exhibiting the performance issues, trying to understand whether any of possible changes in the configuration file might have caused the interruption in service, and figuring out how to mitigate the problem as quickly as possible.

With version control in place, the solution might be easier – and faster. System administrators still might need to do a lot of work until they can isolate the issue, but then, rolling back might be a simple matter of pulling an older configuration file from the version control repository. If proper documentation is in place, it might even be possible to know *why* each change has been made.

However, despite obvious administrative advantages, version control still does not help us maintain a tidy and uniform environment, because there could still be big discrepancies in the data center deployment, there might be dozens of software configurations on the production servers, and no easy way to analyze and compare them all. Furthermore, there might be other, unknown changes introduced on the hosts, which could further complicate things.

# CONFIGURATION MANAGEMENT

The second critical piece of the ITSM CM service is, you guessed right, configuration management. Configuration management software completes the missing piece of managing a uniform environment, without relying on the human factor to achieve the necessary balance.

Configuration management software normally works in the client-server model. An agent is deployed on target platforms. It runs as a background service and occasionally polls a central repository, comparing the software under its control with the master template stored on the remote server. New policies are downloaded onto the platform and executed. If there are any changes detected that do not match the templates, they are overrun, effectively making the platform behave the way the policies dictate.

For people coming from the Windows world, the closest analogy would be Group Policy Management, although configuration management tools are also widely available in Windows, including native Microsoft tools. In large high-performance compute environments running Linux, there are numerous third-party tools available, sometimes with commercial support.

## BE LAZY: AUTOMATE

Configuration management has an added bonus of helping automate deployments. Imagine you have 1000 servers, all of which need to be provisioned in an identical manner. In small companies, you just may hire a number of system administrators who would then install and set up these machines by hand, sometimes using their own scripting to simplify and speed up the process. But, the great risk in having people involved in any configuration is that every step along the way is an opportunity to make a mistake and deviate from the baseline.

Time and money being of critical importance, in large deployment scenarios, companies cannot afford the luxury of using brute force to overcome the problem of numbers. Configuration management becomes an ideal substitute because it offers all the required benefits of automation, with reduced risk for mistakes – although when they do happen, they tend to be of much bigger scope. A typical deployment would occur as follows:

- Servers are manually placed inside the data center.
- Installations are initiated over the network (using PXE boot), and installation images are downloaded onto the hosts. In most cases, auto-install configurations will be used, so there is no need for human input during the setup. For instance, the partition table is initialized using preset values, default users and groups are created, and so forth.
- The next step is to deploy software, and this is done using configuration management. Depending on the software of choice, the agent pulls packages, recipes, or modules from the central server.
- It then parses the rules (policies) by which the packages should be deployed, and herein lies one of the great advantages of configuration management

software. For example, a recipe may dictate that all servers labeled as Web servers should have Apache installed, or that servers with disks 1 TB in size may need an additional partition and a mount point. Fine-grained rules can be used to create and provision a significant number of different scenarios and needs.

- The agent will continue running and will, often on hourly basis, contact the main server again. New and changed packages will be downloaded, and existing content on the disk compared. Any custom-made tweaks will be overwritten, effectively restoring server changes to the known and expected baseline.

Configuration management is normally used for reversible changes that do not require reboots or service interruption. But, it can also be used for firmware updates, BIOS/UEFI updates, virtualization or Linux containers, and many other use cases. The automation aids in provisioning, and also makes servers builds and data center setups deterministic and predictable.

## ENTROPY IN LARGE ENVIRONMENTS

Using configuration management is a great tool for trying to minimize variation so that the data center operation runs the way it has been designed. However, invariably, there will be new issues cropping up that do not seem to be addressed by existing rules and policies, or they might come to bear in a way that you may not immediately understand. This does not mean your setup is broken, it just emphasizes that you can use configuration management to aid in profiling your environment.

Since configuration management software allows for rapid mass deployments, you can test changes in a controlled manner. You can start by deploying new configurations on test servers first, followed by machines that are nearing their warranty date, batch servers, only affecting infrastructure hosts the last. You can also stagger deployments by functionality, location, and many other factors, all of which allow you to run sort-of design of experiment on data center scale. In many cases, to be able to succeed with this kind of work, you will need a directory service such as NIS (Network Information Service, n.d.) or LDAP (K. Zeilenga, 2006) managing the environment.

Through configuration management, you will be able to track down critical elements that affect your environment, test your hypotheses, and then change your setup and tune your monitors accordingly. In this way, the whole system becomes a closed circle with inputs and feedback, whereas you retain visibility and control.

## MASTER THE CHAOS

Sometimes, configuration management will help you detect problems in an indirect manner. This is somewhat similar to our understanding of the dark matter (Dark matter, n.d.) in the universe. We learn about it through gravitational lensing of galaxies, and by observing the speeds and rotation of other objects in the vicinity of the dark matter through inconsistencies in mass–energy equations. In the data center, if you come to realize that, despite rigorous configuration management of kernel tunables and system parameters, you still observe significant, unexpected issues with your operating systems and applications, you will know that you may be doing the wrong thing.

In complex setups, configuration management will be more about what not to do and not to check – what *is not* there – rather than the pieces that you do cover, and the greatest overall usefulness will be in driving standardization across the environment, which is always a welcome step from both the actual technical perspective and managerial involvement.

If you try to achieve a very high level of uniformity in your data center, when problems do occur, it will not be so much a matter of investigation; you will just search for changes in the configuration and make sure that any "rogue" servers are aligned to the template. Solving problems that lie outside the expected boundaries of norm can be fun and challenging, but ultimately, it will not yield any meaningful contribution to the health and stability of the overall environment. Despite the temptation, such work should be suppressed. It will also free system administration time for other, more productive tasks known to directly affect the critical parts of your business.

## CONFIGURATION MANAGEMENT SOFTWARE

There are many programs available, with their own distinct advantages and capabilities. Your decision for the right tool will revolve around pricing, deployment size, operating system versions and flavors, type of changes that you want to control, available skillset in your company, and others. To name a few, there are several popular tools that you might want to consider for your first, high-level exploration in this field:

- Chef (Chef, n.d.) is designed to treat infrastructure as code. Business logic is translated into recipes, which are deployed on target systems, known as nodes. Clients then poll the server periodically and pull the latest updates, keeping the environment standardized. The software also offers integration with analytical tools, and it comes with its own management console.
- CFEngine (CFEngine, n.d.) is a configuration management and automation framework, designed for networks up to 50,000 nodes. Here, the necessary logic is encapsulated inside packages, which are then distributed and executed based on classes.
- Puppet (Puppet, n.d.) offers a similar approach, using its descriptive language to define manifests, which are then used on target systems. Much like the other two tools, it offers integration with cloud solutions, Linux containers, and other technologies, with scale and cross-platform operability in mind.

## THE CORRECT WAY OF INTRODUCING CHANGES INTO THE ENVIRONMENT

Even if you have all the right tools and methods in place, you still need to exercise caution when changing your production environment. Essentially, every single change is an opportunity to deviate from a well-established, clearly understood status quo into unknown, forcing you to exercise your problem-solving expertise. Being able to maintain a stable and predictable work setup is probably the greatest testament to your problem-solving skills, in that you may never have to exercise them. Or rarely.

## ONE CHANGE AT A TIME

If you have to introduce new software or configurations into your data center, the best way to do it is by making sure all other components remain unchanged for some time before and – especially after – you have made the change. Too often businesses and organizations pile things together, to save time and cost, because downtime and maintenance are counterproductive, which in turn significantly complicates matters when things go wrong. The worst part is that some problems result from interaction between components, and it takes a long while to troubleshoot and isolate them, whereas normally related issues would be simple and straightforward or nonexistent. Worse yet, even if you plan well, and you have a change control board in place, and you follow the ITIL framework to the boot, you can still not account for random and unannounced changes that someone may initiate in the environment. If you can ensure that there is only one free dimension in your matrix, it will be much easier to monitor the deployment, track changes, identify problems, and – most importantly – roll back when necessary.

Now, this may be unpractical for large data centers, but in that case, you need to treat complex systems as individual components. If you must perform a change that involves 10 different networks and routers, then the entire chain becomes one unity. The scope and complexity of potential problems will grow, but all elements must be considered, ensuring you can prepare for the worst.

The ability to withstand a huge, sudden outage following a change is a great indicator how well prepared your environment is. In some cases, it will also reflect on your backup and restore capabilities, as well as disaster recovery (DR). If you run a mission-critical high-performance compute setup, then you must plan changes with total catastrophe in mind to cope with any kind of problem across the spectrum.

Furthermore, this ability is also an indicator of your operational readiness. You may have version control and configuration management tools deployed with a great deal of automation and excellent monitoring, but it will often realistically cover *only* a subset of your environment: Linux but not Windows; storage appliances and networking gear will have their own vendor-locked operating systems that may not permit the use of third-party tools; your utilities may rely on certain pieces of the data center to always remain in use.

If you factor in all these pieces, combine them into a single functional entity, and then work on how to recover and restore services as quickly as possible upon failure, you will have created a robust ecosystem that can withstand changes, both planned and unplanned. Tools such as Git and Puppet will help you drive standardization when you discover operational gaps, and good monitoring tools will alert on any lack of standards and compliance.

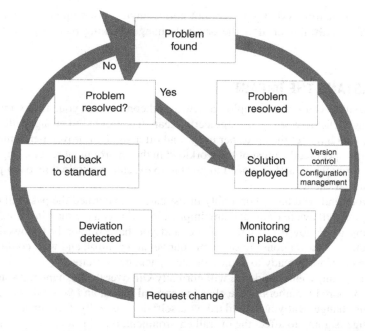

**FIGURE 9.1** Problem-Solving Cycle, With Version Control, Configuration Management, and Monitoring in Place

Again, going back to what we have discussed earlier, monitoring and change control software should be used as *whitelist* tools. They should only track *known* baselines and alert when things deviate from thresholds. You should not try to fix problems that reside outside the norm, as their number is effectively unbounded and will always defeat your workforce and knowledge, whereas a limited subset of clearly established rules can be maintained and controlled. Thus, operational excellence becomes a circle, as shown in Fig. 9.1.

## DO NOT RUSH TO MEET THE DEADLINE

One of the great enemies of the system administrators and engineers is the project timetable. Real or optimistic, it exists to define when things should be done, and sometimes, you will be forced to make tough decision against the clock, even when some of the technical pieces may still be missing. Quite often, changes pushed through without necessary diligence and testing will result in an unexpected, often negative outcome.

If you are unsure that you have prepared sufficiently, or that there are still pieces and components that have not been covered, you should not make any changes.

The worst situation is that you may not notice anything wrong at first, and issues may surface only longer after the original change, making recovery all the more difficult.

## UNDERSTAND THE IMPACT

Let us assume you need to deploy a new sysctl.conf file on your Linux machines. After long, delicate work, your engineering team has decided to change half a dozen settings, which reflect the customer usage and offer some improved performance for your hosts. Specifically, most of the workload in the environment requires significant network throughput, and you need to be able to execute multiple threads in parallel, with minimal latency.

On your end, you have thoroughly investigated and defined the pass/fail criteria, and you are well aware of all and any implications this change may involve. You are now going to deploy the sysctl.conf file, and you have diligently followed all the best practices. Old versions are saved in your version control, and your configuration management team is ready to deploy the new package or recipe.

At this point, your confidence will normally win over the hesitant and sometimes clueless or bored members of the change approval board, and you will steam ahead with your change. But you should ask yourself: do you really, fully understand how this change is going to affect the overall environment, on all levels? A small local fix on a Linux host does not look important enough to warrant any extensive involvement with other experts, from other domains.

However, if you discuss the change with your colleagues, you may discover that there could be some gaps in your work. Or you may consider them yourself. Will the increased network load affect the switching and routing equipment? Are there going to be any bottlenecks? If you are going to increase the parallelism of execution, do you have sufficient software licenses that may be required for the task? If your clients are going to use additional data, more frequently, are your storage systems equipped for the task? Have you tested *all* your customer flows to make sure the configuration change does not adversely affect them?

## NO PROBLEMS REPORTED MEANS NOTHING

After you have deployed your new change, you will ready yourself for any potential issues. Blessedly, there may be none, in which case you will briefly follow up with monitoring teams and then go back to other, more interesting work. However, in reality, you may merely be ignoring possible new problems.

There will often be positive bias in the organization, a desire to get things done. When people expect a change that is going to make everyone's lives better, they will want it to succeed. This means that negative signs may be ignored or missed. Alternatively, your monitoring software may not be equipped to cope with new symptoms that may arise from your change. It is possible that you have not anticipated them, or they may affect another domain.

Common sense and experience will drive how and when you conclude work in your environment. A *clear* methodology of deployment also helps. There are some good, general practices that are always useful, like avoiding any configuration changes before the weekend or toward the end of the day, deploying changes in a slow, staggered manner, continuous communication with the customers, and effective monitoring of well-correlated, well-understood critical parameters of the environment. However, if you do not have the necessary situational awareness into the scope of the original problem or the reason for the change, what it may cause, and how you are expected to measure it, then you will struggle completing the last piece.

## RIPPLE EFFECT

In big, complex setups such as high-performance compute data centers, it is very easy to deviate from normal, peaceful behavior into chaos. Human errors, configuration problems, and false alarms can often trigger a headless chicken race, with one bad action leading to another, compounding the situation. Decisions made in haste and without all the facts will muddy the understanding of the problem, and you may find yourself just trying to get everyone to work together before any real problem fixing can be done.

Once again, it is important to stick to a strict discipline and adhere to established policies that can help reduce the damage. Technically minded people may tend to treat the ITIL framework with disdain, but good, effective incident management and problem management can help reduce the unnecessary workload and focus the energy where it is required. However, even under stress and pressure, it is important not to neglect the proper techniques and tools of problem solving.

## CONCLUSION

We started our problem solving with technical tools, but we finish it with methodology and process. Previously, we learned how to handle data through concepts such as statistical engineering and design of experiment, we discussed monitoring and its pitfalls, and in this chapter, we learned about following through on environmental changes and controlling the environment.

Our tools of the trade are version control and configuration management software. Just as importantly, we make sure to retain a careful, methodical approach to how changes are introduced into our environment, with focus on critical components and situational awareness, in the same way we handled problem solving in the first place.

## REFERENCES

Apache subversion, n.d. Available at: https://subversion.apache.org/ (accessed April 2015)
CFEngine, n.d. Available at: http://cfengine.com/ (accessed April 2015)

Chef, n.d. Available at: https://www.chef.io/chef/ (accessed April 2015)

Dark matter, n.d. Available at: http://en.wikipedia.org/wiki/Dark_matter (accessed April 2015)

Git, n.d. Available at: http://git-scm.com/ (accessed April 2015)

K. Zeilenga, E., 2006. RFC 4510: lightweight directory access protocol (LDAP). Available at: http://tools.ietf.org/html/rfc4510 (accessed April 2015)

Network Information Service, n.d. Available at: http://en.wikipedia.org/wiki/Network_Information_Service (accessed April 2015)

Puppet, n.d. Available at: https://puppetlabs.com/ (accessed April 2015)

# Fine-tuning the system performance

# 10

So far, we have mostly focused on fixing problems in the environment through the use of various technical tools and by adhering to strict methodology in problem solving. The next logical step in mastering the domain of high-performance computing is to optimize and improve the processes, make our work setup more robust, and streamline the workloads so that they run faster and more efficiently. We will now work through several practical examples that highlight situations in which there is no specific technical problem, but which could eventually become pressing issues. Making the necessary adjustments and tweaking the environment to match the demand will allow you the necessary operational flexibility and allow you to avoid having to work in a "firefighting" mode.

## LOG SIZE AND LOG ROTATION

Logs are valuable. Logs are important. But if we let them blow up unnecessarily, they can undo the very advantage they provide us in scanning and understanding the environment. In general, if log parsing and analyzing becomes a task that tolls a significant amount of system resources and interferes with the normal work flows, then it becomes effectively meaningless.

## SYSTEM LOGS TEND TO GROW ALL THE TIME

There is a somewhat (un)healthy degree of paranoia among system administrators and security experts. They like to retain data as long as possible, even when it is no longer necessary or useful. We mentioned data clutter and housekeeping in Chapter 7. Indeed, we want to avoid hoarding information for the sake of it, as well as retaining logs that serve no purpose beyond a certain date. For instance, server messages from a previous boot cycle might be important, but those saved three or four reboots back are definitely of no value except possibly for detecting trends and for statistics collected by business intelligence (BI) systems. But for those, it is possible to keep reduced database entries. On the systems in your environment, there is no reason to store ancient data logs.

Linux systems come with a neat log rotation mechanism, which allows log files to be closed and archived once they reach a certain size. The mechanism is aptly named logrotate (logrotate(8), n.d.). By default, the service is configured to run daily (from within /etc/cron.daily). The process reads its configuration file, stored under /etc/logrotate.conf, and if any log that matches the size criteria is found, it is rotated into a compressed archive with incremental numbering. Normally, up to five archives are kept, after which they are permanently deleted. A sample logrotate configuration may look like

```
# see "man logrotate" for details

# rotate log files weekly

weekly


# keep 5 weeks worth of backlogs

rotate 5


# create new (empty) log files after rotating old ones

create


# uncomment this if you want your log files compressed

compress


# uncomment these to switch compression to bzip2

#compresscmd /usr/bin/bzip2

#uncompresscmd /usr/bin/bunzip2


# RPM packages drop log rotation information into this directory

include /etc/logrotate.d


# system-specific logs may also be configured here.
```

Per-task configurations are stored under /etc/logrotate.d directory. For instance, for process accounting, which can easily become a system hog, especially on busy hosts, with a very large number of tasks created every second:

```
#cat acct

/var/account/pacct {

    size=+200M

    missingok

    create 640 root root

    postrotate

    /etc/init.d/acct force-reload >/dev/null 2>&1

    endscript

}
```

## BE KIND, REWIND

If we may borrow the reference from a popular Hollywood movie, rotating logs is a healthy practice, but it also gives you peace of mind when it comes to retaining old stuff. We do want to keep our partitions tidy and clean, but we also do not want to throw away everything. Sometimes, archived information can be useful, and having older log files available may serve a purpose.

One practice that is definitely overlooked is a periodic analysis of how often system administrators and engineers in the environment access archived data and the use of it to troubleshoot problems. If you have the ability to run this kind of correlation, you will effectively come at the optimal time window for system data retention. For example, you may keep logs up to 3 months back but discover that in the resolution of last 20 critical environment problems, your technical staff only used data from the last week. In that case, it is possible to configure a more aggressive cleaning policy that matches the expectations and use of the available information.

## WHAT GOES INTO MESSAGES?

Another aspect that can definitely be streamlined is the way system messages are written. There are two reasons for this: (1) the amount of information and (2) the ability to separate useful pieces of data from unnecessary distractions. The real trick is to analyze your environment and decide on the minimal (or rather maximal) useful subset that provides you with the needed logs to maintain situational awareness and efficiency.

## Make it fast(er)

In Chapter 3, we talked about several types of systems logs, which aided us in the initial steps of our investigations and problem solving. The next step is to dictate what gets logged in the first place, and to allow for fast logging that does not slow the system when high volumes of information are written to disk.

One of the ways to speed up logging is to use asynchronous writes for less critical data. For the Linux syslog facility, this is done by prepending a minus sign to the log name, for each defined directive in the /etc/syslog.conf file. For instance

```
kern.*              -/var/log/kernellog;

cron.*              -/var/log/cron;

*.info;mail.none;   -/var/log/messages;

mail.*              -/var/log/maillog;

*.emerg             *

*.alert             root
```

## Useful information versus junk

The subtitle of this section implies a certain amount of courage. Are you willing to call data in your environment junk? But sometimes, this kind of attitude is necessary in order to improve your work methods. Like everything in life, system data obeys Sturgeon's law (Gunn, 1995), and it is critical to separate crud from important pieces of information. Not only will you lighten the computational load involved in collecting and processing this data, you will allow yourself to focus on real problems. But, the initial inclination to accept the fact is already an important step.

## Make sure you log what you need

This is, of course, easier said than done. There are two approaches to mapping the environmental necessities. You can start by logging everything and then narrowing down, pausing between changes to see whether anyone is going to complain. You can also start with the smallest of subsets and expand as your needs grow, hoping that your planning and technologies are scalable enough to cope with future challenges.

The first method is preferred because it involves less risk and allows people to define the envelope for their work. The second requires forward thinking, strategic vision, and this also means you might have to cope with new vectors of data without having the right resources, and that will always happen when you most need the logs.

The optimal way is probably somewhere in between. That said, it is critical to evaluate your ability to respond to issues at the end of scale (i.e., everything is logged all the time) to build robust systems that can cope with the torrents of data. For instance, if you have a hundred servers in your environment, you might build data logging facilities to match the size of your setup. However, 3 years from now, you might experience a huge business boom, the environment could be running 10,000 servers, and your single database, stored on a slow local disk, might be struggling. You will experience degraded service and performance, and scaling up might not be immediately possible, if ever.

Cost plays its part. It would be overkill to use a hundred logging servers as a contingency for a situation in which they might be needed a decade from now. But solutions need to be designed to account for this eventuality and allow for a seamless, transparent, gradual transition to accommodate higher volumes of data.

Therefore, the most balanced approach is to establish a framework for a large, flexible environment with infinite growth, then build the minimal set that matches the existing requirements, and slowly build from there.

## FILESYSTEM TUNING

Optimization of filesystem used for work areas and system partitions, such as /tmp, /var, /work, and others, can sometimes improve the performance and execution tasks of your machines, or at the very least, reduce the load for specific, targeted applications and use cases. While hardware improvements are often more desired, in some cases it might not be possible to introduce platform changes, and you will have to restrict yourself to software tweaks and mount options.

In general, most of the common filesystems used in Linux have a variety of advanced mount options, which can sometimes help reduce access times and improve short-burst write and read throughput. Sustained operations will eventually be capped by the I/O bus and properties of block devices.

### EXT3/4 FILESYSTEM

We cannot possibly go into every option, nor should anyone assume that there is a golden standard that matches all workloads and usage profiling. However, familiarity with what the technology can do may aid you in certain situations. Filesystem format and mount options can also be used to benchmark operating systems, as you may achieve different performance with seemingly identical settings in the I/O stack.

At this point, you may simply read the main pages and test various flags and values. However, filesystem optimization also presents a good opportunity to consider the typical or expected workload profiles running in your environment. Indeed, by examining what the filesystem can do and correlating to your tasks, you might find the right optimization formula. Blindly tweaking filesystem options will probably not yield any meaningful results. All that said, let us briefly look at some of the more common settings:

- -T – this formatting option specifies how the system will be used. The list of available usage types can be found under /etc/mk2fs.conf. For instance, -T news will change the default inode block size from 128 bytes to 4 KB, because it is tuned for a very high number of small file operations typical of a newsgroup or mail server.
- Extent – the extents scheme for storing the location of data blocks in an inodes is supposed to be more efficient than the indirect block scheme, especially when working with large files. Similarly, if you expect to have directory trees with a large quantity of objects, using the *dir_index* option can speed up lookups.

Mounting options are a far more popular choice because they allow for a nondestructive way of filesystem optimization, as opposed to formatting. Moreover, very often, standard operating systems used in large high-performance compute environments will use default options provided by enterprise vendors. Indeed, in most cases, the defaults will be more than sufficient for a wide range of use cases.

For Ext3/4 filesystems, there are several useful mount options to consider. Data and metadata commits are probably the most beneficial settings that system administrators and engineers can change to benchmark and improve the performance of their filesystems. There are three major options available: data = journal, data = ordered, and data = writeback.

- data = journal – data is committed into the journal before being written into the main file system.
- data = order – data is forced directly out to the main filesystem before its metadata being committed to the journal.
- data = writeback – this mount option allows journaling data commits into the filesystem after actual data has been written, which could lead to an improvement in performance. The downside is that there might be some filesystem data corruption following a crash, so the best option is to use it with battery-backed storage.
- commit = XXX – this option changes the default 5-second delay in journaling data commit to a user-specified value. Higher values will potentially improve performance, but also increase the risk of data loss in case of sudden power outages or system crashes.

Many other options exist, and they are beyond the scope of this book. But, the specified subset is sufficient enough as a starting point. It is also important to consider different permutations, as well as workload types.

## XFS FILESYSTEM

The XFS filesystem is less of a default choice in most Linux distributions; nevertheless, it is almost universally supported. XFS is designed to perform best in the execution of I/O operations, through the use of allocation groups (AG), a type of subdivision of the physical volumes in which XFS is used. This design capability gives XFS scalability and bandwidth, and it makes it a great potential candidate for high-load systems, such as databases, version control servers, and the like, as well as possible optimization.

Once again, there are two major types of options, including formatting and mounting. The former are destructive, but they may lead to increased performance. Moreover, because XFS is less often used by default, and because it is normally tailored for specific uses, there is a better opportunity to set up options other than default, even on standard enterprise Linux images.

- Lazy-count – this changes the method of logging various persistent counters in the superblock (mkfs.xfs(8), n.d.). Under metadata-intensive workloads, these counters are updated and logged frequently enough that the superblock updates become a serialization point in the filesystem. With lazy-count = 1, the superblock is not modified or logged on every change of the persistent counters. Instead, enough information is kept in other parts of the filesystem to be able to maintain the persistent counter values without needing to keep them in the superblock. This can give significant improvements in performance on some configurations. Essentially, the functionality is similar to the writeback option used for the Ext3/4 filesystems, except that it is set during the format stage.
- Size = XXX – this value changes the default internal journal size to a higher value.
- Agcount = XX – this value controls the number of allocation groups. It determines how many concurrent accesses are allowed to the filesystem. In general, a typical format command would include the following:

```
-f -l internal,lazy-count=1,size=256m -d agcount=16
```

In general, mount options should correlate to the selected formatting options. The full list is too long and detailed for this book, but you may want to consider the following:

- Logbufs = X – this option increases the number of log buffers used for storing journaling information into memory.
- Logbsize = X – this value defines the size of the log buffer.
- Allocsize =X – this option sets the buffered I/O end-of-file preallocation size when doing delayed allocation writeout. Increasing the value may help under heavy disk loads, especially if the lazy-count option is enabled.

At this point, much like with the Ext3/4 filesystems, you should check different permutations of the format and mount options, increment values by a factor of x2, and measure the impact on expected workloads.

## THE SYSFS FILESYSTEM

A close sibling of the /proc pseudo-filesystem is the sysfs filesystem, normally mounted on Linux under /sys. This filesystem exports information about various kernel subsystems, hardware devices, and associated device drivers from the kernel's device model into user space. Some of the variables are writable, like tunables, allowing administrators to manipulate the way the system behaves. Again, much like /proc, working with /sys comes with a significant responsibility, and an intimate understanding of the kernel internals is required to avoid damage.

### HIERARCHY

The /sys tree includes several subsystems (Mochel, 2005), namely

```
drwxr-xr-x 12 root root    0 Feb  8 14:22 ./

drwxr-xr-x 27 root root 4096 Feb 19 12:09 ../

drwxr-xr-x  2 root root    0 Feb  8 14:24 block/

drwxr-xr-x 14 root root    0 Feb  8 14:22 bus/

drwxr-xr-x 37 root root    0 Feb  8 14:22 class/

drwxr-xr-x  4 root root    0 Feb 19 12:18 dev/

drwxr-xr-x 16 root root    0 Feb  8 14:22 devices/

drwxr-xr-x  5 root root    0 Feb  8 14:22 firmware/

drwxr-xr-x  3 root root    0 Feb  8 14:22 fs/

drwxr-xr-x  6 root root    0 Feb  8 14:22 kernel/

drwxr-xr-x 84 root root    0 Feb  8 14:22 module/

drwxr-xr-x  2 root root    0 Feb  8 14:22 power/
```

Full exploration of sysfs goes beyond the scope of this book. However, system administrators and engineers should familiarize themselves with the tree structure and the purpose of some of the directories, because they will eventually have to make tweaks and changes to tunables, as part of their investigation and problem solving.

## BLOCK SUBSYSTEM

This tree contains directories for each enumerated block device discovered on the system. Examples would be SCSI or SATA devices. For each device, it is possible to examine and change a large number of tunables, including the maximum number of I/O requests that can be handled simultaneously, the highest number of pages read by the readahead (Corbet, 2010) algorithm, and others. However, the most important one is the ability to change I/O scheduler used for the device, which can affect the way I/O workloads are handled:

```
cat /sys/block/<device>/queue/scheduler

noop deadline [cfq]
```

The choice of the I/O scheduler (Budilovsky, 2013) may affect the system responsiveness under heavy loads. This could be of high importance for Web servers, mail services, databases, and similar services. For batch computational hosts executing CPU-bound tasks, the difference will be minimal or negligible. Nevertheless, it is important to know about the available tunables, study them, and then apply changes when running profiling tasks or optimization in isolated setups.

## FS SUBSYSTEM

This is a relatively new addition in the kernel, and it is normally used as the top-level mount point for the control groups (cgroups) (Chapter 1. Introduction to Control Groups (Cgroups), n.d.) mechanism, which allows a virtual partitioning of the system resources such as CPU, memory, swap, network, block I/O, and others. Imagine you have two users, and one of them executes twice as many tasks as the other. Without cgroups, over time, the user with more tasks will proportionally utilize more resources than the other. Cgroups allow the resource space to be divided into fair or weighted groups and allow the system administrator to fine-tune the portion of each relevant resource for each user and their tasks.

## KERNEL SUBSYSTEM

This is the most interesting piece of the /sys tree. Through the files in this part of the pseudo-filesystem, it is possible to tweak memory behavior and other critical portions of the system. Among the more important subdirectories, we have

- Mm – this directory contains various and highly powerful tunables related to memory management. We will see a very useful example later on.
- Security – this filesystem is meant to be used by security modules, such as AppArmor, SELinux, and others. It is possible to change and manipulate variables, and thus to affect the way security modules work. In some situations, this could be useful, especially if you suspect these modules might be affecting the performance or consistency of user application runs.
- Slab – this directory contains a snapshot of the internal state of the SLUB allocator (Corbet, 2007) for each cache. Certain files may be modified to change the behavior of the cache.

## MODULE SUBSYSTEM

Finally, this directory contains a listing of all the modules loaded into the kernel, each being separated in its own subdirectory. The information displayed by the lsmod command reflects the contents of these subdirectories. However, it is also possible to change attributes for some of the loaded modules, modifying their behavior, with all the associated risks.

## PROC AND SYS TOGETHER

When you combine the power of tunables under /sys and /proc, it is possible to derive solutions for very complex issues, which may not be immediately apparent from the initial symptoms. Indeed, let us present three examples that highlight the usefulness of these filesystems. As mentioned, both require a very deep understanding of Linux internals, but this kind of problem is common in large high-performance compute environments.

### MEMORY MANAGEMENT EXAMPLE

Someone reports a system with a weird behavior whenever memory utilization reaches 100%. In other words, whenever the physical memory capacity is exhausted by running processes, the host begins exhibiting very high levels of %sy usage, which affects the performance of actual running tasks, as well as interactive responsiveness. Troubleshooting this kind of problem is not easy, but assuming you have done your homework and followed all the text in the previous chapters, you will eventually reach the conclusion that the phenomenon is related to the way the kernel handles transparent huge pages (THP). With the option turned on for all the processes, the defragmentation of memory pages causes an unnecessary system load. Resolving the issue requires disabling the THP use to a less rigorous regime. This is affected by changing a pair of tunables under the /sys/kernel/mm tree:

```
echo "advise" > /sys/kernel/mm/transparent_hugepage/defrag

echo "advise" > /sys/kernel/mm/transparent_hugepage/enabled
```

## CPU SCHEDULING EXAMPLE

The second example takes us into the realm of CPU scheduling. We discussed this at some length in Chapter 7. After profiling a customer application that runs for a very long time, you discover that a significant portion of system calls result in timeout errors (strace –c)

```
% time     seconds  usecs/call     calls    errors syscall
------ ----------- ----------- --------- --------- -----------------
65.22 22150.280501          38 583070684 190983354 futex

34.29 11645.525802      154865     75198           nanosleep

...

100.00 33961.356957           1235739375 192275032 total
```

If we trace the execution, we get

```
42909 15:00:58 futex(0x7fffffffed11c, 0x189 /* FUTEX_??? */, 1, NULL, 2aaaab9171e0) =
-1 EAGAIN (Resource temporarily unavailable) <0.000004>
```

This type of error indicates a possible race condition between children spawned by the parent process. Furthermore, checking the per-process scheduling statistics under /proc, we see

```
#cat /proc/37635/sched

comp_engine.bin (37635, #threads: 3)

-----------------------------------------------------------

se.exec_start                              :      510725977.671344

se.vruntime                                :       88286931.224305

se.sum_exec_runtime                        :       10678332.196011

se.statistics.wait_start                   :              0.000000

se.statistics.sleep_start                  :              0.000000

se.statistics.block_start                  :              0.000000

se.statistics.sleep_max                    :         628031.486623

se.statistics.block_max                    :            466.273931

se.statistics.exec_max                     :              4.661808

se.statistics.slice_max                    :             11.968168

se.statistics.wait_max                     :             12.748935

se.statistics.wait_sum                     :          29332.184719

se.statistics.wait_count                   :               5916002

se.statistics.iowait_sum                   :           4288.113797

se.statistics.iowait_count                 :                   862

se.nr_migrations                           :                  2388

se.statistics.nr_migrations_cold           :                     0

se.statistics.nr_failed_migrations_affine:                       0

se.statistics.nr_failed_migrations_running:                   9828
```

```
se.statistics.nr_failed_migrations_hot:          15042

se.statistics.nr_forced_migrations :               140

se.statistics.nr_wakeups         :             4966577

se.statistics.nr_wakeups_sync         :            16662

se.statistics.nr_wakeups_migrate    :              2168

se.statistics.nr_wakeups_local      :             22704

se.statistics.nr_wakeups_remote     :           4943873

se.statistics.nr_wakeups_affine     :               214

se.statistics.nr_wakeups_affine_attempts:       4926620

se.statistics.nr_wakeups_passive    :                 0

se.statistics.nr_wakeups_idle       :                 0

avg_atom                         :            1.805490

avg_per_cpu                      :         4471.663398

nr_switches                      :             5914367

nr_voluntary_switches            :             4943410

nr_involuntary_switches          :              970957

se.load.weight                   :                1024

policy                           :                   0

prio                             :                 120

clock-delta                      :                 176
```

From the output, we can derive that there were a high number of failed hot migrations between CPU cores (se.statistics.nr_failed_migrations_hot), as well as a relatively high number of involuntary switches (nr_involuntary_switches) compared to the voluntary ones.

This is a good opportunity for an attempt to improve the system performance and the application runtimes using the CPU scheduling tunables under /proc. If we consult the documentation (14.4 Completely Fair Scheduler, n.d.) on scheduling tunables under /proc/sys/kernel, we get

- sched_compat_yield – this parameter enables the aggressive yield behavior of the old O(1) scheduler. For instance, Java applications that use synchronization extensively perform better with this value set to 1. It is advisable to change it only when you observe a drop in performance. The default value is 0.
- sched_migration_cost – this tunable specifies the amount of time after the last execution that a task is considered to be "cache hot" in migration decisions. A "hot" task is less likely to be migrated, so increasing this variable reduces task migrations. The default value is 500,000 (ns). If the CPU idle time is higher than expected when there are runnable processes, we should try reducing this value. If tasks bounce between CPUs or nodes too often, we try increasing it.
- sched_latency_ns – this parameter defines the targeted preemption latency for CPU bound tasks. Increasing this variable increases a CPU bound task's timeslice. A task's timeslice is its weighted fair share of the scheduling period. The task's weight depends on the task's nice level and the scheduling policy. Minimum task weight for a SCHED_OTHER task is 15, corresponding to nice 19. The maximum task weight is 88761, corresponding to nice -20. Timeslices become smaller as the load increases.

This value also specifies the maximum amount of time during which a sleeping task is considered to be running for entitlement calculations. Increasing this variable increases the amount of time a waking task may consume before being preempted, thus increasing scheduler latency for CPU bound tasks. The default value is 20,000,000 (ns).

- sched_wakeup_granularity_ns – likewise, we need to consider the wake-up preemption granularity. Increasing this variable reduces wake-up preemption, reducing disturbance of compute bound tasks. Lowering it improves wake-up latency and throughput for latency critical tasks, particularly when a short duty cycle load component must compete with CPU bound components. The default value is 5,000,000 (ns).

At this point, we should run some kind of a design of experiment, and execute several runs with different permutations of the above tunables. Since it is impossible to "guess" the right number, the simplest way of conducting the test would be by increasing or decreasing the parameters by a factor of 2, rerunning the application and testing whether there is a change in the number of futex errors, as well as the overall impact on performance.

## NETWORK TUNING EXAMPLE

Our third case is the most complex one. The scenario you are facing is as follows. One of your customers has recently migrated their SQL server to a new operating system version, as part of the standard environment refresh. Making things worse is also a business decision to move away from a virtual machine to a dedicated physical host with significant computing resources.

Unfortunately, your customer is phoning, complaining about the poor performance of the new server, and blaming it all on the modern operating system. The SQL server is not coping well with the workload, and connections are timing out. The server also seems to be heavily overloaded, and it never completes the torrent of tasks sent its way.

Resolving this kind of an issue can be extremely difficult, even without the human factor, as it also covers numerous changes that go beyond the kernel itself and into the application space. But, it could be a valuable lesson in system optimization. If we apply all that we have learned so far, we want to minimize our investigation to as few changes as possible, and then test them one a time. The first step is to understand the work flow.

In our example, the customer application is firing roughly 1500 connections to the SQL server in a very short sequence (a matter of seconds), pulling small pieces of data, each of which is then passed to a separate script, running on the server itself, processed, and then logged both remotely and into a file stored on the local hard disk.

At this point, a comparison between the good and the bad system is mandatory, including both the operating system and the application stack. For the former, this means comparing the values under /proc. For the latter, this means comparing SQL server configurations, and making sure they are identical – or at least proportional, as some of the settings are related to server resources, such as the memory size, the number of CPU cores, and so forth.

Even without access to the actual physical hardware and software, we can still ask important questions that could determine the next lead in our investigation:

- How long does it take the virtual machine to process the 1500 requests?
- How long does it take to process a single request?
- What is the number of concurrent requests in the process table?
- What is the average system load while the tasks are running?
- How does the SQL configuration affect the load and times, that is, if certain parameters are decreased or increased (preferably by a factor of 2 each time), how does the overall execution change?

Another important clue is the obvious error of connection timeouts, pointing to the fact that the SQL server is not configured to handle the expected throughput of connections. For the same setting, the problem does not manifest itself on the virtual machine, which could be an indication that the database requests are processed more *slowly* on the virtual machine, avoiding the bottleneck.

With all these parameters being taken into consideration, the next step is to profile the server workload. In our example, each connection triggers a script that runs for about 4–5 seconds before existing. Overall, this gives us a good indication of what the server total throughput is, and then how we can tweak it. Some of the options include the following:

- Increasing the number of connections above the maximum application load.
- Changing or increasing the SQL server I/O table cache sizes.

- Physical tweaks may also include turning hyperthreading on, and then matching the SQL thread concurrency to the number of CPU threads.

However, at this stage, we are mostly interested in what we can achieve in the /proc and /sys space. Indeed, since we have observed that the server is not handling the network throughput well, and the connections are timing out, we could potentially reduce the load. Some of the options that come to mind include the following:

- Echo 1 > /proc/sys/net/ipv4/tcp_abc – increase congestion window (tcp(7), n.d.).
- Echo 1 > /proc/sys/net/ipv4/tcp_adv_win_scale – the socket receive buffer space is shared between the application and kernel. TCP maintains part of the buffer as the TCP window, which is the size of the receive window advertised to the other end. The rest of the space is used as the application buffer, used to isolate the network from scheduling and application latencies. The tcp_adv_win_scale default value of 2 implies that the space used for the application buffer is one fourth that of the total. Changing the value could improve performance under heavy workload, either for the kernel or for the application itself.
- Echo 1 > /proc/sys/net/ipv4/tcp_tw_reuse – this tunable allows reuse of TIME_WAIT sockets for new connections when it is safe from the viewpoint of the protocol.
- Echo 1 > /proc/sys/net/ipv4/tcp_tw_recycle – similarly, this variable enables fast recycling of TIME_WAIT sockets, although this option is not recommended in some network environments. However, for large data centers, where network address translation (NAT) is normally not used, it could be useful, as in our case.
- Echo 1 > /proc/sys/net/ipv4/tcp_max_syn_backlog – this parameter specifies the maximum number of queued connection requests that have still not received an acknowledgement from the connecting client. If this number is exceeded, the kernel will begin dropping requests. On most modern Linux systems, with sufficient memory, the value can be increased safely.
- Echo 1 > /proc/sys/net/core/netdev_max_backlog – this value sets the maximum number of packets allowed to queue when a particular interface receives packets faster than the kernel can process them. Doubling the number and testing could help in our scenario.

## CONCLUSION

Sometimes, Linux kernel tuning does take a form of a black magic, mostly because there is no one way that systems can be optimized. Most of the time, the variations and inefficiencies in the applications, as well as the imprecision of the runtime environment, will negate all and any changes under /proc and /sys. That said, in some scenarios, optimizations can be highly useful, and it can also help detect issues in the data center setup, if not necessarily outright boost the performance of your systems. Log handling and filesystem tweaks can also lead to improved throughput and shortened execution times of your tasks.

In the end, tuning system performance is mostly about understanding specific workloads and tailoring the environment to match them, if possible. Often as not, you will discover which tweaks are best left alone rather than being applied. These results will give you a better understanding of your systems, and ultimately lead to a better, more robust, and more productive work setup.

## REFERENCES

14.4 completely fair scheduler, n.d. Available at: https://www.suse.com/documentation/sled11/book_sle_tuning/data/sec_tuning_taskscheduler_cfs.html (accessed March 2015)

Budilovsky, E., 2013. Kernel based mechanisms for high performance I/O. Available at: http://www.tau.ac.il/~stoledo/BudilovskyMScThesis.pdf (accessed March 2015)

Chapter 1. Introduction to control groups (Cgroups), n.d. Available at: https://access.redhat.com/documentation/en-US/Red_Hat_Enterprise_Linux/6/html/Resource_Management_Guide/ch01.html (accessed March 2015)

Corbet, J., 2007. Available at: http://lwn.net/Articles/229984/ (accessed March 2015)

Corbet, J., 2010. Improving readahead. Available at: http://lwn.net/Articles/372384/ (accessed March 2015)

Gunn, J., 1995. Addendum: Sturgeon's law. Available at: http://www.physics.emory.edu/faculty/weeks//misc/slaw.html (accessed March 2015)

logrotate(8), n.d. Available at: http://linux.die.net/man/8/logrotate (accessed March 2015)

mkfs.xfs(8), n.d. Available at: http://linux.die.net/man/8/mkfs.xfs (accessed March 2015)

Mochel, P., 2005. The sysfs filesystem. Available at: https://www.kernel.org/pub/linux/kernel/people/mochel/doc/papers/ols-2005/mochel.pdf (accessed March 2015)

tcp(7), n.d. Available at: http://linux.die.net/man/7/tcp (accessed March 2015)

# Piecing it all together

# 11

We have reached the end of the road, in a sense. It is time to wrap up all our hard work and develop a strategy that will last through the passage of time and the change of the technology landscape. A well-designed, flexible policy will help you handle all kinds of planned and unplanned problems, and it will not be rendered obsolete by the time you implement it in your organization.

## TOP-DOWN APPROACH

Problems can be solved in many different ways. Many system experts are highly technical people, with great expertise in a narrow field. Moreover, many are keenly focused on the stuff they love and do, which inherently limits their vision. And it is the vision that you require to be a good problem solver.

## KEEP IT SIMPLE: START SIMPLE

A crucial part of the top-down approach is that you try to see the whole picture, from afar, with few details, looking for discernible patterns. You observe the whole system, you try to understand its mechanisms, and then, you dive in only when it is relevant. Not only will this method save time, it will also render more effective results.

Therefore, when you encounter an environmental issue, do not attack with all the force, vigor, and technical skills you have. Attempt to use simple tricks and tools first. It takes much experience and intuition to find the correction solution on the first go, and if you are not sure about the current problem, step back and do some basic, preliminary checks.

## UNDERSTAND YOUR ENVIRONMENT FIRST

One of the key components to making the best educated guess to what you should do, whether it is just a collection of simple commands that check the health of the system or a more detailed investigation, is to know how your environment behaves. Without understanding this, your work will not only be riddled with mistakes, you may even cause damage and accentuate the problem.

To make things even worse, some people may even misinterpret the very meaning of this statement. For them, understanding the environment might be all about mastering all the title tools, the flavors of operating systems, and programming

277

languages. However, in reality, the real challenge is finding the relations between different parts of your ecosystem. If you understand the cause and effect between your data center technologies and their implementations, you will be able to significantly improve your investigative work.

## IT IS LIKE AN ONION: LAYERED AND IT WILL MAKE YOU WEEP

The step of mastering one's environment is often more difficult than it appears. Certainly, you have a bunch of servers, centralized storage, a complex network infrastructure with a firewall, and maybe several customer applications. But, the delicate relations are often far more complex than that.

Long-term support and backward compatibility, dependence on old technologies, lack of desire and budget to move on to new solutions, and the stark fear of breaking things that work often force companies and organizations to maintain a dreadful legacy status quo, piling on new solutions as hacks and patches rather than complete solutions. Even highly flexible environments that start as state-of-the-art industry examples stagnate over time, becoming bogged down in their own mission statement. Often, new technologies are implemented to resolve a shortcoming in an older incarnation of a related technology, introducing unnecessary complexity that only grows worse in time.

When you try to fix issues, your problem solving should also account for the legacy leftovers and make sure they are accounted for in the solution. Otherwise, you will merely be patching the same old leaky boat.

## PROBLEMS THAT "RESOLVE THEMSELVES" COME BACK WITH INTEREST

There is no such thing as problems that go away on their own. In the best case, an unknown component in your data center changes, causing the manifestation of the issue to vanish temporarily. But this is a wicked scenario. You do not control the environment, you are neither aware of what caused the problem to occur nor the reason it supposedly went away. This means the problem will recur, often with increased impact.

After you have gained a solid situational awareness of your ecosystem, you must invest time in excellent monitoring and complete solutions that handle the problem across the entire spectrum, even if this means protracted engagement with third-party vendors and follow-up months after the original issue surfaced. Otherwise, there is a very good chance that your woes will return.

## NO SHORTCUTS: PHYSICAL LAW OF CONSERVATION OF EFFORT

Perhaps you will not find the above equation in any of Newton's books, but it is as real as Murphy's Law. Sometimes, you may get lucky – you will nail the problem down on the first strike and your data center will quickly resume normal operation.

Sometimes, your educated guess will be so intelligent that you will be amazed at your own intuition. Good knowledge of the environment and a robust monitoring infrastructure will certainly help you make the best decisions. However, most of the time, you will have to invest much time in finding the root cause to the problem and designing efficient, useful solutions.

Business urgency, workforce attrition, boredom, and many other factors may affect how well you work around the problem. You might be tempted to just let things slide, but ultimately, they will come back.

"No shortcuts" does not mean you will not work fast and efficiently, with automation and scripting instead of hard manual labor. But, it does mean you will not compromise, you will not neglect proper methods, rigorous data collection, and analysis, and you will use an objective approach to truth. You will also make sure the fixes are thoroughly tested before being implemented. Trying to save time in these critical pieces of the investigation will only yield more damage and confusion in the long run.

## METHODOLOGIES USED

All of the above cannot happen using just goodwill and luck. You need to be thorough and methodical about it, and it is best if certain standards and well-known best practices are applied to assist you in your work.

### DOCUMENTATION

Keeping tabs of what you do and how you do things is a good first step and an excellent close to problem solving, regardless of the size and scope of the investigation. Whether you are handling a small, isolated outage or a big issue with major customer impact, if you can translate the problem into words and provide business continuity through clear directions, you will have helped the organization in the long run.

Information control is the most volatile link in the chain. The same solutions are often redone and rehashed time after time simply because people are unaware of the existing effort, there is no coordination of work among groups, and people are loath to put their ideas into words. Finally, a robust search system is another great challenge, and it is only effective on the Internet, never within companies. Open-sourcing the knowledge is probably the most useful way of harnessing this vast pool of data.

### A CLEAR APPROACH

When coping with critical business problems, constrained by financial and bureaucratic rules of the game, with tight schedules and no margins for error, you must make your problem solving effective and focused. This means starting with simple things before moving to more complex ones, using only numbers to sway your judgment and that of others, and carefully correlating between causes and effects you observe in your environment.

## Y TO X SHOULD BE YOUR MOTTO

We go back to the lessons learned in Chapter 7. The detrimental abundance of data, complexity, and lack of search ability will compel you to be very careful about utilizing your time and resources. It is all too easy to get lost with a hundred and seven different permutations of some experiment, each taking a week. Or, you may have this beautiful spreadsheet with 61 MB worth of measurements that no one understands.

While you may be very smart and skilled in your domain, and every one of your peers exercises a similar mastery of their subject, it is still virtually impossible to analyze the effect of changes in an environment based on the tweaking of input parameters. However, if you observe the outputs, or rather, the variations in output, you will be able to more easily find the critical parameters that influence the system the most.

For most engineers, the Y to X approach is counterintuitive, but it is extremely effective. It also allows you to have a good coverage and good confidence in your tests even if the reality does not permit you to run all the permutations you want and all the conditions you seek.

## STATISTICAL ENGINEERING IS UNDERAPPRECIATED

On the same note, most if not all of the tools and methods available in the branch of statistical engineering are heavily underused in the industry. One, they go against the common practices. Two, few people have the required mathematical knowledge to analyze the variances and to interpret the collected samples, using the Y to X approach with focus.

Investing in this field can greatly benefit your organization. Even on the individual level, it can help your problem-solving strategy become more effective. Pairwise comparisons and component search can also assist you in making the right choice when it comes to software and hardware selection, and the Design of Experiment tests, combined with statistical engineering, ought to provide you with a robust mechanism for analyzing highly complex problems in the data center.

## MATHEMATICS IS POWERFUL, BUT NO ONE USES IT

However, it all funnels down to mathematics. Most engineers have a decent intuition, some knowledge of scripting tools and programming languages, and a relatively good understanding of their environment. They are not very good at numbers, though.

Most people can make useful graphs and calculations, but they miss the necessary background for statistical calculations. What is the minimal size of your test pool to get the right confidence level? How many times must you rerun the experiments?

How long should the test last? Pit all that against the nervous program manager, fidgety manager, the stressed operations shift supervisors, paying customers who do not care about your little woes, and a huge global environment running 24/7, and you are in a bit of a spot. Throw in your own limited time, numerous projects, and you will realize why so much of the problem solving comes down to running a bunch of tools and hoping for the best.

Escaping the realm of mathematics in favor of pure system administration is very easy. Everyone can understand log outputs, CPU values, and the like. Few can make the necessary links between seemingly unrelated problems. But, most of the answers hide in the unexplored waters of mathematics.

## TOOLS USED

After you have gained a good understanding of your environment, and you are pretty confident in your statistical skills, you still need to be well versed in your actual tools of the trade. It is easy to go overboard as well as to make wrong assumptions just because your ecosystem allows you all the wrong maneuvering.

### OVERVIEW OF THE TOOLS USED

Problem solving happens on many levels, and accordingly, the software utilities you are going to use will come in a variety of shapes and colors. You have the basic information tools and logging as your first layer. Application tracing and profiling comes next. After that, you might want to invest in step-by-step debugging, in user space and on the kernel level. Stepping out of a single system, you connect the dots using environmental monitoring, developing situational awareness needed for the solution.

When handling problems, you must avoid being enamored by any one tool, no matter how modern and powerful it sounds. You must ask yourself what you are trying to achieve. Specific problems will require a delicate approach, and sometimes, no one tool will be good enough; maybe only by using all of them will you be able to fix the issue. In other scenarios, nothing will help because you have an inherently broken work model, and it is important to learn that also. Here, the tools will be the method used to expose the weaknesses and help you resolve them strategically in the long run.

### THE ADVANTAGES AND DISADVANTAGES OF SELECTED COMPONENTS

This brings us to the question of relevance and efficiency. Any program you choose for your problem solving becomes a part of the problem. It is important that you be aware of this and avoid bias. Do not focus on familiar software, focus on the *right* software. And if it is missing, obtain it, learn how to use it, and make good use of it in your setup. You have to be aware of the strengths and weaknesses of each selected program, and how they come to bear in the bigger picture. For example, if your software logs 10 GB worth of data, it might not be the best software to analyze disk I/O bottlenecks. You will have to account for timing, availability and granularity of information, the level of intrusiveness – all this in addition to the purely technical capabilities.

## FROM SIMPLE TO COMPLICATED

Just as important as using mathematics, proper methodologies, and the right tools for the job is the gradual application of your intellectual force during troubleshooting. It is all too easy to dig right into the kernel and try your mightiest utilities. But often as not, you will find that a large number of problems can be resolved using more basic tools. There will be situations in which you will need a kernel profiler or a debugger. However, in most scenarios, you should examine your environment first, compare "bad" systems to "good" ones, and start with some simple troubleshooting.

### DO NOT OVERREACH – KNOWLEDGE IS YOUR ENEMY

A corollary of this challenge is that too many people will often assume the worst and invest a disproportionate amount of their time trying to fix a problem, and the more they know, the more they will be at risk of choosing the wrong bit of knowledge from their vast pool of past experience. Few people have the knack for always making the right intelligent guess, and many will stray before circling back to the solution.

If you only have basic familiarity with a handful of system administration tools, your investigation will always be relevant. However, if you are a very skilled problem solver, then you must exercise restraint before unleashing your powers. It is all too easy to be overconfident and make mistakes because you just see too broad of a picture.

### A STEP-BY-STEP APPROACH

One thing that can help keep you stay focused is using an almost template-like approach to handling problems. You may call it a recipe. But, your investigation will start with clear instructions – to yourself – which will help you remain on track.

### DO NOT BE AFRAID TO STEP BACK

Problem solving includes an undocumented element of emotional involvement. Some people find the investigation thrilling and engaging, and they can be blinded by their own success or frustration. If you realize your work is not taking you down the results highway, you may want to consider letting go, stepping back, and reevaluating your ideas and suggestions. This can be especially hard if you have already spent a long time trying to fix a problem.

### SOMETIMES YOU WILL ONLY MITIGATE

Despite your best efforts, certain problems and their resolution will remain outside your reach, especially in big, complex setups such as data centers. You will have found the fix for an issue, only to be forced to wait 3 months for your vendor to produce an official patch, or your customer groups to allow the necessary downtime for the implementation.

In these scenarios, even your best technical skills will not help much. However, this is a great opportunity to exercise organizational capabilities and thinking in terms of a long-term vision. If you can mitigate the problems by driving toward a change on the infrastructure level, you may benefit your environment by making it more flexible and resistant against future problems.

## OPERATIONAL CONSTRAINTS

As you may well know, the technological limitations will be the least of your worries. You may find an excellent, practical solution to a significant challenge in your environment only to learn that human factors, financial considerations, and project timetables are considered more important by the management. You will be forced to adapt and adjust your strategy.

### MONEY, MONEY, MONEY

As an unspoken lemma to Murphy's Law, between flexible solutions that offer zero downtime to customers and status quo, your customers will always choose the cheapest option. Few people will have the vision to see the long-term benefits of proposed solutions, especially since the current management approving the change may not be the one to reap the benefits, and vice versa. Your leadership may decide to focus on the short-term ideas and projects that can be easily marketed, rather than invest in long-arching technologies.

This means your fix for the storage problems or resource management may be brilliant, but it could take 2 years or two extra million dollars to implement, and it is that much easier to have the IT staff work a few hours more every week. Again, in the long term, your idea would have paid off, but the quarterly report will show immediate savings from a short-term solution.

Although shortcuts rarely work, and you need to fight them without compromise to achieve the best results, you must acknowledge the situation and act accordingly. This means the monetary factor will play a critical role in how you design your solutions, and you must be prepared to discard excellent tools and practices and to choose lesser ones. However, that makes your ability to meet the business needs with less than an ideal work set into an even greater challenge.

### YOUR CUSTOMERS CANNOT AFFORD DOWNTIME, EVER

To make things worse, your customers will always complain about any proposed downtime schedule, even if it may benefit them. This is a normal human reaction, and it is often rooted in legitimate business constraints. Once again, you should not compromise, but plan accordingly. If you know your customers will not let you reboot their servers, then you ought to plan all and any future solution for the data center to allow for seamless upgrades and fixes and uninterrupted services.

Practically, this may mean you ought to invest in high-availability technologies, cloud, distributed file systems, clusters, and other decentralized and redundant solutions that allow partial downtime without service degradation. The real challenge will be in achieving the best results within the limited framework dictated by your customers and the budget.

## YOU WILL HAVE TO COMPROMISE

If we have not stressed this enough, then here it is: operational excellence focused on problem solving will revolve around intelligent compromise. You will never have the ideal conditions, people, and tools to work with. There will always be something missing, something wrong.

People will have their own agenda, their own schedule, and their own skill set. Your hardware refresh will get delayed, the customers will clamor for more changes while never allowing for them, and the sheer complexity of your environment will make everything 10 times harder. But as long as you plan to work under these conditions, you will be able to design robust and flexible solutions. In this regard, problem solving is as much about fixing the actual technical glitch as it is in making sure the proposed fix is actually practical and usable in your environment. For instance, in many cases, upgrading to a newer kernel might be what you really need, but that might never come to be because no one will let you do it. You will have to go back to the drawing board and think of a new solution.

## SMART PRACTICES

If you stack all the ifs and maybes that could come about in your data center, you will realize that the problem space is virtually endless, and that you can spend your career digging through a never-ending stream of recurring problems without ever coming out on top. Your time and experience are limited, so you must carefully apply them to manage the problems in your environment.

### SHARING IS CARING

When you are tight on time and resources, it is very easy to ignore the needs of others, especially if you are being pressured, you are behind schedule, and your customers do not care about your woes. Naturally, many system administrators and engineers will try to isolate themselves and find the niche wherein they can operate with a modicum of quiet and control. Unfortunately, this is also the best recipe for making your life harder.

There is a reason why data centers often employ many workers, and it is more than just the legal restrictions on your work hours. Skill set diversity is a necessity in complex environments. However, few people take advantage of the situation and work mostly alone, on their own, with little to no sharing of information and knowledge.

It is almost too naïve to expect system administrators and programmers to just sit together and discuss their problems, but there is a middle ground between isolation and happy work groups. Sharing your findings and experience with your colleagues is a great way to build good work relationships, earn trust, and most importantly, help yourself. There will always be someone with better coding or debugging skills than you, or a different perspective that could solve the issue that much more quickly.

Information sharing is one of the biggest challenges in most organizations, and there is significant overhead of people doing identical work without ever knowing about the effort of their peers. You may not solve the whole data pyramid, but you could definitely make your life easier by sharing some of your work experience and practices with your cubicle neighbors.

## CONSULT WITH OTHERS: THEY HAVE SEEN IT BEFORE

The added bonus of improved cooperation is that you will be able to solve your issues more efficiently. You can go beyond the boundaries of your team or your department. Out there, on the Internet, someone will have already seen and fought the same problem you are facing now.

Most large companies will be more conservative in the adoption of new technologies, which means they will be using relatively older technologies and operating systems. On the other hand, young and small startups and the academy will normally be spearheading the bleeding edge of art and science, and they will have already encountered, wrestled with, and resolved some of the issues you could be facing currently. Good cooperation may also lead to new ideas, and it will certainly make your work more productive.

## JOB SECURITY IS NO SECURITY AT ALL

Too many people will, when faced with a situation in which someone else might be able to do exactly the same task they are doing at pretty much the same cost and quality, defensively bunker down and refuse to cooperate. Colloquially, this is known as job security, an unspoken and sometimes subconscious philosophy to refuse to share practices and data that could render you redundant.

A significant chunk of any respectable IT organization is contained in isolated personal silos, by people who find the notion of exposing their domains of responsibility a direct threat to their position. It is one of the chief reasons why projects can often take so long, and why you have to beg for information when trying to fix problems. Some system administrators or engineers will simply not share.

If you are in a position where you can impart your data to others, or choose not to, so that you remain the critical point of contact, consider the implications of your actions, even beyond the immediate business needs. You will retain the skill, supposedly, but you will also remain dependent on your existing knowledge. Soon enough, though, your knowledge will gradually become irrelevant, as the organization embraces new solutions and moves on to other, more cooperative people. Furthermore, because you have limited yourself to what you know, you will not learn any new skills. Eventually, you will become unnecessary.

It is wrong to assume that knowledge is static and that its value does not depreciate over time. On the contrary, the only real job security is to solve the eternal problems of the data center that do not age or change with time – financial and operational constraints, the customer demands, the difficulty in sharing information with other people. If you can maintain an edge in one or all of these domains, you will have gained the job security you seek. This means adopting a flexible mindset and seeking solutions that will benefit everyone, in addition to buying yourself time to invest in learning new technologies for a future challenge. Staying put with your ancient skills is the best way to make yourself obsolete.

## GIVE A MAN A FISH – OR TEACH HIM TO FISH

So how does one go about their job security? The simple answer is, do not withhold information, do not make yourself into a necessary cogwheel, because they are so easy to replace. Given the choice between feeding others snippets of information or teaching them the whole doctrine of how to do something, you should choose the latter.

Problem solving can be methodic, but it cannot be a recipe. People are not robots, and most issues you encounter in data center environments will require a dose of healthy thinking and intuition. If you go about problem solving armed with only a bunch of tools without a higher meaning or purpose, you will fail. And so will others, if you only give them the tools and not the whole toolbox, which also includes the *why* and *how* of problem solving.

Finally, when you are forced to teach others what you know, you will realize that the task is more difficult than you imagine. In fact, this should be the real test of your knowledge. You cannot claim you are the subject matter expert unless you can teach others.

## ONLY YOU KNOW WHAT IS BEST FOR YOUR ENVIRONMENT

So far, we have talked much about compromise and consideration and working with other people. Hand in hand with flexibility comes great responsibility. Yours. If you are the domain owner, then it is up to you to devise the best plan to fix the problems and provide a sane operational environment for your customers. This means learning from others, sharing willingly, being a team player, but also not compromising when it comes to accountability.

Closure is just as important as every other step in the whole problem-solving strategy. Sometimes, it is very easy just to move on to a new challenge once you have found the technical bit, but you must see it to the end. This is probably the least interesting and most boring part of the whole affair. But it is your responsibility. Do not assume others will know or care about your constraints, or that they will share your motives for the problem and its solution. Sharing knowledge is great, but you are still the owner of the issue, and you are the one who must see it all the way through. Only then will you be able to claim your problems have been resolved.

## CONCLUSION

We have reached the end of our journey. We started it by looking at the data center, through the eyes of an explorer facing a jungle, uncertain, wary, maybe even confused. Carefully, we blazed our path through problem solving, using a methodical, step-by-step approach in our investigations, trying to avoid the classic mistakes and traps along the way.

Some of the problems we faced are purely technical, and indeed, there is a lot to be said and done on the technical side, as we have learned in Chapters 1–6. But, equally importantly, we handled the softer side of problem solving: the mathematical models and best practices, the monitoring and configuration management, and we pieced it all into a single, effective continuum, which allows us to tackle new challenges with confidence, and maybe, the reason why you joined the world of IT, and to have fun doing so.

# Subject Index